Development Discourse and Global History

The manner in which people have been talking and writing about 'development' and the rules according to which they have done so have evolved over time.

Development Discourse and Global History uses the archaeological and genealogical methods of Michel Foucault to trace the origins of development discourse back to late colonialism and notes the significant discontinuities that led to the establishment of a new discourse and its accompanying industry. This book goes on to describe the contestations, appropriations and transformations of the concept. It shows how some of the trends in development discourse since the crisis of the 1980s – the emphasis on participation and ownership, sustainable development and free markets – are incompatible with the original rules and thus lead to serious contradictions. The Eurocentric, authoritarian and depoliticizing elements in development discourse are uncovered, whilst still recognizing its progressive appropriations. The author concludes by analysing the old and new features of development discourse which can be found in the debate on Sustainable Development Goals and discussing the contribution of discourse analysis to development studies.

This book is aimed at researchers and students in development studies, global history and discourse analysis as well as an interdisciplinary audience from international relations, political science, sociology, geography, anthropology, language and literary studies.

Aram Ziai is a Heisenberg-Professor of the German Research Foundation (DFG) for Development and Postcolonial Studies at the University of Kassel, Germany. He previously taught at the Institute for International Development (IE) at Vienna University.

Development Discourse and Global History

From colonialism to the sustainable development goals

Aram Ziai

Routledge
Taylor & Francis Group

LONDON AND NEW YORK

First published 2016
by Routledge

2 Park Square, Milton Park, Abingdon, Oxon OX14 4RN

711 Third Avenue, New York, NY 10017, USA

Routledge is an imprint of the Taylor & Francis Group, an informa business

First issued in paperback 2017

British Library Cataloguing-in-Publication Data
A catalogue record for this book is available from the British Library

Library of Congress Cataloging-in-Publication Data
Ziai, Aram, author.
    Development discourse and global history : from colonialism to the
sustainable development goals / Aram Ziai.
        pages cm
    1. Economic development—Philosophy.   2. Development economics—
Philosophy.   3. Sustainable development—Philosophy.   I. Title.
    HD75.Z53 2016
    338.9001'4—dc23
    2015010396

ISBN: 978-1-138-80325-1 (hbk)
ISBN: 978-1-138-73513-2 (pbk)

Typeset in Goudy
by Apex CoVantage, LLC

Contents

Acknowledgements

Various chapters have already been published in earlier versions and they have all been revised for this volume. I acknowledge the kind permission of the publishers and copyright holders for the following texts: Chapter 2 has appeared in *Globale Strukturpolitik? Die Nord-Süd Politik der BRD und das Dispositiv der Entwicklung im Zeitalter der Globalisierung* (Münster: Westfälisches Dampfboot 2007), 14–37. Chapter 3 has appeared as 'Imperiale Repräsentationen. Vom kolonialen zum Entwicklungsdiskurs' in *Blätter des iz3w* Nr. 276, 15–18. Chapter 5 appeared in 2013 in *Development in Practice* 23(1), 123–136. Chapter 6 is based on 'Negotiating 'Development': Constitution, Appropriation and Contestation' which will appear in: Dhawan, Nikita/Fink, Elisabeth/Leinius, Johanna/Mageza-Barthel, Rirhandu (eds.) 2015: *Negotiating Normativity. Postcolonial Appropriations, Contestations and Transformations*. A version of chapter 7 appeared in 2014 as 'Progressing towards incoherence: Development discourse since the 1980s' in: *Momentum Quarterly* 3(1), 3–14. Chapter 8 appeared in 2010 as 'From development discourse to the discourse of globalisation. Changing forms of knowledge about change and their political repercussions' in: *Sociologus* 1/2010, 41–70. Chapter 10 appeared in 2009 as 'Development: Projects, Power, and a Poststructuralist Perspective' in: *Alternatives – Local, Global, Political* 34(2), 183–202. Chapter 11 appeared in 2011 as 'Millennium Development Goals: Back to the Future?' in *Third World Quarterly* 32(1), 27–43. Chapter 12 appeared in 2014 as 'Justice, not development: Sen and the hegemonic framework for ameliorating global inequality' in *Global Justice: Theory, Practice, Rhetoric* 7(1), 28–38. A downsized version of chapter 15 appeared as a Working Paper of the Department of Development and Postcolonial Studies at the University of Kassel. Chapters 1, 4, 6, 9, 13 and 14 have not been published before.

I was writing this book while on a Heisenberg-grant and a Heisenberg-professorship funded by the DFG and am very grateful for that, also to those who supported the application (Christoph Scherrer, Uta Ruppert and Cord Jakobeit) and those who made sure the professorship for Development and Postcolonial Studies was established at the University of Kassel (Christoph!). A 'thank you' also goes to Khanam Virjee, Bethany Wright and Margaret Farrelly at Routledge and the anonymous reviewers. Their work also made this book become real. The same holds true for Silke who looks after the kids half of the time.

I would like to thank all my students as well as my wonderful colleagues in various places from whom I have learnt a lot during the past decade: Christoph Scherrer, Sonja Buckel and the Hegemony Colloquium and many others and especially Daniel Bendix in Kassel; Gerald Hödl, Karin Fischer, Uli Brand and the others from IE in Vienna; Joe Hill, Conrad Schetter, Katja Mielke and the others from ZEF in Bonn; Chris Methmann and Jörg Meyer in Hamburg; Chandra Danielzik and Kwesi Aikins in Berlin; Sally Matthews in Grahamstown; Akosua Adomako Ampofo and Nana Akua Anyidoho in Accra; Sara Mazinani Shariati and Yaser Bagheri in Tehran; Oscar Vega Camacho in La Paz and Friederike Habermann who is probably more fellow in struggle than colleague. Special thanks for inspiring discussions and emotional support go to my flatmates Friz, Mart and Sarah; to Regina, Armin, Jürgen, Harry, Josephine and Daniel and to all those I forgot here; to Enno and the BUKO; to my great kids (are you actually reading this book?) and of course to Franziska, whom I hope will always recognize me. This book is dedicated to my parents Seid Hossein Ziai Ardastaninejad and Lisa Rosemarie Ziai Ardastaninejad (born Dänecke), who will probably never read it but made it possible a long time ago.

1 Introduction
The discourse of 'development'

On January 9, 2015, the EU launched the 'European Year for Development 2015 (EYD 2015)' and declared it 'a year dedicated to raising awareness, engaging Europeans everywhere in the EU's development cooperation and sparking a debate around the motto "Our world, our dignity, our future"'.[1] The press release informs us that the 'EYD 2015' was proposed by the European Commission and unanimously adopted by the European Parliament and Council, what the EU International Cooperation and Development Commissioner has to say about it, and what events and creative opportunities for involvement across the member states are being prepared – but it does not actually explain what is meant by 'development' and 'development cooperation'. The terms are assumed to be self-evident: everyone knows that they are about something like projects for poverty eradication in Africa, Asia and Latin America.

On January 20, 1949 – 66 years earlier – when US President Truman announced a 'program of development' for the 'underdeveloped regions', this was different: he had to explain what he actually meant by these words, what he planned and why this endeavour was necessary and even useful to those who had just elected him as president. This difference shows that somewhere between 1949 and 2015, 'development had achieved the status of a certainty in the social imaginary' (Escobar 1995: 5), that people know what to think when they hear the word *development*.

This book is concerned with just that: what people think when they hear or speak or write *development*, what politicians try to achieve when they launch development programmes, what aid workers imagine they are doing when working in development projects – and with what all this has to do with relations of power between North and South. Its topic is the discourse of development, the structures that can be found in the speaking and writing on it. This implies a theoretical approach that deems discourse to be relevant, that assumes it makes a difference whether we designate an entity as an *underdeveloped* country, as a newly industrialising country, as an age-old civilisation or as a rogue state, because each of these expressions evokes different images, allows for different political measures and enables different perceptions and constructions of identity.

In particular, the book is interested in the historical transformations that this way of speaking has undergone during the 20th century and until the present. Of course, the book can be only very selective here and does not claim to cover its object comprehensively. Yet it does try to trace the changes in the discourse of development during different periods by examining empirical material coming mostly from international organisations. It is in this respect, and in this respect only, that it deserves the title of global history. It cannot claim to be global in the sense of comparing local perspectives on *development* from different continents. Similarly, it cannot claim to be postcolonial in the sense of reconstructing the voice of those oppressed by colonialism and neocolonialism, but it is quite concerned with elements of colonial discourse that have survived in contemporary development discourse.

In a way, the book can be seen as a continuation of my PhD thesis (Ziai 2004) which analysed what I called the classical paradigm of *development* as well as the Post-Development critique. This paradigm is an arrangement of assumptions on different levels: on a philosophical level, the assumptions of Cartesian rationality (separating the subject of knowledge from the object to be dissected into parts), the idea of *Homo oeconomicus* (we are all pursuing material interests and utility maximisation) and a Baconian view of nature as something to be analysed in order to be subdued; on a meta-theoretical level the assumptions that a good society is *developed* and all societies can become like this, and that there is one state and one process of *development* which can be identified by experts on *development*; on a theoretical level that industrialised societies are the norm for this state and process and that societies deficient in comparison to this norm need modernisation, economic growth and technology; on the level of methodology that comparative analysis allows us to identify more and *less developed* societies and that *development* can be measured through quantitative indicators; on the level of methods that states are the units to be compared and measured and the most important indicator is economic performance in terms of GDP/GNP and per capita income; on the practical level that *development* can be achieved through planned interventions in society based on expert knowledge carried out by states or development organisations and that negative side effects have to be accepted for the sake of *development*.

This last assumption was demonstrated memorably by a representative of the Indian consulate in Bonn, Germany, when in August 1999 demonstrators protested against the Sardar Sarovar dam and the flooding of several hundred villages (and some resisting villagers). In response to the protesters' slogan 'No human sacrifices for development!', he replied: 'So you want our country to remain underdeveloped!' Obviously, he deemed the sacrifices necessary and the objective worth the cost – just as Nehru had, when he told those villagers who would be forcibly resettled for the Hirakud dam in 1948, that they were to 'suffer in the interest of the country', for the sake of national development (Roy 1999). What is this *development*? Who decides what it actually is? How it can be defined and achieved? The question has never left me since – and spoiled my planned career in development aid.

Instead, I spent the next years reading and writing on this question, and some of the results have been assembled here in this volume. But, one might ask, is there not enough literature on the topic? So why now this book? Because, I would argue, a perspective building on the work of Foucault, on his concepts of discourse and power, on his methods of archaeology and genealogy, can contribute to our knowledge of the topic by highlighting aspects so far unnoticed. Whether the book lives up to this claim remains of course for the readers to decide.

The first part is concerned with theory and chapter 2 ('Poststructuralism, discourse and power') will lay the meta-theoretical, theoretical and conceptual foundation for the rest of the book. The next part is entitled 'Archaeology' and will dig into the constitution of development discourse. Chapter 3, 'From "civilising mission" to "development"', starts with analysing the discursive similarities and differences of the two discourses. Chapter 4, 'An archaeology of development knowledge', analyses *development* as a discursive formation and its specific rules regarding its objects, concepts, subject positions and strategies. Chapter 5, 'The concept of "development" and why the concept should be abandoned', explores the Eurocentric, depoliticising, and authoritarian implications of the concept. In chapter 6, 'Development discourse: appropriation and tactical polyvalence', I examine how elites in postcolonial states have used the concept for their own ends in national and international arenas.

'Genealogy' is the title of part III, and these chapters investigate the historical change of the discursive formation of *development* at the end of the 20th century. The first two of these chapters deal with different aspects of the transformation of development discourse after the 'crisis of development' in the 1980s. Chapter 7, 'The transformation of development discourse: Participation, sustainability, heterogeneity', examines the effects of the inclusion of these three concepts into the discourse of development agencies and finds that they lead to incoherence and contradiction because some of their elements are incompatible with the rules of formation of the discourse. Chapter 8 ('From "development" to "globalisation"') deals with the rise of neoliberalism and the discourse of globalisation which is found to operate according to new rules and lead to new policies in the realm of North-South relations. Chapter 9 examines documents of one of the institutions often identified with neoliberalism, the World Bank, and analyses the massive shifts that have occurred in the representation of poverty and the corresponding strategies in this institution between the 1970s and the 2000s ('World Bank discourse and poverty reduction').

Chapter 10 ('"Development": Projects, power and a poststructuralist perspective') looks at different programmes and projects of development of the 1980s, 1990s and 2000s and finds that there has been a shift in relations of power concomitant to the transformation of development discourse and that *development* functions as an empty signifier that can be filled with various contents. In chapter 11 ('MDGs: back to the future?'), the story lines of the central Millennium Development Goals documents are analysed and compared with a similar document: the declaration of the Second Development Decade of 1970. Chapter 12 – entitled 'Justice, not development: Sen and the hegemonic framework for ameliorating global inequality' – is concerned with one of the most influential approaches in development theory in the beginning 21st century, with Amartya Sen's *Development as Freedom* – and with its relation to development discourse.

In Chapter 13, 'Migration management as development aid?', the focus is on the nexus of the two discourses of migration and development and specifically the International Migration and Development Initiative. Chapter 14 ('The post-2015 agenda and the SDGs: The persistence of development discourse') discusses one of the most important reports on the Sustainable Development Goals and compares it to the first announcement of a development programme by US President Truman, in order to ascertain continuity and change in the discourse between 1949 and 2014. Chapter 15 will deal with the question of what discourse analysis can contribute to development studies. First recapitulating and assessing some criticisms of this perspective, it proceeds to list what I deem to be significant arguments and insights it has brought the discipline, before closing with those points that the preceding chapters might add to this ('Conclusion: The contribution of discourse analysis to development studies').

Note

1   https://ec.europa.eu/europeaid/sites/devco/files/eyd2015-press-release-20150109_en.pdf (March 1, 2015)

Bibliography

Escobar, Arturo 1995: *Encountering Development. The Making and Unmaking of the Third World*. Princeton: Princeton University Press.
Roy, Arundhati 1999: The Greater Common Good. Online http://www.outlookindia.com/article/The-Greater-Common-Good/207509 (March 1, 2015).
Ziai, Aram 2004: *Entwicklung als Ideologie? Das klassische Entwicklungsparadigma und die Post-Development Kritik*. Hamburg: Deutsches Übersee-Institut.

Part I
Theory

Part I
Theory

2 Poststructuralism, discourse and power

No one, not even a social scientist, has an unmediated access to social reality. All of us are influenced by socialisation, experience, assumptions, cultural conventions, a certain knowledge interest, etc. – you could say we perceive reality from a certain perspective constituted in this manner, through a pair of glasses. A theory is nothing more than a deliberately crafted pair of glasses which should provide us with a more systematic or thorough view on reality, a perspective on our topic which makes sense for us.[1] This chapter is concerned with clarifying and justifying the glasses that are being used in this book: the epistemological and theoretical foundation and the central concepts and methods built on this foundation. This foundation can be described as social science informed by poststructuralism, the central concepts (inspired by Michel Foucault) are discourse and power, and the method is archaeology and genealogy.

Epistemological and theoretical foundations: structuralism, poststructuralism and social science

In order to argue why precisely this epistemological foundation was chosen, it is necessary to clarify what is meant by structuralism, poststructuralism and poststructuralist social science.

Structuralism

Structuralism, at least in the meaning used in the arts and humanities, is based on the structural linguistics of Ferdinand de Saussure (see for the following Saussure 1983a, 1983b, Münker/Roesler 2000, Stäheli 2000). Its objective was the description of the general structures of language. Saussure differentiated between *langage* (the universal ability to speak), *langue* (a certain language system) and *parole* (an applied language). According to him, the sign, defined as the smallest unit of a linguistic structure carrying meaning, is composed of signifier and signified – e.g. in the English language the word 'bread' and the concomitant concept of a loaf of bread. Saussure highlights the arbitrariness of the sign, i.e. he emphasises the arbitrariness of the relation between signifier and signified: there is no natural connection between the word 'bread' (or *Brot* or *pain* in other language systems) and the thing it designates, it is an arbitrary convention. However, if there is no inherent relation between the level of signifiers and the level of signifieds, linguistic meaning cannot be constructed with reference to something beyond language, but only within language. The meaning of the signs is thus the results of differences within the language system: only because the word 'bread' differs from the words 'bed' and 'head' (or 'cake' and 'cookie') can it fulfil the function of designating a certain thing (bread). 'What counts is not the signs' reference to something beyond language, but their relation, to be precise: the mutual difference of the signs' (Münker/Roesler 2000: 4, translation AZ). According to Saussure, the sign is social by nature, i.e. it is independent of the individual's will, as the linguistic structures predate each individual act of endowing something with meaning. Thus an objective, scientific analysis of language systems is possible.

A central legacy of Saussure's structural linguistics is the focus on the relation of the elements of a structure. Saussure's thought was universalised beyond the horizon of linguistics. The 'linguistic turn', maybe the most important paradigm change in 20th century philosophy (see Rorty 1967), can basically be seen as the application of Saussure's ideas to other areas and systems of meaning.[2] Its starting point is the assumption that these other systems are (just like language) structured as systems of difference and that they exhibit certain laws or principles. Meaning is produced by the relation of the elements of the structure and can thus objectively be identified. Thus the subject is seen in structuralism not as the agent who endows things with meaning, but rather as an effect of these structures – which is why sometimes the 'disappearance' or even the 'death of the subject' was proclaimed. The universal structures of the human mind thus constitute structuralism's object of inquiry, and questioning this claim became the starting point for poststructuralism.

Poststructuralism

Poststructuralism[3] is best portrayed not as a coherent school of theory, but rather as a philosophical current that emerged from the critique of structuralism – which came in part from the structuralists themselves (on the following see Münker/ Roesler 2000, Stäheli 2000, Belsey 2002).[4] It criticised the idea of a closed system of language structures, of a rigid order which assigns one signified to each signifier, and the claim of complete scientific explanation. Instead, the poststructuralists describe the incompleteness of language structures which allows for ever new meanings through contextual or historical shifts of the unstable relation between signifier and signified and reveals the idea of discrete, orderly systems as imprecise. In contrast to structuralism, the relations between signifiers and signifieds do not constitute a rigid structure, this structure exists only insofar as it is reproduced continuously and is thus (at least potentially) characterised by constant change. For poststructuralists, the structure of language not only precedes individual speech acts, but is impossible to catch up with for theory, it is not organised around a centre and can never be described completely and unambiguously, which renders the theoretical claims of structuralism illusory. Furthermore, this claim results in the systematic exclusion of that which cannot be grasped by the method, the structure's Other. To capture meaning and create an orderly system of signifiers and signifieds, other possible meanings have to be excluded.

Thus poststructuralist philosophy is a 'vindication of difference' (Münker/Roesler 2000), for engaging with the excluded Other to counter the totalising tendencies of structuralism. Still, poststructuralism is based on some central theoretical tenets of structuralism and examines structures which produce meaning, so it should not be seen as the abandonment of structuralism, but its radicalisation and reflexive continuation. Poststructuralism's important assumptions can be described as follows:

- Reality can only be perceived through language structures or other systems of representation producing meaning in which reality is constructed. Language is not merely the description of reality, but the means by which it is created.
- The smallest units of these structures are signs comprising signifiers and signifieds, their relation is arbitrary and unstable (but usually temporarily and contextually fixed, which enables communication).
- Meaning and knowledge are thus effects produced by differential relations within these structures, they cannot be based on nonlinguistic objective foundations (such as religion, rationality, science, the knowing subject, etc.).[5]
- In each structure there is something which cannot be grasped by this structure and is excluded.
- The subject is the effect of the structures constituting it. Our subjectivity is the product of different discourses that shaped it. However, unlike in structuralism, subjects are not merely determined by these structures. As there are competing discourses, there is agency in following one discourse instead of another.

These characteristics have consequences for a social science informed by poststructuralism.

Social science informed by poststructuralism

The concept of poststructuralist social science seems imprecise on a closer look because social science is usually linked with the claim to a truthful description of social reality – a claim rejected by poststructuralist philosophy. Social science which still clings to the claim of correctly describing social reality (though without an objective claim to truth) and which bases itself on the assumptions described above can be called inspired or informed by poststructuralism.[6]

According to its philosophical orientation, social science informed by poststructuralism can be described as constructivist and anti-essentialist, i.e. it regards reality as socially constructed and declines to attribute a specific nature to social actors and phenomena ('democracy is . . .', 'women are . . .', 'African culture implies . . .'). Furthermore, it exhibits the following traits:

- It regards society in analogy to language as a system of differences in which the identity of actors and phenomena is described through the opposition to others, through their position within a structure.

- It does not base itself on a foundation which exists beyond any systems of representation. Thus there are no laws determining the relation between elements of society,[7] merely by definition limited and unstable relations. So in poststructuralist terminology, the field of the social is one of undecidability, or more precisely, one of contingency.[8]
- The subject is not the origin of social relations, but is constituted by them. The plurality of social structures intersecting in the subject produces a plurality of possible identities or subject positions (Laclau/Mouffe 2001: 114ff). The subject can thus be seen as the difference between the possible and the actual positions, the difference between undecidability and decision.
- Meanings, i.e. relations between signifiers and signifieds, are never stable and unchanging, but are temporarily fixed, otherwise communication and society would not be possible.[9] While it is possible to prove regularities within society, they are 1) merely immanent and not the manifestation of a determinant external to the structure (e.g. the walk of history or human nature) and 2) they are (in contrast to natural laws) limited and subject to change. Still, the elements of society are not linked merely by coincidence, certain logics can be observed. And a temporarily coherent system of elements thus linked can be called a social formation (Laclau/Mouffe 2001: 136).
- In such a paradigm truth cannot be conceived as correspondence between statement and reality, because there is no perception beyond systems of meaning. Truth can only be analysed as produced within a structure, as socially produced.[10]

Why should we base research on such an admittedly complex and problematic epistemological foundation? My proposition is: because only this foundation is able to adequately accommodate the construction, complexity and historicity of social reality. Essentialisms reducing the complexity of reality are not accepted as explanations in the perspective of poststructuralism. As identities are constructed through difference, this shall be illustrated by some examples of different theoretical foundations.[11]

A central premise of liberal economic theories is the assumption of *Homo oeconomicus*: human beings are naturally inclined to further their own (above all material) interests. So the empirical observation that many people act according to this pattern is explained by reference to a prediscursive human nature, instead of examining, in which societies, in which groups or at which points in time this kind of behaviour was less or not at all dominant, and which social circumstances have supported the spread of this behaviour (Etzioni 1990, Habermann 2008).

In realist theory of international relations, an image of human society based on Thomas Hobbes plays a similar role. The absence of an institutional order endowed with a monopoly of violence on the international level is assumed to lead to a security dilemma: allegedly the security of actors (states) is principally endangered through the existence and there is a situation of threat and rivalry which renders stable international cooperation nearly impossible (Ashley 1986, Wendt 1992).

In Marxist theory there are similar essentialisms, above all in the conception of the economy as a social mechanism functioning according to objective laws independent of human behaviour and in the category of objective (class) interest, which assumes a logical – instead of a political – link between a certain position in the process of production and the mentality of the people (Laclau/Mouffe 2001).

In all three examples there is reference to some knowledge on society or human beings which renders a detailed engagement of specific social phenomena and their historical transformations superfluous and can serve as a legitimating ideology for certain types of domination. This kind of knowledge about reality constitutes a foundation which is beyond theoretical and political contestation – and beyond the historical and contextual shifts of the relation between signifier and signified. A sceptical posture towards this type of knowledge, however, leads to a social science informed by poststructuralism.

Yet the poststructuralist foundation also has its problematic aspects, which need to be dealt with. The most important of these are the methodological exclusion of the referent, the neglect of the subject and its agency and the focus on difference and microstructures.

The methodological exclusion of the referent results from the insight that in the perception of reality we cannot do without systems of meaning. From the perspective of poststructuralism statements on reality are strictly speaking not possible, merely on the representation of reality. This confinement, however, is ultimately not acceptable for a social science. A possible way out of this dilemma, marking the difference between poststructuralism and social science informed by poststructuralism, is to be aware of the perspectivity of any and all statements on reality, and to present one's own theoretical and normative glasses as the result of (hopefully) well-founded but always contingent decisions – and not as universally valid. This is the purpose of this section.

The exclusion of the subject in the poststructuralist perspective seems almost equally problematic in the light of the object of social science, as subjects do seem to play a role in society. Yet in order to remain theoretically coherent, neither the existence nor the influence of the individual actions of individual actors must be disputed. It is however of central importance to analyse subjects as products of structures and not idealise them as the origin of these structures.

Another problematic aspect is the focus on singularity, difference and microstructures. The omnipresent suspicion derived from poststructuralist philosophy that theoretical constructs homogenise differences and flatten discontinuities, in order to appear as a coherent explanation of reality, renders its usefulness as a theoretical foundation for the analysis of society's macrostructures rather doubtful. Nevertheless, even with a microsociological theory there is always an even more differentiated view on social and political phenomena, and the ever more detailed description of an infinity of singular phenomena does not seem to be a reasonable objective of theory. The construction of coherence (which is to a certain extent always arbitrary),[12] the ordering of the empirical material, is a condition of theory-building in social science.[13] Again, the point is to be aware of this construction and ordering and to give reasons for its underlying contingent decisions.

Analytical categories: discourse and power

In a poststructuralist perspective on society, language, or more general representation, is ineluctable: only through systems of language or representation do we
have access to reality. Discourse, preliminarily defined as a system of meaning,
in which relations between signifiers and signifieds are fixed, is thus one of the
central theoretical categories of this study. The second category is a result of poststructuralism's effect to demonstrate the contingency and historicity of seemingly
self-evident categories as well as their exclusions – in a more political view: their
involvement with relations of power. Power is thus the second central theoretical
category. The two concepts are being defined in this section based on the work
of Michel Foucault.[14] My proposition is that an analytics of discourse and power
based on Foucault is able to illuminate relations of power invisible to other theoretical approaches,[15] primarily those that result from discursive structures or that
are not repressive but productive.

Analysis of discourse following Foucault

Discourse theory following Foucault is confronted with the question which works
exactly to follow. A closer look reveals certain differences between his original
methodology of discourse analysis in the *archaeology of knowledge*, the shorter and
more accessible *order of discourse*, and his usage of the term discourse in the context of his analyses of power in later works.

The discourse analysis in the *archaeology of knowledge* is strongly influenced
by structural linguistics and can be sketched as follows: discourse is defined as
'a group of statements in so far as they belong to the same discursive formation'
(Foucault 1972: 117). According to Foucault, these discursive formations are *not*
necessarily characterised by a common topic or common concepts, but by regularities in the formation of objects, types of statements and concepts, by common
rules of formation:

> *Whenever one can describe, between a number of statements, such a system of disper-*
> *sion, whenever, between objects, types of statement, concepts, or thematic choices,*
> *one can define a regularity (an order, correlations, positions and functionings, trans-*
> *formations), we will say . . . that we are dealing with a discursive formation. . . .*
> *The conditions to which the elements of this division (objects, mode of statement,*
> *concepts, thematic choices) are subjected we shall call the rules of formation.*
> (Foucault 1972: 38, emphasis in the original)

'System of dispersion' means that there may be deviance from the norm and
yet a systematic regularity of the discursive dispersion, so rules must not be
conceived as determinants in the structuralist sense. The unity of a discourse
is thus not given through a common topic, but 'a group of *rules* that are
immanent in a practice, and define it in its specificity' (ibid.: 46, emphasis in
the original) and which order the relations between statements and groups of
statements (29). Archaeology is thus defined as the systematic description of

'the regularity of a discursive practice' (145), which does not, in contrast to the history of ideas, try to find the notions 'behind' the discourses, but merely analyses the set of conditions of the existence of statements, their linkages and accumulations (125, 145).[16]

These discourses constitute 'practices which systematically form the objects of which they speak' (Foucault 1972: 49), which reveals the constructivist perspective: Discourses are not representations of an objective reality, but the bricks with which we build social reality. Foucault emphasises, however, that he does not want to treat discourses as 'groups of signs (signifying elements referring to contents or representations)' (ibid.), i.e. as systems of relations between signifiers and signifieds. Not because this would be wrong, but because he is interested in something else: 'Of course, discourses are composed of signs, but what they do is more than use these signs to designate things . . . It is this "more" that we must reveal and describe' (ibid.). This 'more' is the rules of the discourses.

Although Foucault occasionally mentions societal influence on discourse – he writes about specific 'forms of articulation' 'between discursive formations and non-discursive domains' (162) and that theoretical choices of a discourse are dependent of its function in a 'field of non-discursive practices' (68) – he usually conceives of discourses as anonymous, subjectless and autonomous entities (62f, 86f, 117, 121f, 169). Their rules of formation are according to him 'not the result, laid down in history and deposited in the depth of collective customs, of operations carried out by individuals' (63). In the archaeology of knowledge, 'the rules of formation operate not only in the mind or consciousness if individuals, but in discourse itself; they operate, therefore, according to a sort of uniform anonymity, on all individuals who undertake to speak in this discursive field' (ibid.).

Thus Foucault assumes discourses to be entities that are autonomous regarding societal influence and individual actions and defined by certain regularities, the rules of formation. They construct the objects of which they speak and should not be analysed as systems of representation, but merely as positive realities. In this, he neglects that their constructive operations are possible only because they are systems of meaning and their linking of signifiers and signifieds is crucial for analysis. Further, the positive and objective description of discursive reality he envisions is not possible: even the discourse of discourse analysis constructs its objects and is unable to 'say it like it is'. Finally, his concept of discourses as autonomous is theoretically and politically problematic. If the rules of the discourse actually were entirely independent of individual practices, they would have to originate in some other, metaphysical level – which would of course be opposed to Foucault's philosophical location. And this concept is unable to focus on the doubtlessly existing and most asymmetrical influence of social actors on discourses. Dreyfus and Rabinow thus criticise Foucault's 'illusion of autonomous discourse' with good reason (1983, Part I).

Already two years after the publication of the archaeology of knowledge, in his popular inaugural lecture 'L'ordre du discourse' (English as 'The Discourse on Language' in Foucault 1972: 215–237), a shift in Foucault's concept of discourse can be observed. Here, he describes rules of exclusion, systems for the control and delimitation of discourse and procedures for the rarefaction among speaking subjects. This means for each discourse only certain objects, statements and speakers are allowed as legitimate. Not only the opposition between reason and madness, but also that between true and false operates in this perspective as rules of exclusion which change in the course of history. Foucault illustrates this point with the example of 19th-century biologist Gregor Mendel, whose hypotheses are true from the perspective of today's biology, 'but he was not *dans le vrai* (within the true) of contemporary biological discourse: it simply was not along such lines that objects and biological concepts were formed' (224) – Mendel did not obey 'the rules of some discursive "policy"' (ibid.). Scientific disciplines are defined by 'groups of objects, methods, their corpus of propositions considered to be true, the interplay of rules and definitions, of techniques and tools' (222).[17] According to Foucault, religious, political or philosophical doctrines function in a similar manner: they are also defined by the recognition of the same truths while at the same time they indicate the adherence to a certain group (class, nationality or party): 'Doctrine effects a dual subjection, that of speaking subjects to discourse, and that of discourse to the group, at least virtually, of speakers' (226).

In statements like these, the social character of discourses is being recognised, their entanglement with social (and economic and political) relations of power, in contrast to his earlier work they are 'the very object of man's conflicts' (216). Yet Foucault still criticises that in Western thought, discourse was merely seen as 'thought, clad in its signs and rendered visible by words' or as 'structures of language . . . producing a certain effect of meaning' (227). The justified critique that language is not an innocent representation of objective reality again turns into a rejection of a theoretical and methodological perspective which examines the production of meaning through the interplay between signifiers and signifieds. One can only wonder why.[18]

The motive of the entanglement of discourse and social relations of power (and the corresponding abandonment of the 'illusion of autonomous discourse' (Dreyfus/Rabinow 1983) is dominant in the following works of Foucault. He stresses the close relation between knowledge and power, that: 'power and knowledge directly imply one another; that there is no power relation without the correlative constitution of a field of knowledge, nor any knowledge that does not presuppose and constitute at the same time power relations' (Foucault 1977a: 27). Certain relations of power render possible certain discourses and discourses engender and support relations of power (1978: 97). Thus: 'Each society has its régime of truth, its "general politics" of truth: that is, the types of discourse which it accepts and makes function as true' (1980: 131) and truth is 'linked in a circular relation with systems of power which produce and sustain it, and to effects of power which it induces and which extend it' (133). Therefore Foucault is not concerned with revealing ideology and promoting nonideological truths (a 'battle on behalf of truth') and with 'changing people's consciousness', but with the 'political, economic and institutional régime of the production of truth' (132f). In line with the assumption of a close relation between knowledge and power, he does not any longer claim objectivity, but is aware of the perspectivity of the knowledge he produces ('affirmation of knowledge as perspective', 1977b: 156). And although he no longer perceives discourses as completely autonomous, he still perceives them (and not knowing subjects) as the main actors and thus maintains that the 'subjects of knowledge' are merely 'effects of these fundamental implications of power-knowledge and their historical transformations' (1977a: 28) – of discourses.

So in contrast to his earlier work, the social character of discourses and the relations of power in their production become the central focus of Foucault's analyses. However, he mentions that these entanglements are sometimes not straightforward, emphasising what he calls the 'tactical polyvalence of discourses' (1978: 102): the same discourses can be employed in different political strategies: 'we must not imagine a world of discourse divided between accepted discourse and excluded discourse, or between the dominant discourse and the dominated one; but as a multiplicity of discursive elements that can come into play in various strategies' (ibid.).

To productively use Foucault's heterogeneous theory of discourse for social science, we have to carefully reflect which elements we refer to and which others should rather be neglected. In doing so, I would argue that for social science informed by poststructuralism: 1) a perspective which stresses the social character of discourses and their entanglement with power is more useful than the concept of autonomous discourses; 2) acknowledging the perspectivity of one's own knowledge is more useful than the positivist claim of merely describing reality; 3) locating the theory in poststructuralist reflections on the constitution of meaning is more useful than rejecting this connection.

In this context Foucault's category of the 'non-discursive' needs to be discussed. In the light of poststructuralist reflections on the constitution of reality through discourses as systems of representations (which can also be found in Foucault's work)[19] it is strictly speaking not possible to designate a nondiscursive area of reality: we perceive reality only mediated by discourses. What Foucault refers to as nondiscursive, buildings, institutions, physical practices, are rather nonlinguistic phenomena which are perceived to have a different materiality than texts or utterances.[20]

So, taking all of the above into account, we can define discourse – partly building on Foucault's work, partly modifying or rejecting it – as follows: discourses are systems of meaning, in which certain relations between signifiers and signifieds are fixed, certain assumptions are considered true, certain mechanisms for the production of truth are accepted, certain elements are linked and in which certain rules guide the formation of objects, statements, enunciative modalities and topics. They constitute identities by providing the subjects with certain concepts and ways of speaking, certain types of constructing reality and producing statements. Discourses are open systems constituted by regularities, there are manifold overlaps between them and their number is limitless. Discourses are the result of individual and collective practices and thereby unstable and subject to historical change.

Analysis of power following Foucault

In the area of power we have to similarly clarify which elements of Foucault's theory can be usefully taken up, because differences and contradictions can be found here as well. In his most explicit presentation of his analytical method regarding power (1978: 81–102), Foucault describes power as relational, decentered, ubiquitous, intentional, nonsubjective and above all productive, all in all as a 'multiplicity of force relations immanent in the sphere in which they operate' (92). Following Foucault, power must not be conceived as something that powerful persons or institutions possess. Rather, they are nodes in a web of power relations. The powerful state does not possess a monopoly of violence, but power manifests itself in social relations at the microlevel which lead to a situation in which the state appears to have this monopoly – or in which it does not, depending on whether individuals accept this claim. So in this perspective, state apparatuses and hegemonies are 'institutional crystallization[s]' (93) of decentered power relations and thus their effects, not their origins.[21]

The ubiquity of power is already a result of its close relation to knowledge. As mentioned, there is no relation of power without corresponding knowledge and no field of knowledge which does not presuppose and constitute relations of power (Foucault 1977a: 27). So there are no spaces 'outside' of power (1980: 141). However, this does neither mean that power is always negative (there is no normative judgment involved) nor that there is no possibility for individual action.

The description of relations of power as simultaneously intentional and nonsubjective implies that these relations correspond to a certain observable logic and rationality. So an objective or even an intentionality can be presumed (actually the latter term may be misleading) which cannot be traced back to 'the choice or decision of an individual subject' (1978: 95). An example which illustrates this quality of power (which does not come from Foucault though) can be seen in the economic relations in capitalism, which take place according to a certain rationality and lead to certain results, but without anyone planning or coordinating these relations.

Relations of power are productive, according to Foucault, because they are not confined to a repressive function (e.g. limiting what can be said, outlawing practices, censoring truths) – they are generating or giving rise to fields of knowledge and types of practices: 'power produces; it produces reality; it produces domains of objects and rituals of truth' (1977a: 194). This productive function does not only refer to the mind. Through the disciplinary techniques of surveillance (which renders visible) and normalisation (which controls, sanctions and homogenises) (170, 183f), power influences the body of the individual or, through the control of birth rates or the health system, the whole population. Foucault refers to these techniques for disciplining bodies and regulating populations as bio-power, as power which is directed at biological processes of life (1978: 139).

In his later works Foucault thus demonstrates the shortcomings of juridical, repressive concepts of power operating with the categories of sovereignty, law and prohibition (see also Rehmann 2003). According to him, these are not only unable to grasp the modern, productive and disciplinary operations of power (1978:

89f). Linked with the discourse and techniques of right, they have 'efface[d] the domination intrinsic to power in order to present the latter at the level of appearance under two different aspects: on the one hand as the legitimate rights of sovereignty, and on the other, as the legal obligation to obey it' (1980: 95). Thus domination appears as a stabilisation of power relations trying to appear legitimate by legal claims. In contrast to this, Foucault suggests a strategic concept of power, which conceives 'politics as war pursued by other means' (1978: 93), and which – as a 'micro-physics of power' (1977a: 26ff, 138ff) – describes the manifold, unstable, productive relations of power tied with fields of knowledge which together constitute a 'complex strategical situation' in a particular society (1978: 93).

The task of genealogy then is to provide a history of knowledges and discourses and their relations of power without reference to a historical subject or other teleological categories (Foucault 1980: 117). It should examine the historical change of these relations, yet 'must record the singularity of events outside of any monotonous finality' (1977b: 139) and 'oppose . . . itself to the search for "origins"' (140). The focus on singularity, heterogeneity and difference is a genuinely poststructuralist element in Foucault's theory.

The term 'dispositif' (apparatus) finally links discourses and nonlinguistic elements. Foucault describes it as an 'ensemble consisting of discourses, institutions, architectural forms, regulatory decisions, laws, administrative measures, scientific statements, philosophical, moral and philanthropic propositions', among which there is a system of relations. This apparatus possesses a strategic function at a given historical moment and arises as a reaction to a strategic necessity (1980: 194f).

However, Foucault's approach to analysing power has certain problems as well: in the literature it has been accused of reductionism, because processes of socialisation are perceived merely as conditioning (e.g. Rolshausen 1997: 75). Similarly legal structures appear only as instances of domination, which sidelines the problem of collective decision-making and government (Lemke 1997: 122). And resistance of course occurs in Foucault's concept, but is not explained theoretically. On the other hand, the focus on microrelations neglects the state's contribution in organising relations of power (120f).

Partly in response to these criticisms, Foucault coined the concept of governmentality, which reflects the role of freedom within relations of power and tries to bridge the gap between micro- and macro-level (Burchell et al. 1991). Governmentality denotes a specific relation of power which aims at the 'conduct of conduct', and to govern from this perspective is 'to structure the field of possible action of others' (Foucault 1982: 221). This relation of power leaves the individuals untouched as subjects of their action although it influences and governs them – they are free to act as they will. The art of governmentality is how to guide the usage they make of their freedom and the term links the act of governing (*gouvernement*) with the way of thinking (*mentalité*), focusing on the relation between forms of domination and processes of subjectivation (Foucault 1991, Lemke 1997).

Foucault thus differentiates between three different types of power,[22] a sovereign, a disciplinary and a governmental type. Sovereign power, sometimes denoted as the repressive or juridical model of power, is 'identified with a law that says no, power is taken above all as carrying the force of a prohibition' (1980: 119). It oppresses or censors or conceals, and its mechanisms can be administrative acts as well as exclusions from or in discourse (1977a: 194, 1972: 216).

Disciplinary power, in contrast, is productive, it produces reality, generates knowledge, induces pleasure, gives rise to certain practices, abilities and even subjects (1980: 119, 1977a: 170, 194). It employs – as a 'political anatomy of the body' – hierarchical observation and normalising judgment (1977a: 170). As 'bio-politics of the population' its main instrument is the regulation of the sum of bodies, the calculated transformation of human life and its mechanisms (1978: 139, 143).

Governmental power, identified in the art of governing, operates through structuring the field of action of free subjects. It manifests itself in 'action upon an action' (1982: 220), in 'guiding the possibility of conduct' (221) or, to use the most commonly used phrase, in the conduct of conducts.[23] Its objective is the governing of individuals by shaping their free will, their subjectivity. Government is then 'the art of exercising power in the form of and according to the model of the economy' (1991: 92) – the capitalist economy, one should add. In another text, Foucault curiously identifies government with relations of power based on claims to truth (1992: 15).

Problems, ambiguities, contradictions

This is not the place to contrast Foucault's theory with his concrete analyses, asking whether he has or has not implemented his methodological principles. Here, we are merely concerned with his most important theoretical categories sovereign, disciplinary and governmental power, and with the problems, ambiguities and contradictions that can be found here which require clarification before we can decide which elements of Foucault we can build on and which have to be modified or discarded.

1)   The definition of governmental power as 'structuring the field of action' is not identical with its other definition of 'conduct of conduct'. The shaping of subjectivities and of the subject's preferences which is implied in the latter definition *may* be a long-term result of a structuring of the field of action, but is by no means a necessary one. We have to differentiate between a (successful) act upon the field of action and a (successful) act upon the preferences for action, i.e. the subjectivity of a person. This point marks the difference between a deterministic concept which conceives power as a conditioning which succeeds by definition and a concept which takes into account the freedom of the subjects.

2)   However, the structuring of fields of action is precisely what Foucault described in *Discipline and Punish* as characteristics of disciplinary power. How else would it be possible to discipline prisoners? In Foucault's example of the Panopticon the field of action of the inmates is structured by surveillance and possible sanction: within a certain space they are free to act as they will. The ideal outcome of this structuring, i.e. the internalisation of surveillance and a subjectivity which exhibits conformist behaviour even after the

surveillance ceases, manifest a successful act upon the preferences for action as a result of productive, disciplinary mechanisms of power.

3) The example also illustrates that the exercise of power does not presuppose an acting subject, as seems to be suggested in the definition of power as an 'action upon actions'. Impersonal entities and apparatuses can likewise constitute such relations of power. When Foucault stresses the nonsubjective character of relations of power, he implicitly rejects a definition of power which is closely intertwined with acting subjects.

4) Sovereign power actually functions in the same manner. The existence of laws and prohibitions is nothing but a structuring of fields of action which can by no means guarantee that individuals will respect and abide by them. They can merely be threatened with sanctions if their deviant behaviour is noticed by state institutions. But their behaviour cannot be determined – breaking the law is a possible alternative of action.

5) Therefore even Foucault's example of a chained slave ('slavery is not a power relationship when a man is in chains', 1982: 221) has to be differentiated. He argues that there is a relation of physical constraint, not of power. But according to his definition of governmental power this is not quite the case: regarding the order to row there is merely a structured field of action. The slave can decide not to – although the sanctions are presumably unpleasant enough to render this alternative unattractive.

6) Strictly speaking even a situation where someone threatens me at gunpoint to do something constitutes no qualitative difference to one where the person threatens merely to hit me in the face if I refuse. Of course there is a significant difference between life-threatening and other sanctions, but we can draw no objective line here: Which kind of threat is perceived as massive enough as to subjectively cut off alternatives of action, is dependent on the values and emotions of a person.

7) A relation of force is constituted then by acts of physical violence. In the case of the galley slave, the alternative of flight is excluded by iron chains. In this regard, there is no relation of power because this would presume a subject which is free to act.

8) Another problem is the delimitation of sovereign power from productive power. Laws and prohibitions not only pursue the same objective as disciplinary power (the production of docile subjects), they also use the same mechanism (structuring fields of action). One could argue that the specificity of sovereign power lies in the codification of its norms and sanctions and in its claim to legitimacy in using violence to implement its sanctions. Yet regarding the prison, which is one of Foucault's prime examples for disciplinary power, this would lead to its categorisation in the area of sovereign power.

9) The production of true knowledge, which has also been mentioned as a characteristic of governmental power, cannot function to separate the categories either. Sovereign and disciplinary power are also relying on the constitution of knowledge – e.g. knowledge about the correct behaviour in school or knowledge about what is right and just.

Therefore it can be maintained that the structuring of fields and action and the production of true knowledge are mechanisms employed by all three types of power. The categories seem to blur. It is hard to assert that the analytical frame has been unambiguously enhanced by the category of governmentality and the separation of sovereign and disciplinary power is not convincing. Discursive power, on the other hand, which limits what can be said or produces fields of knowledge and constructions of reality, appears somewhat neglected in Foucault's writings on analysing power. His 'agency turn' in these writings, defining power as 'action upon actions' does seem somewhat inappropriate regarding the relations of power immanent in discursive structures. In earlier writings Foucault demonstrated that anonymous discourses can become subjects of the exercise of power and subjectivities and constructions of reality its objects. And it is still not quite clear, whether and how relations of power in the field of the economy can be grasped with Foucault's instruments.

A systematisation of Foucault's analysis of power could, in a first step, differentiate between:

- power as a structuring of fields of action which influences actions (one could call it *conditioning* power);
- power as a shaping of preferences for action which influences subjectivities (*subjectivising* power); and
- power as a structuring of constructions of reality which influences thinking (discursive or *representing* power).

Classical examples of Foucault's analyses could then be rephrased as follows: a discursive exercise of power which limits what is sayable and provides certain conceptualisations of an object while excluding others, is primarily a structuring of constructions of reality, thus an instance of representing power. It has repressive (a certain kind of knowledge is prevented and oppressed) as well as productive effects (a certain kind of knowledge is generated). By offering certain subject positions within the discourse and portraying certain ways of behaviour as just and legitimate, it can also influence fields of action and even preferences for action (conditioning and subjectivising power).

A disciplinary exercise of power which prescribes behaviours and threatens refusal with sanctions is primarily a structuring of fields of action, thus an instance of conditioning power. Again, we find both repressive (certain acts are prohibited) and productive elements (certain acts are trained). In some cases, this exercise of power may lead to a shaping of preferences for action – the trained behaviour is internalised and subjectivities are shaped. In other cases, the trained behaviour is dropped as soon as there is no surveillance or no conditioning anymore. What Foucault describes as sovereign power is a special case of disciplinary power operating with the demarcation legal/illegal and the claim or threat of a monopoly of violence.

A governmental exercise of power which through commercials or generally the media aims at the efficiency- or market-oriented conduct of individuals out of their own free will, is (if successful) primarily a structuring of preferences for action, thus an instance of subjectivising power. However, it is linked with representing power as well. It is productive in the sense of creating a certain subjectivity and has a repressive dimension insofar as other types of subjectivity are sanctioned.

It becomes clear that a rigid separation between repressive and productive ways of exercising power is hard to maintain. What can also be observed is the entanglement of the levels of thinking (constructions of reality), agency (fields of action) and subjectivity (preferences for action).

Poststructuralism, archaeology, genealogy: brief remarks on method

So which methodological consequences follow from the above discussion of theoretical foundations and analytical categories?

A poststructuralist analysis is not concerned with reality as it is, but the way it is represented and constructed, primarily in texts. It focuses on the production of meaning in discourse, and this means: on the relation between signifier and signified. Which contents are attributed to which concepts in which contexts? And which words or phrases are treated as synonymous, which signifiers are linked in chains of equivalences? These are the questions that guide poststructuralist methods.

Archaeology is the analysis of discursive formations. It thus looks for the rules of formation that constitute the unity of a discourse. These rules concern the objects, concepts, enunciative modalities and strategies of a discourse. It also examines the limits of what can be said within the discourse and what is excluded – the repressive dimension of representing power. Its productive dimension is also relevant: which objects are created, which statements are provided possible, which realities are constructed in the discourse? In archaeology, texts are being analysed not as statements produced by individual subjects, but by the structures of the discourse, by rules which impose themselves on anyone who speaks in this discursive field.

Further, what is of interest is the way that discourses may be connected with institutions and practices to constitute an apparatus (dispositive) which produces regular effects and organises relations of power. This apparatus arises from a strategic necessity and has a strategic purpose which can be identified through its effects, although this strategy is independent of the intention of the individuals operating within this apparatus.

If archaeology provides a synchronic analysis of discourses, genealogy provides the diachronic analysis. It examines the history and transformation of discourses and in particular of the relations of power inherent in them: Which relations of power gave rise to this discourse and which effects of power are produced by this discourse? The aim is to be aware of singularities and discontinuities and to avoid the homogenisation of discourse.

Notes

1 Of course this representation of the relation between science and reality is not neutral either, but an expression of a certain philosophy of science which will be discussed in this chapter.

2 Examples are structuralist anthropology which was founded by Claude Lévi-Strauss, the structuralist revision of psychoanalysis by Jacques Lacan, or Roland Barthes' semiotics, which takes any context of meaning as a topic of structuralist analysis. Michel Foucault's archaeology can at first also be seen as an application of structuralist methods on the field of the history of ideas, but poststructuralist elements can be found here as well.

3 Following poststructuralism, it is not possible to say 'what poststructuralism is'. Münker and Roesler put it this way: 'Writing about poststructuralism means inventing it' (2000: ix). So all that can be done here is to describe one interpretation of poststructuralism which links the concept with certain contents. Defining the concept is not an act of representation, but a performative act.

4 In the works of Barthes, Lacan and Foucault a transition from structuralism to poststructuralism can be observed.

5 This is why poststructuralist approaches are sometimes referred to as postfoundational. Marchart (2002: 11) defines postfoundationalism as follows: it rejects approaches which assume that knowledge can be anchored in a universal, objective foundation such as God or rationality (see also Stäheli 2000: 9).

6 Stäheli (2000: 15) also points to the impossibility of a poststructuralist sociology and postulates all that we could have were 'poststructuralist perspectives on the social'.

7 Laclau and Mouffe state: 'If society is not sutured by any single unitary and positive logic, our understanding of it cannot provide that logic. A "scientific" approach attempting to determine the "essence" of the social world would . . . be the height of utopianism' (2001: 143). This means it is inadequate to describe the essence of our society as 'capitalist', because it is not merely determined by this single logic (Gibson-Graham 2006).

8 Undecidability refers to situations in which there can be no scientific analysis or decision on which elements of society will be articulated according to objective laws. Of course these articulations do take place, based on contingent processes and decisions – the situations are in fact 'decidable', but not rationally or universally, therefore the second term seems more appropriate (cf. Laclau/Mouffe 2001: xif).

9 If Laclau and Mouffe talk about the 'impossibility of society', they refer to a rigid social totality which appears impossible from the poststructuralist perspective because of the instability of the relations. In the statement here the point is a different one: that the unrestrained floating of signifiers would render social interaction impossible.

10 On the concept of truth in poststructuralism see also Stäheli 2000: 271.

11 The following description of some social theories is necessarily simplified and merely serves to explain the specificity of the poststructuralist position – it cannot substitute a thorough engagement with these theories.

12 The construction of coherence refers to poststructuralism's perspective that the empirical material never possesses an order in itself, but that it has to be constructed through categorizations, classifications and the like.

13 This is a point made by Christine Hanke. In her discussion of Foucault's discourse analysis she raises the question how we can combine the construction of coherent formations with the recognition of discontinuity and claims: 'Maybe the question is whether we want to demonstrate the power of discursive formations – this requires to act big and to gloss over differences – or whether in our work with texts we want to focus on fragments and details and go against the grain, linger at their margins, make them move and deconstruct their alleged coherence' (Hanke 1999: 117, translation AZ). Thus the question is one of academic policy.

14 This implies that I disagree with a reading of Foucault (e.g. in Dreyfus/Rabinow 1983; Sawyer 2003) that sees theoretical incompatibilities between the earlier works of discourse analysis and the later works focusing on power.

15 Strictly speaking it is not the case that these relations exist on a prediscursive level of reality and the said analytics (functioning as a nonideological view on reality) merely 'sees' them. Based on the epistemological foundation discussed above, it provides only one perspective, the plausibility of which is for the reader to decide. The order of discourse is constructed.

16 Later Foucault also described archaeology as a method which examines the 'system of acceptability', which legitimates a certain knowledge as acceptable and true (1992: 33f).

17 There are clear parallels to Thomas Kuhn's concept of paradigms (Kuhn 1962).

18 A possible though admittedly speculative explanation for Foucault's strange rejection of the idea that social relations of power manifest themselves in language and the approach of examining signifiers and signifieds could be seen in the fact that both were quite *en vogue* in Paris around 1968, there were strong currents of Marxism (and the critique of ideology) on the one and hermeneutics and semiotics on the other hand and he wanted to emphasise their shortcomings and neglects. Maybe this is also a case of the academic necessity for researchers to distance themselves from prevailing schools of thought and present a new innovative approach which tends to lead to an overstatement of cases and novelties.

19 '[W]e should not imagine that the world presents us with a legible face, leaving us merely to decipher it . . . We must conceive discourse as a violence that we do to things or, at all events, a practice that we impose upon them' (Foucault 1972: 229, see also 49).

20 Of course, one could also argue about the latter: texts and utterances also possess physical materiality, just as nonlinguistic practices also possess a dimension of meaning.

21 Here we can see parallels to the work of Nicos Poulantzas.

22 Although Foucault claims that '[w]e live in the era of governmentality' (1991: 103), he stresses that the other two types of power relations are still in operation today as well (102).

23 The phrase 'conduire des conduites' ('conduct of conduct') does not appear in the English translation, but only in the French original (Foucault 1994: 237). However, it has become the most common description for governmentality since Colin Gordon's introduction (Gordon 1991: 2).

Bibliography

Ashley, Richard K. 1986: The Poverty of Neorealism. In: Keohane, Robert (ed.) *Neorealism and its Critics*. New York: Columbia University Press, 255–300.

Belsey, Catherine 2002: *Poststructuralism: A Very Short Introduction*. Oxford: Oxford University Press.

Burchell, Graham/Gordon, Colin/ Miller, Peter (eds.) 1991: *The Foucault Effect. Studies in Governmentality*. Chicago: University of Chicago Press.

Dreyfus, Hubert L./Rabinow, Paul 1983: *Michel Foucault – Beyond Structuralism and Hermeneutics*. 2nd ed. Chicago: University of Chicago Press.

Etzioni, Amitai 1990: *The Moral Dimension. Toward a New Economics*. New York: Free Press.

Foucault, Michel 1972: *The Archaeology of Knowledge & The Discourse on Language*. New York: Pantheon.

Foucault, Michel 1977a: *Discipline & Punish. The Birth of the Prison*. New York: Random House.

Foucault, Michel 1977b: Nietzsche, Genealogy, History. In: Foucault, Michel (ed.) *Language, Counter-Memory, Practice: Selected Essays and Interviews*. Ithaca: Cornell University Press, 139–164.

Foucault, Michel 1978: *The History of Sexuality, Volume 1: An Introduction*. New York: Random House.

Foucault, Michel 1980: *Power/Knowledge: Selected Interviews & Other Writings 1972–1977*. New York: Random House.

Foucault, Michel 1983: The Subject and Power. In: Dreyfus, Hubert L./Rabinow, Paul (eds.) *Michel Foucault: Beyond Structuralism and Hermeneutics*. 2nd ed. Chicago: University of Chicago Press, 208–228.

Foucault, Michel 1991: Governmentality. In: Burchell et al. (ed.) *The Foucault Effect. Studies in Governmentality*. Chicago: University of Chicago Press, 87–104.

Foucault, Michel 1992: *Was ist Kritik?* Berlin: Merve.

Foucault, Michel 1994: *Dits et Ecrits IV*. Paris: Gallimard.

Gibson-Graham, J.K. 1996: *The End of Capitalism (As We Knew It): A Feminist Critique of Political Economy*. Oxford: Blackwell.

Gordon, Colin 1991: Governmental Rationality: An Introduction. In: Burchell, Graham et al. (ed.) *The Foucault Effect. Studies in Governmentality*. Chicago: University of Chicago Press, 1–52.

Habermann, Friederike 2008: *Der Homo Oeconomicus und das Andere: Hegemonie, Identität und Emanzipation*. Baden-Baden: Nomos.

Hanke, Christine 1999: Kohärenz versus Ereignishaftigkeit? Ein Experiment im Spannungsfeld der foucaultschen Konzepte 'Diskurs' und 'Aussage'. In: Bublitz, Hannelore et al. (eds.) *Das Wuchern der Diskurse: Perspektiven der Diskursanalyse Foucaults*. Frankfurt: Campus, 109–118.

Kuhn, Thomas 1962: *The Structure of Scientific Revolutions*. Chicago: University of Chicago Press.

Laclau, Ernesto/ Mouffe, Chantal 2001 (1985): *Hegemony and Socialist Strategy: Towards a Radical Democratic Politics*. 2nd ed. London: Verso.

Lemke, Thomas 1997: *Eine Kritik der politischen Vernunft: Foucaults Analyse der modernen Gouvernementalität*. Berlin: Argument.

Marchart, Oliver 2002: "Gesellschaft ohne Grund: Laclaus politische Theorie des Post-Fundationalismus", in: Laclau, Ernesto 2002 (1996): Emanzipation und Differenz. Wien: Turia+Kant, 7–15.

Münker, Stefan/Roesler, Alexander 2000: *Poststrukturalismus*. Stuttgart: Metzler.

Rehmann, Jan 2003: Vom Gefängnis zur modernen Seele. Foucaults 'Überwachen und Strafen' neu besichtigt. *Das Argument* Nr. 249, 45(1), 63–81.

Rolshausen, Claus 1997: *Macht und Herrschaft*. Münster: Westfälisches Dampfboot.

Rorty, Richard (ed.) 1967: *The Linguistic Turn. Essays in Philosophical Method*. Chicago: University of Chicago Press.

Saussure, Ferdinand de, 1983a: The Object of Study. In: Lodge, David (ed.) 1987: *Modern Criticism and Theory: A Reader*. London: Longman, 2–9.

Saussure, Ferdinand de, 1983b: Nature of the Linguistic Sign. In: Lodge, David (ed.) 1987: *Modern Criticism and Theory. A Reader*. London: Longman, 10–14.

Sawyer, R. Keith 2003: Archäologie des Diskursbegriffs. *Das Argument* Nr. 249, 45(1), 48–62.

Stäheli, Urs 2000: *Poststrukturalistische Soziologien*. Bielefeld: Transcript.

Wendt, Alexander 1992: Anarchy is what states make of it: the social construction of power politics. *International Organization* 46(2): 391–425.

Part II
Archaeology

3 From 'civilising mission' to 'development'

The way the relations between North and South, the West and the rest, metropolis and periphery are represented is imbued with relations of power. These representations are structured by certain discourses which serve to produce knowledge and construct identities. During the middle decades of the 20th century, the colonial order of discourse was pushed aside by that of 'development'. Yet some continuities can be observed.

Colonial discourse

Whether Cecil Rhodes raves over the blessings of British world rule, the French foreign secretary Hanotaux announces to spread civilisation in barbarian lands, German Kaiser Wilhelm II proclaims his intent to win over other continents for Christian morality, US politician Beveridge talks about divine providence, the All-German Association talks about the rights of master races or Belgian King Leopold II talks about a crusade against darkness: the legitimisations of imperial policy and conquest of different colonial powers at the end of the 19th century are largely interchangeable. The basic structure of colonial discourse is the division of the world into 'civilised' peoples or nations and 'uncivilised' tribes or masses. And the basic claim is that the latter are unable to effectively govern their own affairs, so that the former come to help them, because they are by nature or the will of God destined to rule or even obliged to do so for the sake of humanity. So far, so simple.

However, this system of representation does not merely function to justify imperial policy, the knowledge produced here also serves to construct identities, i.e. it exerts not only representing but also subjectivising power. Yet the European, Western or occidental identity can only be constituted as progressive, liberal and civilised, as the ideal norm of human existence, by distinguishing itself from a backward and barbarian Other, which is constructed as deficient deviance from this norm (Hall 1992). Certain discursive constructions enable the designation of the Self as civilised, even when engaging in the colonies in torture and similar practices normally rather perceived as uncivilised. Commenting on such practices of the US in the Philippines, regional expert Foreman argued in 1898: 'In common with many other non-European races, an act of generosity or a voluntary concession of justice is regarded [by the Filipinos] as a sign of weakness. Hence it is, that the experienced European is often compelled to be more harsh than his own nature dictates' (cited in Doty 1996: 40). In this line of argument, the brutality, cruelty or injustice of colonial practices is caused by the spoiled mentality of the indigenous peoples, and actually runs counter to the rather gentle disposition of the colonisers. The knowledge produced here enables the civilised to employ barbaric practices while at the same time affirms the construction of the perpetrator's identity as civilised and that of the victims as uncivilised.

On top of that, the usage of such practices is designated as entirely rational. Here, just like in countless other instances, colonial discourse constructs an ensemble of differences: superior/inferior, civilised/uncivilised, rational/emotional, guided by reason/guided by instinct, fit to govern/unfit to govern, sovereign/dependent, colonising/colonised, etc. The characteristics attributed to the Self and the Other are linked by chains of equivalence: to be superior means to be civilised, to be civilised means to act rational, to act rational means to be fit to govern, which in turn means to be superior, and so on. The positive and negative characteristics are all linked to one another. The implicit point around which the differences are organised, is the affiliation to a racially defined group, to be more precise: to a group defined primarily by race and gender. The positive characteristics all manifest in the 'white man'. On the collective level, it provides the foundation of the 'master race'. The white man thus constitutes what Laclau and Mouffe (following Lacan) call the 'nodal point' or 'dominant signifier' of a discourse (Laclau/Mouffe 2001: 112): the centre which serves as a point of reference for the differences according to which identities are being constructed. It is the benchmark according to which all other identities are found to be deficient. To be precise, one needs to specify the nodal point as the white adult middle class male, as the poor classes, women and children were in similar ways seen as inferior in a racial hierarchy as the non-Whites: poverty was seen as organic pathology and women were also often seen as a degenerate race, akin to black people and apes, while children and savages were linked by analogy anyway (McClintock 1995: 34–37).

Correspondingly the indigenous, who represent the white man's Other in colonial discourse, are measured according to this benchmark and identified as (at best) children close to nature or (at worst) savage beasts. In any case, they are uncivilised, irrational and unfit to govern themselves. The difference between Self and Other is simultaneously being denied and affirmed, in an interplay of universalism and essentialism: It is being denied, because in the ethnocentric evaluation the indigenous appears merely as an incomplete image of one's own norm of human existence, which is to be educated and assimilated according to this norm. The strange and unknown Other appears as a deficient version of the Self (see also Horkheimer/Adorno 1988: 13f, 18f). It is being affirmed, because despite all education and uplifting the colonised will always remain inferior within the order of discourse and are unable to fully reach the level of civilisation of the white man. Postcolonial critic Homi Bhabha refers to this as colonial mimicry: 'colonial mimicry is the desire for a reformed, recognisable Other, *as a subject of difference, that is almost the same, but not quite'* (1994: 122, emphasis in the original). Its epitome is Macauley's objective of education: to breed 'a class of persons Indian in blood and colour, but English in tastes, in opinions, in morals and in intellect' (ibid.: 124f). Yet the natives will always remain Indian in blood and colour and never be fully regarded as equal.

Nevertheless we already encounter the element of *development* in colonial discourse. Although even in the early 20th century some liberals vehemently reject the idea that 'the negroes are simply not yet as developed as we are' and maintain that they are products of an 'inferior race' (cited in Kößler 1998: 71, translation AZ), we can find others like John Stuart Mill, who already in the 19th century traced back the (unquestioned) inferiority and backwardness of the colonised to historical instead of racial factors: the Europeans were merely more progressed in the 'history of human improvement' (cited in Spurr 1993: 66). This, however, is a manifestation of a Eurocentric theoretical model which originated in Enlightenment thinking and became popular in 19th century evolutionism: that the societies in Africa, Asia and Latin America prior to conquest and settlement by Europeans represent earlier stages of the evolution of mankind in comparison to Europe (Comte 1923: 322). This model is summed up by philosopher John Locke in the phrase 'in the beginning, all the world was America', the continent was 'the childhood of mankind' (cited in Hall 1992: 219). This model is described by Melber as 'chronification of spatial co-existence' (1992: 32, translation AZ) and by Nandy as 'transformation of geo-cultural differences into historical stages' (1992: 146).

Yet in the application of this model the concept of *development* underwent a shift in meaning: it transformed from an intransitive to a transitive verb, i.e. 'to develop oneself' was replaced by 'to develop someone else'. Instead of the indigenous who were perceived as incapable of *developing* the land, the colonial powers assumed the task of 'developing backward areas'. However, to *develop* at first referred to exploiting the economic resources of the region and civilising the colonised – but not to their standard of living. Only in a long and discontinuous process during the first half of the 20th century, the idea gained prominence that *developing* a colony had to be linked with material improvements for the indigenous population (see Alcalde 1987 and the next chapter). The mandate system of the League of Nations was an intermediate step on this way: the legitimation of the trusteeship that some countries exerted over others was connected to the well-being of the latter's population. These countries were, in the words of the League of Nations 'inhabited by people not yet able to stand by themselves under the strenuous condition of the modern world' (cited in Rist 1997: 60) and thus in need of tutelage by others, but only under the watchful eyes of an international organisation: the Permanent Mandates Commission. There is already a hint of universalism in the air: a natural inequality of peoples is no longer mentioned. A new order of discourse is in the making, which after World War II and the second wave of decolonisation became the definitive structure in the representation of North-South relations. In this process, a number of heterogeneous factors played a role: anticolonial movements, the Russian Revolution of 1917, strategic (economic and geopolitical) necessities of the industrialised countries (above all the USA) during and after the wars and the discrediting of openly racist world views through the crimes of Nazi Germany (see Alcalde 1987, Escobar 1995, Cooper 1997).[1] Colonial discourse turned into the discourse of development.

From colonialism to development: discursive discontinuities

The discourse of development which became immensely influential in the second half of the 20th century exhibited fundamental changes in comparison with the discourse of colonialism as outlined in the previous section. The most important of these is certainly that people in colonised countries were no longer represented as unable to govern themselves (and therefore dependent on some benign colonial rule). Colonial racism had been increasingly discredited after World War II and the Holocaust,[2] the right of the peoples to self-determination and universal human rights came to be increasingly accepted as self-evident.[3]

A new order of discourse becomes visible not only in the UN charter, but also in the oft-quoted inaugural address of US-president Truman which he delivered in January 1949:

> [W]e must embark on a bold new program for making the benefits of our scientific advances and industrial progress available for the improvement and growth of underdeveloped areas. More than half the people of the world are living in conditions approaching misery. . . . Their economic life is primitive and stagnant. Their poverty is a handicap and a threat both to them and to the more prosperous areas. . . . The United States is pre-eminent among nations in the development of industrial and scientific techniques. . . . I believe that we should make available to peace-loving peoples the benefits of ours sum of technical knowledge in order to help them realise their aspirations for a better life. And, in cooperation with other nations, we should foster capital investment in areas needing development. Our aim should be to help the free peoples of the world, through their own efforts, to produce more food, more clothing, more material for housing, and more mechanical power to lighten their burdens. . . . The old imperialism – exploitation for foreign profits – has no place in our plans. What we envisage is a program for development based on the concepts of democratic fair dealing.

What becomes clear is the acceptance of a conditional equality of peoples: they are all equal, only some are not as progressed on the universal scale of *development* as others, they are *underdeveloped*. However, after the abandonment of the earlier racism, there is hardly any mention of underdeveloped peoples or individuals, but of underdeveloped regions. This means the object of the discourse is being conceived in the terms of economic geography, not in the terms of biology. The dichotomy civilised/uncivilised is being replaced by the dualism *developed/underdeveloped*. The corresponding ensemble of differences can be sketched as follows: industrial and scientific progress/stagnation, economic growth/stagnation, technology/manual labour, modernity/tradition, high productivity/low productivity, prosperity/poverty, better life/conditions approaching misery, free trade and democracy/old imperialism, nations providing development aid/nations receiving development aid. Again, the individual elements of the ensemble of differences are linked through chains of equivalences: a better life is unthinkable without industrial and scientific progress, this demands high productivity, this in turn demands economic growth and investments, the condition of which is free trade. On the other hand, manual labour is a sign of poverty, it is linked to low productivity and a traditional society, etc. The point of reference for these differences, the nodal point of the discourse, is the *developed* industrial society, above all the US.[4] According to this norm, the countries of the South and the countless heterogeneous ways of life to be found there are classified as deficient: they are poor in terms of their per-capita-income and gross national product, they suffer from a lack of *development*. This diagnosis calls for a certain medicine: they need *development* in terms of modernisation, capital investment and transfer of technology.

In this discourse, the *development* of former colonies becomes a central task which can, now the racist element has been abandoned, no longer be withheld from the 'natives'. Thus the trusteeship for the *development* of the society is given to and taken over by the new elites of postcolonial states. As Cowen and Shenton (1996) showed, the idea of trusteeship was formulated by the followers of Saint-Simon, advocating social technology already in the 19th century. The trustees are those who have the capacity to use society's resources for the betterment of society as a whole, and the modernising elites assuming trusteeship readily adopted the hierarchies of development discourse and were willing to educate, modernise and *develop* their subjects in a similar authoritarian manner as the colonisers had done.[5] Especially indigenous peoples in the postcolonial states were still seen as backward and in need of tutelage.

However, not only the elites, but large parts of the population willingly adopted the discourse of development and the image of the South as *underdeveloped*. The reason is this that this discourse constructs them no longer as inferior subjects, but as equal participants in the 'development race' in the 'economic arena' (Sachs 1990: 3), in the progress of humanity towards growth, who are able to catch up their backlog against the leading nations within a few decades. Yet this discourse simultaneously constructs the identity of the *underdeveloped* as backward and as part of an inferior culture whose deficits can only be compensated by taking over Western ideals of rationality, productivity and modernity and a constant effort to assimilate oneself to the norm.

The identity of the *developed* produced by the discourse is not only linked to the ideals of freedom and democracy, free trade and progress, it is crucially also a 'samaritan' identity which grants development assistance to the peoples suffering from 'conditions approaching misery'. Truman admitted that self-interest also played a role in this, portraying the poverty in the South as a handicap and a threat. It was a handicap for the expansion of the US economy that urgently needed new markets (and old resource providers) after the boom period of World War II, in which it doubled its production – to avoid the impending bust. It was a threat because of the very real possibility of decolonising nations joining the communist camp – the containment of communism being the central imperative of US foreign policy during the Cold War. Therefore there was a strategic necessity first of all to discover the problem of Third World poverty, and second to link it to traditional (noncapitalist) values and practices on the one and to a lack of capital and technology on the other hand.[6] The obvious solution then was abandoning traditional social structures and importing Western values on the one and importing Western capital and technology through investments and integration into the world market on the other hand.

The crucial significance of this way of constructing the problem results from the changed global constellation and the corresponding different, anti-colonial, bias of the development discourse. Contrary to the old imperialism the objective of the discourse was to help produce African, Asian and Latin American subjects who of their own free will support an international order in line with the interests of the metropolises in the First World.[7] 'The "white man's burden" of the colonial period shifted from civilising the uncivilised to global governance, the production of a world in which the US way of life could flourish' (Doty 1996: 83). In theoretical terms, governmental, subjectivising power is at work in the new discourse of development far more effectively than in the discourse of the colonial era, as the use of disciplinary power and violence is increasingly delegitimised.

The postwar discourse of modernisation theory depicted here constructed *development* (as mentioned) as a race in the economic arena, thus assuming that each country's success is determined by its own efforts. During the 1960s and 70s, this view was confronted by dependency theories promoting an alternative conception which pried open this structure of the discourse confining the debate on flawed and successful national policies. They did so through analysing *underdevelopment* and *development* as two sides of the same coin, that is of the capitalist world system. Consequently their recommendation was not integration into the world market, but delinking and self-reliance. However, the dependency theories shared the diagnosis of the problem promoted by development discourse: the industrialised states are *developed* and the *underdeveloped* states have to catch up with economic growth and industrialisation. For example Cardoso and Faletto define real (in contrast to dependent) *development* as 'a reduction of dependence and the change of the economic system from a peripheral to a central economy' (1976: 18). So the aim is the transition towards an industrial metropolis – to become like them. The system of differences of the discourse remains more or less the same.

Another aspect of the new discourse also follows from the changed construction of Southern subjects. After those still designated as savages during colonialism were perceived as equal human beings – and because of the strategic objectives mentioned above – Third World poverty became visible and turned into a new focus of North-South relations. Development aid did not only serve to ameliorate poverty, it also simultaneously served to monitor, administer and manage poverty – in particular regarding its potential threat to a capitalist global order, as can be observed in Truman's address or Kennedy's Alliance for Progress, which started in 1961. Therefore institutions were needed that produced knowledge on the Third World and its subjects, made them visible, calculable and objects of social technology (Escobar 1988, Brigg 2002).[8] The legions of development aid workers that went to Africa, Asia and Latin America – over 200,000 in the Peace Corps alone[9] – contributed to the discursive structure crucial to *development*: there are problems in the South (related to *underdevelopment*) and people from the North possess knowledge to solve these problems (because they are *developed*). Paulette Goudge (2003), a former aid volunteer, clearly observed the role played by race in the attribution of knowledge and expertise in this context. That there might be social problems in the North for which problem-solving knowledge might be available in the South is a statement which has no place in development discourse. It is beyond the limits of what can legitimately been said within it.[10] Here we can observe the category of discursive power.

Summing up, it can be said that in comparison to colonial discourse, the discourse of development is directed to a higher degree towards the production of identity in the South, as it has no place for the violent implementation of metropolitan interests (the old imperialism).[11] This is the logical consequence of the delegitimisation of racist ideologies of inequality which provided the foundation for structures of domination at the international level. So from this perspective, the new order of discourse appears to constitute progress in emancipation.

From colonialism to development: discursive continuities

Apart from these numerous changes, we can also observe constant elements in the comparison between the two orders of discourse. These concern the basic structure of discourse, the philosophy of history and the social technology, the latter two leading as a consequence to Eurocentrism and potential for violence.

The basic structure of discourse is the division of the world into a progressive, superior part and a backward, inferior part. As this division takes place from the point of view of the North, it defines the Self (one's own developed society) as the norm which is used to objectively prove the inferiority of the Other. Therefore, no measurement of *development* has ever tried to operationalise hospitality, crime, suicide, social networks or a noninstrumental relation to nature as indicators of a good society. Instead, what counts are life expectancy, years spent in school and above all, the GNP. The system of differences of the development era therefore ties in with that of the colonial era – both are derived from the same norm – and its divisions and dichotomies appear self-evident also because they can build on the preceding discourse.

The element referred to as philosophy of history consists in a concept taken over from 19th century evolutionism in social science, and that is the idea of a universal scale of *development* for the whole of humanity, along which the industrialised countries of Western Europe and North America are more progressed than the non-Western countries. This means that in this type of thinking, the

countless possibilities of human beings organising their coexistence and cooperation are being reduced to following the footsteps of the West, whose past (awash
with violence and environmental destruction) is being romanticised as a necessary progress in human history. If ethnocentrism means that our interaction with
others is governed by the patterns of perception and evaluation predominant in
our culture (Melber 1992: 10f), then the discourse of development is imbued with
a specific type of it, it is thoroughly Eurocentric.[12]

The element referred to as social technology, i.e. the intent to shape the societies in the South (and the people therein) according to rational criteria, has
also been present already in colonial discourse. As mentioned, the trusteeship
shifted from the colonisers to the elites in the postcolonial states, supported by
development organisations of all kinds. But that the trusteeship – and the concomitant legitimation to define how a good society looks like and how it can be
achieved – has been transferred from the colonisers to development experts from
both North and South has done nothing to decrease its potential for violence.
Therefore the record of authoritarian measures conducted (also by postcolonial
states) in the name of *development* is long indeed. It spans from the violent smallpox vaccination of Indian villagers in the 1960s (Apffel-Marglin 1990) to the
'punishment by six strokes' for 'not participating in development projects' in Tanzania's Handeni district in 1962 (Potter 2000: 287) and the regional president
of Southern Sudan, who summed up the principle in the slogan: 'If we have to
drive our people to paradise with sticks, we will do so for their own good' (Alvares 1992: 108). According to cautious estimates, in India alone over 30 million
people have been displaced by dam projects (Roy 1999). The list could go on, the
violence in the history of *development* has been documented by Berger (1974),
Nandy (1994, 1995, 2004), Norberg-Hodge (2009), Seabrook (1993) and Sittirak (1998) and lately (and surprisingly) even Easterly (2013).[13]

This relation between violence and *development* is no coincidence, but a
result of the authoritarian element in development discourse. Knowledge about
development is knowledge about the falsehood of others' ways of living and their
necessary correction. It grants legitimacy to interventions in these ways of living, it allows them 'to be sanctified in the name of a higher, evolutionary goal'
(Sachs 1990: 6). This authoritarian element is due to one rule of formation of
the discourse: a statement in the discourse presupposes knowledge about what
development in the sense of an improvement, a step towards a good society, looks
like and how it can be achieved. This implies the subordination of other ideas
about a good society. Statements not claiming this kind of knowledge have no
place in the discourse. (On the rules of formation see the following chapter.)

Prominent theorists of *development* have proven that the elements of Eurocentrism and social technology are still present at the turn of the century. They
proclaim as the goal of development theory the 'globalisation of the "project
of modernity" in a European Anglo-Saxon fashion' (Lühr/Schulz 1997: 11),
they talk about 'backward societies' (Senghaas 1997: 59) or they identify as
objective the establishment of modern societies with the 'foundational institutions of competitive democracy, market economy, welfare state and mass

consumption' and demand the transformation of individuals into 'mobile, flexible, performance-oriented personalities' (Zapf 1997: 31, 34). The mission of civilising the uncivilised has been replaced by the global establishment of social institutions in a European fashion and the transformation of the people into performance-oriented individuals, but these intentions do not seem entirely novel. Just like in colonialism, the Northern experts still know how the South has to be remodelled: in their image and according to their values.

Notes

1 Concerning the latter point (the discrediting of racism through the Holocaust), Aimé Césaire has claimed that 'at bottom, what he [the Christian bourgeois of the twentieth century] cannot forgive Hitler is not . . . the crime against man, it is not the humiliation of man as such, it is the crime against the white man, the humiliation of the white man, and the fact that he applied to Europe colonialist procedures which until then had been reserved exclusively for the Arabs of Algeria, the coolies of India, and the blacks of Africa' (1972: 174). In fact, the international discrediting of racism and the Universal Declaration of Human Rights came into being not after the colonial genocides committed by whites against people of colour in America, Africa and Asia, but after a genocide committed by whites against whites (Jews were seen as 'internal others') in Europe.

2 As William Easterly points out, this racism was increasingly contested already during World War II, e.g. when the British Colonial Office for West Africa forced the BBC to apologise after Ghanaians had complained vehemently about the use of the word 'nigger' in a broadcast (Easterly 2013: 85).

3 Of course, the respect for the right of the peoples to self-determination and human rights had certain limits. Yet the counterinsurgency of the US in Latin America and Asia, for example, that openly disregarded these rights, is characterised by the employment of discursive strategies of the colonial era. This concerns in particular the alleged inability of the Filipinos, Vietnamese, Chileans, etc., to govern themselves responsibly, so that in their own interest military interventions were necessary. Just like in contemporary 'humanitarian interventions', the decision of the necessity of such interventions is primarily discussed among the *developed* industrial nations, and only rarely among the United Nations.

4 Although this nodal point of the discourse might seem gender neutral at first sight, the values associated with it (modernisation, rationality, productivity, technology) clearly have a masculine connotation.

5 Easterly (2013) provides numerous examples for this practice.

6 The strategic necessity then gave rise to the establishment of the apparatus (Foucault's dispositive) of the development industry.

7 So the development apparatus used both conditioning power (aid projects and loans) and representing power (the discourse of development) to achieve the desired subjecivisation.

8 In this context, the political role of social science also deserves critical scrutiny (Gendzier 1985).

9 https://en.wikipedia.org/wiki/Peace_Corps (September 17, 2014)

10 In other discourses, such problem-solving knowledge from the South has been accepted in the North, think of Yoga, Buddhism, acupuncture, Ayurveda or Hare Krishna.

11   To be sure, this does not mean that such a violent implementation has not taken place during the era of development, but it has usually been legitimated with discursive strategies of the preceding colonial era (trusteeship in the interest of the 'natives').

12   Melber (1992: 12) sees the specificity of Eurocentrism in contrast to other ethnocentrisms that it even went so far as to construct a theory of the necessary disappearance of difference, as the deficient others (the *underdeveloped*) would become like the Self in due time.

13   While Nandy (1988) and especially Easterly (2013) stress the linkage between violence exerted in the name of *development* and state power (Nandy observes that *development* has become the third 'reason of state' in the South, next to national security and scientific progress), it has to be pointed out that a great deal of the examples of destruction given in the works cited above refer to the workings of corporations or simply the world market.

Bibliography

Alcalde, Javier Gonzalo 1987: *The Idea of Third World Development. Emerging Perspectives in the United States and Britain, 1900–1950*. Lanham, MD: University Press of America.

Alvares, Claude 1992: *Science, Development and Violence: The Revolt Against Modernity*. Delhi: Oxford University Press.

Apffel-Marglin, Frédérique 1990: Smallpox in Two Systems of Knowledge. In: Apffel-Marglin, Frédérique/Marglin, Stephen (eds.) *Dominating Knowledge: Development, Culture and Resistance*. Oxford: Clarendon, 102–144.

Berger, Peter L. 1974: *Pyramids of Sacrifice: Political Ethics and Social Change*. New York: Basic Books.

Bhabha, Homi K. 1994: *The Location of Culture*. London: Routledge.

Brigg, Morgan 2002: Post-Development, Foucault, and the Colonisation Metaphor. *Third World Quarterly* 23(3), 421–436.

Cardoso, Fernando H./Faletto, Enzo 1976 (1969): *Abhängigkeit und Entwicklung in Lateinamerika*. Frankfurt: Suhrkamp.

Césaire, Aimé 1972 (1955): From Discourse on Colonialism. In: Williams, Patrick/Chrisman, Laura (eds.) 1994: *Colonial Discourse and Post-colonial Theory: A Reader*. New York: Columbia University Press, 172–180.

Comte, Auguste 1923 (1842): *Soziologie, Band I*. Jena, Germany: Gustav Fischer.

Cooper, Frederick 1997: Modernizing Bureaucrats, Backward Africans, and the Development Concept. In: Cooper, Frederick/Packard, Randall (eds.) *International Development and the Social Sciences: Essays on the History and Politics of Knowledge*. Berkeley: University of California Press, 64–92.

Doty, Roxanne Lynn 1996: *Imperial Encounters: The Politics of Representation in North-South Relations*. Minneapolis: University of Minnesota Press.

Easterly, William 2013: *The Tyranny of Experts. Economists, Dictators, and the Forgotten Rights of the Poor*. New York: Basic Books.

Escobar, Arturo 1988: Power and Visibility. Development and the Invention and Management of the Third World. *Cultural Anthropology* 3(4), 428–43.

Escobar, Arturo 1995: *Encountering Development. The Making and Unmaking of the Third World*. Princeton, NJ: Princeton University Press.

Gendzier, Irene 1985: *Managing Political Change: Social Scientists and the Third World*. Boulder, CO: Westview.

Goudge, Paulette 2003: The Whiteness of Power. Racism in Third World Development and Aid. London: Lawrence & Wishart.
Hall, Stuart 1992: The West and the Rest. In: Gieben, Bram/Hall, Stuart (eds.) Formations of Modernity. London: Polity Press, 276–320.
Horkheimer, Max/Adorno, Theodor W. 1988 (1944): Dialektik der Aufklärung: Philosophische Fragmente. Frankfurt: Fischer.
Kößler, Reinhart 1998: Entwicklung. Münster: Westfälisches Dampfboot.
Laclau, Ernesto/Mouffe, Chantal 2001 (1985): Hegemony and Socialist Strategy: Towards a Radical Democratic Politics. London: Verso.
Lühr, Volker/Schulz, Manfred 1997: Einleitung. In: Schulz, Manfred (ed.) Entwicklung. Die Perspektive der Entwicklungssoziologie. Opladen: Westdt. Verlag 7–28.
McClintock, Anne 1995: The Lay of the Land. In: Charad, Shari/Corbridge, Stuart (eds.) 2008: The Development Reader. London: Routledge, 31–43.
Melber, Henning 1992: Der Weißheit letzter Schluß: Rassismus und kolonialer Blick. Frankfurt: Brandes & Apsel.
Nandy, Ashis 1988: Introduction: Science as a Reason of State. In: Science, Hegemony and Violence: A Requiem for Modernity. Tokyo: Oxford University Press, 1–23.
Nandy, Ashis 1992: Traditions, Tyranny and Utopias: Essays in the Politics of Awareness. Delhi: Oxford University Press.
Nandy, Ashis 1994: Culture, Voice and Development: A Primer for the Unsuspecting. Thesis Eleven 39, 1–18.
Nandy, Ashis 1995: Development and Violence. Trier: Zentrum für europäische Studien.
Nandy, Ashis 2004: Revisiting the Violence of Development: An Interview with Ashis Nandy. Development 47(1), 8–14.
Norberg-Hodge, Helena 2009: Ancient Futures: Lessons from Ladakh for a Globalizing World, 2nd ed. San Francisco, CA: Sierra Club Books.
Potter, David 2000: The Power of Colonial States. In: Allen, Tim/Thomas, Alan (eds.) Poverty and Development Into the 21st Century. Oxford: Oxford University Press, 271–288.
Rist, Gilbert 1997: The History of Development. From Western Origins to Global Faith. London: Zed Books.
Roy, Arundhati 1999: The Greater Common Good, Frontline 16, no. 11. Online http://www.outlookindia.com/article/The-Greater-Common-Good/207509 (September 17, 2014).
Sachs, Wolfgang 1990: The Archaeology of the Development Idea. Interculture 23(4), Nr. 109, 1–37.
Schulz, Manfred (ed.) 1997: Entwicklung. Die Perspektive der Entwicklungssoziologie. Opladen: Westdt. Verlag.
Seabrook, Jeremy 1993: Victims of Development: Resistance and Alternatives. London: Verso.
Senghaas, Dieter 1997: Die Entwicklungsproblematik. Überlegungen zum Stand der Diskussion. In: Schulz, Manfred (ed.) Entwicklung. Die Perspektive der Entwicklungssoziologie. Opladen: Westdt. Verlag, 47–64.
Sittirak, Sinith 1998: The Daughters of Development: Women in a Changing Environment. London: Zed Books.
Spurr, David 1993: The Rhetoric of Empire: Colonial Discourse in Journalism, Travel Writing, and Imperial Administration. Durham, NC: Duke University Press.
Zapf, Wolfgang 1997: Entwicklung als Modernisierung. In: Schulz, Manfred (ed.) Entwicklung. Die Perspektive der Entwicklungssoziologie. Opladen: Westdt. Verlag, 31–45.

4 An archaeology of development knowledge[1]

The field of discourse analysis is inevitably linked to the work of Michel Foucault. However, whereas often Foucauldian discourse analysis is characterised by the analytical strategy of tracing the interconnectedness of power and knowledge, this has surprisingly little to do with Foucault's methodological reflections in *The Archaeology of Knowledge*. Here, the analysis of discourses is specified as the positivist description of formal rules and regularities in speech and writing which are explicitly characterised as anonymous structures independent of the influence of powerful actors – rather surprising and disappointing for many who turn to discourse analysis as a more fashionable substitute for the critique of ideology.

Nevertheless, as I shall argue in this chapter, Foucault's archaeology can be usefully applied within social science to provide original perspectives and sensitivity for the contingency and the relations of power implicit in discursive constructions. Yet to that end, some parts of his methodological rules have to be modified or left aside. To make this point, the chapter will take the discipline of development theory and policy as an example and submit it to an analysis of its discourse inspired by Foucault's archaeological method, but deviating from it when deemed necessary.

In the first part of the paper, the analytical approach presented in *The Archaeology of Knowledge* and the methodological rules that follow will be (briefly) discussed and modified according to the requirements of a critical social science. Then, this modified approach will be applied to the field of development theory and policy in order to point out the structures of development discourse in the postwar era of the 20th century. In the last part, the emergence of development discourse and the transition from colonial to postcolonial development knowledge will be examined from this perspective, using several policy documents as empirical examples.

Discourse analysis and its problems according to Foucault

In this section, I will briefly reconstruct the methodological rules of Foucault in a fairly simplified form and later discuss their consequences. In *The Archaeology of Knowledge*, Michel Foucault (1972) provides a methodological framework for the analysis of discourses which he proposes as an alternative to the traditional history of ideas. Against the latter's emphasis on the themes of continuity, origin and the sovereign subject, Foucault stresses discontinuities, transformations and structures in the fields of knowledge he examines (1972: 3–17). This should be taken as a methodological guideline, especially the attempt to identify structures in discourse, which are independent of individual actors.

These discourses or discursive formations, Foucault argues, are not united by common objects, statements, concepts or thematic choices themselves, but by their formation and interrelation, not primarily by their content, but by the way this content is generated and ordered: 'Whenever . . . between objects, types of statement, concepts or thematic choices, one can define a regularity (an order, correlations, positions and functionings), we will say . . . that we are dealing with a discursive formation' (1972: 38). These rather abstract rules of formation of a discourse are thus its core, according to the archaeological approach, not the assumptions he takes for granted which can change over time.

In order to identify these rules, Foucault proposes an analysis of discourses based on 'a pure description of discursive events' (27) and distinguishes this from an 'analysis of the language' (ibid.) centring on linguistic signs as well as from an 'analysis of thought' looking for the meaning of what was said or written (27f). Here, we are confronted with the adoption of a positivist epistemological stance and the rejection of a hermeneutic position dealing with questions of meaning and the evasion of a related poststructuralist position examining the relations between signifier and signified. Thus the early Foucault wants to analyse 'discourses as practices obeying certain rules' (138), rules which originate in discourse itself – and not in extra-discursive relations of power such as capitalist relations of production, for example (47, 69). These rules are the rules of formation of objects, enunciative modalities, concepts and strategies, and according to his structuralist methodological position he claims that these rules 'are not the result, laid down in history and deposited in the depth of collective customs, of operations carried out by individuals', 'the rules of formation operate . . . in discourse itself; they operate therefore, according to a sort of uniform anonymity, on all individuals who undertake to speak in this discursive field' (63).

How can we analyse these rules of formation? Referring to the formation of objects, Foucault tells us to 'map the first surfaces of their emergence' (41) – when did these objects appear, in which context, under which conditions – 'describe the authorities of delimitation' (ibid.) – which disciplines or institutions can define the object – and to 'analyse the grids of specification' (42) – according to which criteria is the object classified by the discourse? He stresses that 'mutually exclusive objects' can emerge from the same discursive formation. The formation of enunciative modalities is described by answering the questions which individuals are accorded the right to speak, from which institutional sites the discourse is made, and which subject positions it implies in relation to the various objects. The formation of concepts refers to 'forms of succession' (56) and 'forms of coexistence' (57) of statements as well as 'procedures of intervention' (58) that may be applied to them. Finally, the formation of strategies reaches the level of themes and contents. Of interest are the points of incompatibility, equivalence and systematisation in the discourse (incompatible elements are formed according to the same rules) and the 'economy of the discursive constellation' (66) ('A discursive formation does not occupy therefore all the possible volume that is opened up to it of right by the systems of formation of its objects, its enunciations, and its concepts; it is essentially incomplete, owing to the system of formation of strategies' (67)). The strategic and thematic choices are, according to Foucault, also dependent on 'the function that the discourse under study must carry out in a field of non-discursive practices', the 'rules and processes of appropriation of discourse' and the 'possible positions of desire in relation to discourse' (68). With this last rule of formation, Foucault apparently violates his own methodological rule of not paying attention to the relation between discourse and extra-discursive, or to be more precise: nonlinguistic phenomena.

Consequently, the methodological approach needs to be modified in two ways: it has to adopt a constructivist and hermeneutic epistemological stance which allows it to analyse the constitution of meaning through the relation between signifier and signified and it has to move away from the 'illusion of autonomous discourse' described by Dreyfus/Rabinow (1983) as the 'methodological failure of archaeology', in order to trace the interaction between discursive and nondiscursive/nonlinguistic practices. So in fact we should analyse the constitution of meaning in discourses and the interaction between discursive and nondiscursive practices (see also Wodak/Meyer 2009). With these two modifications, one actually takes up threads that can be found in the archaeology of knowledge itself (Foucault 1972: 45f, 69, 71, 162) (and especially in later works of Foucault as well). Conceding the perspectivity of our knowledge we have to acknowledge – contra Foucault's positivist pretensions – the constructivist element in our activity as analysts of discourse: discourses are not objectively discovered.

We can summarise the position taken here as follows: 1) Fields of knowledge or scientific disciplines are to be examined taking account of discontinuities and without homogenising the differences to be found; 2) At the same time, the analysis looks for overarching structures, texts are examined not as products of individual actors, but as manifestations of these structures, of rules that are immanent in discursive practice; 3) The analysis examines the relation between signifiers and signifieds and the interaction between discursive and nondiscursive practice; 4) The analysis tries to identify the rules of formation of the objects, enunciative modalities, concepts and strategies that constitute a discourse – not, at least not primarily, the objects, statements, concepts and strategies themselves. Attention has to be given to the effects of discourse which are independent of the intentions of the subjects (re)producing it.

The structure of development discourse

The standard criticism towards an analysis of development discourse argues that the singular is inappropriate, in the face of the diversity of concepts of *development* we should be speaking only about development discourses. If we take our constructivist perspective seriously, this is merely a question of scale: if we are focusing on the discipline of development theory, nothing is easier than finding rivalling approaches differing on the question how *development* can be achieved. But it is possible just as well to find similarities between them, just as it is possible to highlight the differences within different approaches to modernisation or dependency or sustainable development for instance. So whether we talk about a discourse of development or several discourses of development or even different discourses of dependency is dependent on the level at which we are looking for (and able to find, hopefully) common rules of formation.

The analysis presented here is based on research conducted during my PhD (Ziai 2004) and focuses on the similarities in development theory amounting to a discourse of development. The empirical work in my thesis – based on publications of and interviews with staff of different development organisations – resulted in the hypothesis that this discourse of development is being transformed since the 'crisis of development' in the 1980s and the corresponding rise of new discourses in the field of development policy (neoliberalism, sustainability, participation, etc.). However, this transformation will be dealt with later (chapters 7–9). The historical transformation of colonial discourse which led to the emergence of development discourse will be discussed later in this chapter. The following remarks refer primarily to the period of the 1950s to the 1970s, but many of the features encountered are still prevalent today.

Discourses do not emerge on an abstract level, they are formed under specific historical circumstances and, at times as parts of a dispositive (apparatus) which links discursive and nondiscursive practices, in reaction to strategic necessities (Foucault 1980: 194f). Without going into detail (see chapter 2), one could argue that development discourse, drawing on 19th century evolutionism as well as on concepts of social technology, emerged out of colonial discourse during the first half of the 20th century as a problem-solving theory which linked the newly-perceived problem of global inequality to the geopolitical and economic interests of the US and its allies. As a discourse of 'the West and the Rest' (Hall 1992), it provided an analysis of societies of Africa, Asia and Latin America with a focus on their deficiencies in comparison to the ideal Western society and on the interventions necessary to improve them, to implement or induce processes of *development*.

Formation of objects

Correspondingly, the objects of development discourse were sociogeographically defined units (states, but also regions or villages) classified as *underdeveloped* (see also Ferguson 1994). The limitation of these units, mostly according to state borders, forms the basis on which statements on the 'level of development' are being made and has the effect of marginalising the vast differences in standards of living within these units. More specifically, certain aspects of these units appeared as objects of development discourse, aspects which were very heterogeneous – ranging from population growth, the lack of 'achievement motivation', an inadequate savings rate, an insufficiently diversified economy, unsustainable agricultural practices, an inadequate integration of women, to problems of bureaucracy and governance – but they all adhered to a certain rule of formation: they appeared and gained visibility as elements explaining the *underdevelopment* of the societies in question and thus as deficiencies to be corrected by interventions of development policy.

The appearance of the objects is regulated by a pattern of specification which makes visible (Escobar 1988) and registers ways of life deviating from the norm through certain indicators and simultaneously defines them as deficient. Generally, development discourse divides the world into *developed* and *underdeveloped* units, and only the latter become the objects of this discourse. Accordingly, global development institutions classify the units as *developed, less developed* and *least developed* or sometimes as high, middle or low income countries. More concretely, we can recognise what Derrida has termed logocentrism. The non-Western world is subjected to hierarchical dichotomies, it is described solely according to the criteria of and in relation to the West: as non- or less industrialised, non- or less rational, non- or less democratic, etc., all in all as an inferior version of the original. The countries of Western Europe and North America, though, have hardly been seen as *developing* by development theory, they belonged to the realm of logos, of pure and invariable presence in no need of explanation (Manzo 1991). This also explains why development theory and policy have (with few exceptions) been dealing only with those regions where there was no or too little *development*: they are social science disciplines dealing with the Other.

A central part of the rules of formation of the objects of discourse is therefore that the objects are judged not according to what they are but what they are supposed to become one day according to the order of discourse.[2] To achieve this goal, measures founded on knowledge about these objects, their future state and the process of transition are necessary. The rule governing the appearance of objects in this discourse thus implies the diagnosis of a deficit as well as measures to compensate it through knowledge-based interventions. However, because the problem-solving envisioned by the discourse has to fail in terms of transforming the objects according to the norm – on the one hand because of the magnitude of the task, on the other because the order of discourse defines these objects as the Other of the norm[3] – there are at best partial successes and often failures. These give rise to new, modified attempts of problem-solving through making visible, incorporating and treating a new aspect of the object. In the history of development theory, this new aspect was first infrastructure, then the rural poor, basic needs, women, ecology, the market and governance, to name but the most prominent (Escobar 1995, Rist 1997). After admitting the failures of *development* the expansion of the object area to new aspects and new plans for transforming society according to the ideal of 'real' *development* follow. This is possible through the invention of new subdiscourses or the linkage of development discourse to others.

Formation of enunciative modalities

The enunciative modalities in discourse are also governed by certain regularities. The competence and legitimacy to make statements and knowledge claims is confined to development experts – mostly, but by no means necessarily, white men from *developed* countries. The institutional places from which the discourse is possible are on the one hand organisations or institutions of development policy, on the other hand also certain university departments dealing with issues of *development* (often from economics, agricultural science, political science, sociology, anthropology or geography). Truth claims on the objects are usually based on the knowledge production of these experts and institutions.

The most important of the rules of formation regarding the modalities of articulation is the one governing the subject positions. While there might be different subject positions of academics, politicians and practitioners, a statement in development discourse implies the position of a person who knows what *development* is and how it can be achieved. Only from this position meaningful statements within the discourse are possible. Statements from a different position and therefore not claiming this kind of knowledge are outside the discursive formation, and are judged to be useless from the perspective of this discourse. However, because *development* is conceived as the state of a 'good society' and the process of getting there, and because there are in fact different conceptions of how such a society should look like and which measures are necessary to achieve it, the position one has to adopt implies the subordination of other people's views on desirable social change. Development discourse therefore constructs the subject position of a knowing and prescribing expert and thus invariably contains an authoritarian element. This effect of the enunciative modality is independent of the intention of the subject occupying the subject position. Statements from locals, which are nowadays also sometimes to be found in development policy, merely serve to underline the necessity to *develop* by articulating their 'development needs', and thus to support the authority of the experts, but do not question the assumption that there is *development* in terms of a universal conception of a good society and that there is expert knowledge on how to achieve this state.

Formation of concepts

Concerning the formation of concepts in development discourse, there are two main characteristics to be identified: First, in analogy to the object *underdevelopment* problems are conceived as deviations from the norm and the concepts are formed correspondingly: illiterate, malnourishment, unemployment, overpopulation (Escobar 1995: 41). One could add failed states, bad governance, defective democracies and other concepts. The implied norm is that of the *developed* society. This norm is present as well in 'positive' concepts like 'good governance' and 'ownership', the rule is that in *underdeveloped* societies there is a lack – a lack of capital, of knowledge, of entrepreneurship, of technology, of accountability – but always a lack which is responsible for the problems and which is addressed by these concepts.

Second, in the history of development theory and policy, the arrangement of concepts occurs according to a general pattern. An aspect of the objects is identified as a crucial factor leading to *underdevelopment* and a corresponding concept gains significance. The claim is that if this concept is given political priority, the

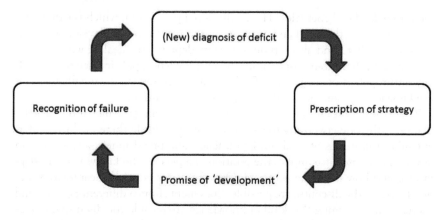

Figure 4.1 The cycle of the 'development' gaze

problem of *underdevelopment* will be solved and *development* will take place. After the desired results fail to appear, the insufficient implementation of the policy advice by institutions and organisations of *development* is made responsible and bemoaned. But soon scientific studies reveal the importance of a new factor hitherto neglected, and a new concept is promoted in development policy, reiterating the promise of well-being and abundance in the future – if the correct policies are applied. There is a cycle of diagnosis – prescription and promise – disappointment – new diagnosis, etc., in which new concepts emerge regularly.

Formation of strategies

According to Foucault, a discursive formation does not occupy the whole space prefigured by the rules of formation of its objects, modalities of articulation and concepts. Its actual content is guided by the formation of strategies or thematic choices, and these are related to historical factors and social functions. The rules of formation outlined so far imply that some countries are seen as the norm, but not which ones. In the case of development discourse, the industrialised societies of North America and Western Europe constituted the norm. (The historical factors and social functions are discussed in the section 'The rise of development discourse'.) Regarding the history and heterogeneity of development discourse, we can discern points of incompatibility, points in which the rules of discourse led to the formation of elements which were incompatible with each other, though still part of the same discourse, and constituted discursive subsets. Incompatible elements were for example the promotion of capitalist or socialist paths to *development*, of export orientation or import substitution, of balanced or unbalanced growth. A great deal of the conflicts in development theory took place between the discursive subsets of modernisation and dependency theories. The latter did not fundamentally break with development discourse, but implied significant modifications mainly on the level of thematic choices (strategies promoted to achieve *development*). The same holds true for most theories of 'alternative development', as the Post-Development critics have correctly pointed out. A critique of development policy demanding better projects or a more equal distribution of resources still remains within the same discursive formation. To a lesser extent, this even holds true for a critique formulating a goal different from modern industrial society. Only a fundamental rejection of the possibility of comparing and evaluating societies according to universal standards, of expert knowledge on *development* constitutes a break with the discourse.

But there is more to be said on the formation of strategies in development discourse. Regarding the interaction between discursive and nondiscursive practices, it seems that there is a dependency or at least a strong relationship of the theories and strategies in development policy with the historical constellation of North-South relations. During the late 1960s and early 1970s, when actors like the G77 and the Non-Aligned Movement were active and influential, development aid gained in importance and the policy recommendations of development institutions were often concerned with regulating markets and 'redistribution with growth' (Chenery et al. 1972). With these actors becoming less significant, with the debt crisis of 1982 and finally with the end of the Cold War, the economic and geopolitical constellation changed: development cooperation became less important and the policy recommendations of development institutions often refocused on growth (without redistribution) and promoted liberalisation – according to critics in the interest of Northern companies and banks. The new concept of good governance which rose to prominence during the 1990s was possible only after the perceived necessity to support anti-communist dictatorships had diminished with the demise of the Soviet Union. Apparently the formation of theories and strategies in development discourse was significantly influenced by nondiscursive practices and specific historical constellations.

In the transformation of development discourse during the neoliberal 'counter-revolution' (Toye), which abandons the Eurocentric and paternalist, but also visionary and somewhat egalitarian prospect of 'developing the underdeveloped regions' through political programmes and interventions (see chapter 8), an aspect is highlighted to which Frederick Cooper has pointed already in his words of caution against the Post-Development critique: that the discourse of development could be read not only as a 'form of European particularism imposed abroad', but also as a discourse of universal rights which lays claim on a 'globally defined standard of living' (1997: 84). This ambivalence becomes even clearer in the context of colonial discourses.

The rise of development discourse: empirical observations

To the above analysis of development discourse, which in a simplified form can be found already in some Post-Development writings, critics have replied that the focus on the second half of the 20th century is misplaced: concept and practice of *development* were older than that and could be found in practices of colonial development or even in 19th century policies to address the problems of capitalist progress within Europe (Cowen/Shenton 1996). While the similarities of practices and their legitimations are certainly relevant, practices in Europe have, however, usually not been based on a discourse of the 'West' and the 'Rest', in the sense that they have not constituted ontological differences between different races or cultures, which is a central point in development discourse. The other criticism deserves closer attention: if practices concerned with 'developing the Other' in Africa and Asia were already a part of colonialism, then an examination of development discourse has to deal with the 1920s and 1930s just as the 1960s and 1970s. One could object that the establishment of a host of organisations, institutions, ministries, university departments, etc., dealing with the issue of *development* and providing jobs for countless 'development experts' – what has been called the development industry, but in Foucault's terms can be described as the dispositive of development, as an ensemble of discursive and nondiscursive practices united by a strategic purpose – took place predominantly after 1950. However, in this section I propose that one could also argue that even on the level of discourse it is possible to discern a number of discontinuities and differences between colonial conceptions of development and the discourse on development in the second half of the 20th century. These will be shown using quotes from influential policy documents and politicians from 1900 to 1960.

During this period, the discourse of development as it was described in the section 'The structure of development discourse') was formed. This formation was characterised by a specific interaction of discursive and nondiscursive practices, the discourse was shaped by its historical context and its social functions. Drawing on Alcalde's (1987) study on the emerging idea of Third World Development, the historical context can briefly be described as follows: the First World War hastened the emergence of the US as the dominant economic power and the decline of Great Britain. It also caused a wave of anti-colonial nationalism in the colonies which Britain sought to appease with measures of economic reform and promises of material well-being. The League of Nations represented a new responsibility of the international community for the welfare of *less developed* countries. The Great Depression of 1929 had several effects which played a role as well: Roosevelt's New Deal as a project of government planning and welfare programs on the one hand and impoverishing effects which led to international comparisons of standards of living on the other. Finally, the aim of drawing the advanced economies out of the recession caused Eugene Staley to conceive of an 'international development program' linking the development of Third World countries with operations of international capital. World War II not only ended US isolationism but gave new strategic value to the *development* and welfare of these countries and provided experience with development assistance as a policy instrument – also for governments in the South. The beginning Cold War restored development assistance after a brief interval (neither in Bretton Woods 1944 nor in San Francisco 1945 was it envisioned as a part of the postwar economic order), mainly triggered by strategic concerns of a geopolitical, but also an economic nature.

In this historical context, the strategic necessity which gave rise to the dispositive of development was to establish and maintain economic relations based on a colonial division of labour in a liberal world economy with countries striving for or having already achieved independence. The promise of material well-being in the discourse of development had the aim to keep Third World states from pursuing a socialist path to progress and at the same time ensured their role as suppliers of raw materials and markets for manufactured products (in particular for a US economy geared to wartime production). Development discourse conceptualised the newly perceived problem of inequality in terms of a lack of capital, knowledge and technology and provided corresponding solutions: financial and technological assistance and development projects based on expert knowledge. A perception of global inequality in terms of exploitation, power relations and hierarchies in the global political economy was thus excluded.[4] Alcalde concludes:

> The first and broadest function of the idea of development was to give economic activity, particularly foreign economic activity, a positive and essential meaning for the lives of less-developed peoples. Whether it was Woodrow Wilson associating American exports with the happiness of mankind, the League Covenant and British colonialists linking development and welfare, New York financiers enticing foreign governments to contract American loans, Eugene Staley proposing a program of industrialization for the welfare of the Third World, or Sumner Welles spreading the creed of peace and prosperity, the aim was essentially the same: enhancing a mental linkage between capitalism and well-being in the South.
>
> (Alcalde 1987: 223)

Now what are the differences I have asserted regarding the discourse of development which emerged under these circumstances and with these strategic functions, and the colonial discourse, which also talked about *development* in Africa and Asia? I believe that significant discontinuities can be identified. They can be found in the constitution of the object of the discourse, the enunciative modalities, the concept and in the strategies and to my mind they allow us to differentiate between colonial and development discourse.

Differences in the formation of the object

Whereas both discourses are dealing with societies in Africa, Asia and Latin America which have to be improved (civilised or *developed* by experts from the North), the crucial difference to the West on the level of ontology which qualifies them as objects of the discourse is based on biological considerations in the one and on economic considerations in the other case: colonial discourse refers not only to uncivilised territories but also to uncivilised peoples, while development discourse predominantly talks about *underdeveloped* regions. The object of colonial discourse is constituted as a biological and anthropological unit, the object of development discourse as a political or geographical unit with certain economic qualities. This can be seen in Article 22 of the League of Nations from 1919 which refers to 'colonies and territories which as a consequence of the late war have ceased to be under the sovereignty of the States which formerly governed them and which are inhabited by peoples not yet able to stand by themselves under the strenuous conditions of the modern world'. These people are thus unable to govern themselves, and require guidance by people from other nations. Therefore, 'the tutelage of such peoples should be entrusted to advanced nations who by reason of their resources, their experience or their geographical position can best undertake this responsibility'. Note that the document does not any longer explicitly assert racial superiority – colonial discourse around 1900 often talked about 'self-governing races' and others (Alcalde 1987: 4) – but still denies that the people in these countries qualify for the principle of self-determination determinedly propagated by US President Wilson.

Thirty years later, in Truman's often quoted inaugural address where as a point four he announced a program of international development assistance, we also hear about territories and peoples: 'we must embark on a bold new program for making the benefits of our scientific advances and industrial progress available for the improvement and growth of *underdeveloped* areas. More than half the people of the world are living in conditions approaching misery. . . . For the first time in history, humanity possesses the knowledge and the skill to relieve the suffering of these people. . . . I believe that we should make available to peace-loving peoples the benefits of our store of technical knowledge in order to help them realize their aspirations for a better life'. The object of the discourse are *underdeveloped* areas, and though the people living there lack science and industrial progress, nowhere do we find a hint that they themselves are backward or inferior or unable to govern themselves. (What we do find is a limitation of the noble efforts to 'peace-loving' – that is noncommunist – peoples.) Instead, we already find a reference to the activity of these peoples (they try to realise their aspirations for a better life and by democracy – probably in the sense of self-determination – will be stirred into 'triumphant action' against hunger, misery and despair). So the doctrine of racial inferiority which appears in the League of Nations document only in a relatively modest version but is still present, has been abandoned in the Truman speech.

Differences in the formation of enunciative modalities

The different formation of the object of the discourse implies a different subject position for non-Western people. Whereas in colonial discourse the subject position of colonised peoples was mainly that of an inferior, backward and uncivilised other in need of education and guidance from the white man, this has changed in development discourse: the appellation is no longer a version of 'you are backward because of your race' but rather of 'you are backward for historical and cultural reasons – and we can help you to become like us and no longer be backward'. In Truman's speech, the people in the South are no longer portrayed as children unable to cope with modernity on their own, but as (future) equal partners in the United Nations whose *underdevelopment* is a matter of their being less fortunate and will be redressed by 'a program of development based on the concepts of democratic fair-dealing'. The technocratic explanation of global inequality identifies 'modern scientific and technical knowledge' as being the key to greater productivity and thus prosperity, and this knowledge can be made available to peace-loving peoples. So the subject position of development experts is opened to nonwhites who acquire this knowledge. *Development* thus becomes a matter of culture and technology: anyone can achieve it now, no one is condemned to remain in the undignified condition of *underdevelopment* – all you have to do is modernise and industrialise and do as the West does. So while the uncivilised are clearly inferior, the *underdeveloped* are also deficient and dependent on the assistance of the West, but they are given the prospect of catching up, they are potentially equal competitors in the race for productivity and growth. This can also be seen in the UN charter, which affirms in Article 1 'the principle of equal rights and self-determination of all peoples'. Of course at that time (1945) many countries were still colonised and the charter includes a declaration regarding non-self-governing territories (Chapter XI). However, it talks about 'territories whose peoples have not yet attained a full measure of self-government' (Article 73) – a statement which does not deny the status quo but no longer legitimates it by referring to an alleged inability of these peoples to govern themselves. This dubious (or, to be frank: racist) claim has disappeared since 1919. A change in the formation of enunciative modalities of the discourse in the shape of a subject position accorded to the South which is almost (but not quite) equal to that of the North is evident.[5] This vastly more attractive subject position offered by the development discourse explains why it was taken up and appropriated in the South far more enthusiastically than the colonial discourse.

Differences in the constitution of concepts

Related to this new subject position and to this appropriation is a difference concerning the central concept of the discourse: while the uncivilised need to be civilised from outside – a weak version is the tutelage by more advanced nations mentioned in the League of Nations – the *underdeveloped* can *develop* by themselves, at least if they are assisted by the US and other *developed* nations. This is the picture drawn by Truman's address where the role of the latter is mostly confined to 'help' the people's 'own efforts' to 'produce more food, more clothing, more materials for housing, and more mechanical power'. Thus to *develop* is within this discourse an activity which is no longer performed by external actors, the verb is no longer exclusively transitive but becomes intransitive (again):[6] countries can *develop* themselves.

Differences in the constitution of strategies

Another difference between colonial and postcolonial usage of *development* implying different strategies can be observed if we trace the relation between signifier and signified. Whereas *development* in colonial discourse predominantly referred to the exploitation of resources and the development of agriculture, industry and infrastructure, in the post–World War II context it evidently included social aspects which were not necessarily linked to the term in former times.[7] This transition can be seen if we compare the British Colonial Development Act of 1929 to the Colonial Development and Welfare Bill of 1940. The former aimed at 'aiding and developing agriculture and industry in certain colonies and territories' and listed 14 different types of activity to achieve these aims, from the adoption of improved machinery in agriculture, the improvement of transport, the construction of harbours, to the supply of electricity and the *development* of mineral resources. Only one of these 14, the promotion of public health, was actually concerned with the well-being of the people living in these areas. In the second edition of this law, presented in 1940, the emphasis has clearly shifted. Not only is the very title changed to explicitly include the welfare of the people, the aim is also reformulated, it is now to 'promote the development of the resources of any colony or the welfare of its people'. It becomes clear that these are taken to be two different objectives united here in this law – a conception that seems rather strange for the student of *development* as we know it. In the postwar era, these two aspects – *development* of resources and industry and social welfare of the people – are usually conflated under the heading of 'economic and social progress and development' (UN charter Article 55, 1945), 'economic and social development' (UN General Assembly Resolution 1710 announcing the first Development Decade, 1960) or simply *development*. However, even though the term *development* is increasingly employed to denote social as well as economic progress, the strategies applied to achieve these aims and the indicators used to measure this progress are predominantly of an economic nature. The focus in concepts and practices of *development* at that time is mostly on economic growth and sometimes the necessary growth rates are exactly specified (see the UN General Assembly Resolutions 1710 and 2626 on the development decades), as are the necessary financial transfers from the developed economies (e.g. UN Resolutions 1711 and 2626) or the necessary savings rates in developing economies (Rostow 1960). This reflects the then dominant belief in the trickle-down effect: economic growth will automatically lead to social welfare and poverty reduction – a belief that was at least badly shaken if not refuted by the results of the Pearson Report 1969 but has in some circles survived until today. So the meaning of *development* has apparently changed between 1929 and 1960: it still refers primarily to economic progress but in the later phase this is identified with social progress as well.

To sum up the results of the analysis in a slightly simplified manner, the discontinuities between two ways of speaking about social change in Africa, Asia and Latin America refer to a different formation of the object of discourse (countries instead of peoples), a different formation of enunciative modalities (almost equal and merely culturally inferior subject position instead of racial inferiority), a different formation of the central concept (intransitive instead of transitive verb) and a different strategic focus (economic and social progress instead of merely economic focus). It can be seen that three of the four differences identified are related to a crucial discursive shift: the ability of peoples in Africa and Asia to govern themselves is no longer denied in the discourse prevalent in later documents, the trusteeship for the *development* of these regions is being transferred to indigenous elites, supported by Northern or multilateral institutions and organisations of development.

Now where does this discursive shift come from? Tracing again the relation between discursive and nondiscursive events, it appears likely that the explicit racism which was central to legitimise colonial rule was largely discredited after World War II and the Holocaust and in the face of anticolonial movements and Cold War rivalry a new way of conceptualising the relation between North and South was seen as appropriate which operated without the notion of racial superiority. The UN charter and the Universal Declaration of Human Rights affirmed the equality of all peoples and in order not to violate this new principle, a transformation of colonial discourse was required. As this transformation consisted of changes in the formation of objects, subject position and concept of the discourse, it seems possible to argue that we are dealing with a new discursive formation: colonial discourse was replaced by a new way of speaking: a discourse of development. To be sure, there is an element of arbitrariness involved in this distinction, which is, however, inevitable if we take a constructivist instead of a positivist stance. Yet the differences listed above seem significant enough to attribute a central role to the transfer of trusteeship and thus to justify this distinction. Of course, it is possible to find in postcolonial texts on development arguments which recur on the alleged inability of people in Africa, Asia or Latin America to responsibly govern themselves – usually in discursive legitimations of military interventions. And it may be possible to find texts from the colonial era which adopt a stance attributed here to a discourse of development. But the majority of texts – this assertion is made here – adheres to different rules and manifests a 'system of dispersion' which allows us to identify two different discursive formations.

It could be argued that both discourses historically still belong to the colonial era, and it is correct that the documents analysed here originate from points in time (1945–1960) where especially in Africa colonialism was well in power. However, the universalism of the declaration of human rights in 1948 and other texts already marks the beginning of a postcolonial era because it delegitimises the justifications which provide the foundation of colonial rule. Therefore we can differentiate between colonial and postcolonial discourses centred on *development* even before the end of (formal) colonialism.

Conclusion

The chapter has examined the methodological rules outlined by Michel Foucault's archaeological approach to discourse analysis. It has proposed to modify it to address its problematic aspects (conception of autonomous discourses, positivist epistemological stance), but to retain its other methodological features (focus on discontinuities, structures and rules of formation). This methodological approach was then applied to the field of development theory and policy in order to identify the structure of development discourse which consists of specific rules of formation concerning the objects, concepts, enunciative modalities and strategies of the discourse. In the last part, the question is addressed whether the discourse of colonial development adheres to the same rules as the discourse on development identified for the second half of the 20th century. On the basis of empirical examples from a number of policy documents,[8] the chapter concludes that the transfer of trusteeship which is evident in the era of decolonisation implies changes in the rules of formation which allow us to speak about a new discourse: a discourse of development.

Notes

1   Chapter 4 is based on a keynote lecture given at the conference 'Developing Africa. Development Discourse(s) in Late Colonialism' in Vienna, January 13–15, 2011.
2   Therefore, policy practices inspired by the Post-Development critique of development discourse have superseded the analysis of 'needs' within a community with an analysis of the 'assets' present (Gibson-Graham 2005).
3   'Inferior alterity, the 'other', is needed for the West's self-construction as *developed*. If it were possible for Western commercial industrialisation to spread the world over, the West would lose its primacy' (Biccum 2002: 39).
4   The renowned economist Kenneth Boulding thus asserted in 1945: 'The black mass of grinding poverty. . . . is not due primarily to exploitation, or to bad distribution of income, or to lack of purchasing power. It is due to the sheer unproductiveness of the mass of human labor. . . . It is not unfair, therefore, to regard economic progress – increase in output per head – as the prime desideratum and to relegate distributional justice to the position of an important side issue as far as the abolition of poverty is concerned' (cited in Alcalde 1987: 151).
5   For the notion of colonized people in the process of colonial education becoming almost the same, but not quite, see Bhabha 1994.
6   In its original use in enlightenment philosophy, the term referred to an intransitive activity.
7   For a more detailed account of concepts and practices of colonial development, see Hodge et al. 2014.
8   As the empirical basis of these conclusions is not too broad, further research is needed to substantiate the claims.

Bibliography

Primary sources:

Charter of the United Nations, 1945.
Colonial Development Act, 1929.
Colonial Development and Welfare Bill, 1940.
Covenant of the League of Nations, 1919.
Inaugural address of President Harry S. Truman, January 20, 1949.
UN General Assembly resolution 1522 (XV). Accelerated flow of capital and technical assistance to the developing countries, 1960.
UN General Assembly resolution 1710 (XVI). United Nations Development Decade. A programme for international economic co-operation, 1961.

UN General Assembly resolution 2626 (XXV). International Development Strategy for the Second United Nations Development Decade, 1970.

Literature:

Alcalde, Javier Gonzalo 1987: *The Idea of Third World Development. Emerging Perspectives in the United States and Britain, 1900–1950.* Lanham, MD: University Press of America.

Bhabha, Homi 1994: *The Location of Culture.* London: Routledge.

Biccum, A. R., April 2002: Interrupting the Discourse of Development: On a Collision Course with Postcolonial Theory. *Culture, Theory & Critique* 43(1), 33–50.

Chenery, Hollis/Ahluwalia, Montek S./Bell, C.L.G./Duloy, John H./Jolly, Richard 1973: *Redistribution With Growth: Policies to Improve Income Distribution in Developing Countries in the Context of Economic Growth.* Oxford: Oxford University Press.

Cooper, Frederick 1997: Modernizing Bureaucrats, Backward Africans, and the Development Concept. In: Cooper, Frederick/Packard, Randall (eds.) *International Development and the Social Sciences: Essays on the History and Politics of Knowledge.* Berkeley: University of California Press, 64–92.

Cowen, Michael P./Shenton, Robert W. 1996: *Doctrines of Development.* London: Routledge.

Dreyfus, Hubert L./Rabinow, Paul 1983: *Michel Foucault: Beyond Structuralism and Hermeneutics.* Chicago: University of Chicago Press.

Escobar, Arturo 1988: Power and Visibility. Development and the Invention and Management of the Third World. *Cultural Anthropology* 3(4), 428–43.

Escobar, Arturo 1995: *Encountering Development: The Making and Unmaking of the Third World.* Princeton, NJ: Princeton University Press.

Ferguson, James 1994 (1990): *The Anti-Politics Machine: 'Development', Depoliticization and Bureaucratic Power in Lesotho.* Minneapolis. University of Minnesota Press.

Foucault, Michel 1972 (1969): *The Archaeology of Knowledge & The Discourse on Language.* New York: Pantheon Books.

Foucault, Michel 1980: *Power/Knowledge: Selected Interviews & Other Writings 1972–1977.* New York: Pantheon.

Gibson-Graham, J. K. 2005: Surplus Possibilities: Postdevelopment and Community Economies. *Singapore Journal of Tropical Geography* 26(1), 4–26.

Hall, Stuart 1992: The West and the Rest: Discourse and Power. In: Hall, Stuart/Gieben, Bram (eds.) *Formations of Modernity.* London: Polity Press, 276–320.

Hodge, Joseph/Hödl, Gerald/Kopf, Martina (eds.) 2014: *Developing Africa. Concepts and Practices in Twentieth-Century Colonialism.* Manchester: Manchester University Press.

Manzo, Kate 1991: Modernist Discourse and the Crisis of Development Theory. *Studies in Comparative International Development* 26(2), 3–36.

Rist, Gilbert 1997: *The History of Development: From Western Origins to Global Faith.* London: Zed Books.

Rostow, Walt Whitman 1960: *The Stages of Growth: A Non-Communist Manifesto.* Cambridge: Cambridge University Press.

Wodak, Ruth/Meyer, Michael 2009: Critical Discourse Analysis: History, Agenda, Theory. In: Wodak, Ruth/Meyer, Michael (eds.) *Methods of Critical Discourse Analysis.* London: Sage, 1–33.

Ziai, Aram 2004: *Entwicklung als Ideologie? Das klassische Entwicklungsparadigma und die Post-Development Kritik.* Hamburg: Deutsches Übersee-Institut.

5   The concept of 'development' and why it should be abandoned

Let me start by juxtaposing two quotes coming both from the broad field of development studies:

> Development research is important. It helps to solve development problems and thus to fight poverty.
>
> (ZEF news nr. 23, editorial, February 2011)

> It seems to us today almost non-sensical to deny that there is such a thing as 'development', or to dismiss it as a meaningless concept.
>
> (Ferguson 1994: xiii)

While the first quote affirms the importance of research about *development* and suggests that the content of the term is concerned with poverty and the struggle against it, the second one considers the possibility of its emptiness and questions its very existence. How can that be? This chapter tries to shed light on this paradox. It discusses the usage of the concept of *development* in development policy and research and its effects and argues that there are good reasons for giving up the concept of *development* and replacing it with various other concepts. However, this should not be misunderstood as a call to dismiss all practices which aim at improving the human condition. Yet there is no need to identify these practices with the term *development*. On the contrary, as numerous practices which have definitely not improved the human condition have been carried out in the name of *development*, it might be a good idea to reject this connection. The chapter argues that these negative phenomena should not be seen as an abuse of a positive concept, but as linked to certain Eurocentric, depoliticising and authoritarian implications of the concept of *development*.

In the first section, the chapter will lay out the theoretical background of the argument and give reasons for the subsequent engagement with conceptual questions, establishing the relevance of discourse analysis. The second section deals with the concept of *development* in the social scientific literature. In the following section I will then argue that development researchers need to abandon the concept because *development* has Eurocentric, depoliticising and authoritarian implications. The fourth section will then deal with the hypothetical and actual attempts to redefine the concept – and with their limits. Subsequently, the fifth section analyses the numerous misunderstandings which result also from these frequent redefinitions. The final section will then try to answer the question of what other concepts can be employed.

Theoretical background: the relevance of discourse

Since the establishment of the linguistic turn in the social sciences, few scholars would still maintain that language merely mirrors an objective reality which is there for all to see. In everyday life, the question of how language represents our reality becomes apparent when different people see different things although they observe the same event: are the combatants of Hamas (of the FARC, of the EZLN, of the PKK, of the LTTE, etc.) freedom fighters or terrorists? Are the military attacks of US forces in Syria (in Afghanistan, in Iraq, in Yugoslavia, in Somalia) an imperialist war or a humanitarian intervention? Of course, one might give definitions and criteria and reasonable arguments, but the decisive point is that it makes a fundamental difference whether we describe reality in one way or another. As a consequence of our perception, some political actions will appear as legitimate, and others as illegitimate or even criminal. In development research, the same pattern applies when we classify China (Brazil, India, South Africa, etc.) as a regional power or as a *developing* country. Language constructs our reality, and the specific way in which it does so has consequences.

Not entering into theoretical debates and differences here (see Keller 2005, Diaz-Bone et al. 2007, Wodak/Meyer 2009), the term discourse usually denotes a structure in the way reality (or a certain aspect of it) is constructed through language. Building on poststructuralism (which itself is based on structural linguistics) (Münker/Roesler 2000, Belsey 2002) the smallest unit in language is the sign, and the sign is composed of the signifier (e.g., the word 'tree') and the signified (the large thing with twigs and leaves under whose shadow we can read romantic poems and get stung by bees). According to structural linguistics, the relation between signifier and signified is arbitrary (in other language systems, different words are used), and the sign carries meaning as a result of differences between the signifiers ('tree' is different from 'bee' and 'sea'). Thus our access to reality is only through language, through systems of representation in which certain signifiers are linked to certain signifieds.

Now poststructuralism maintains that these systems that structural linguistics talks of are by no means unambiguous, discrete and stable. On the contrary, they are sometimes ambiguous and allow for misunderstandings, they cannot be easily delineated, and each relation between signifier and signified is inherently unstable and has to be reproduced continuously. Thus, discourses can be described as systems of relations between words (signifiers) and things (signifieds) which construct a topic in a certain way. They provide certain statements, images and arguments. Following Foucault (1972, 1980), they possess certain rules on what can be said and regarded as true and are linked with institutionalised knowledge production and relations of power.

This poststructuralist perspective implies a postpositivist stance in terms of meta-theory or philosophy of science, that is the positivist principles of objectivism (value neutral knowledge is possible, separation between fact and value and subject and object in research), empiricism (knowledge is based in empirical matters only and empirical testing of hypotheses is the only valid way of generating knowledge) and naturalism (just like the natural sciences, social science should aim to explain and predict reality through universal laws) are rejected (Smith 1996). The methodological consequence is that this chapter is predominantly confined to the meta-theoretical level while being compatible with different theoretical perspectives.[1] The argument proceeds by reviewing the literature and discussing the concept of *development*, it does not seek to establish whether one or the other construction of reality can be empirically verified but primarily explores their political implications. These are important because discourses have significant effects in terms of enabling or legitimating certain practices while rendering others unthinkable.

The concept of *development*

For reasons of space, only a cursory and incomplete review of the literature on the concept of *development* will be provided here. While most surveys on the history of development theory begin in the mid-20th century, a broader perspective proves to be illuminating and allows to draw parallels to earlier conceptions of political economy (see Martinussen 1997, Chang 2003) or social philosophy (Kößler 1998). A thorough examination of these predecessors (Ziai 2004a) yields that development theory has two roots: 19th century evolutionism (and earlier philosophies of history) (Nisbet 1969) and 19th century social technology (building on Enlightenment philosophy and designed to reconcile order and progress in the face of the problems caused by industrial capitalism) (Cowen/Shenton 1996). Evolutionism assumed that social change in societies proceeds according to a universal pattern (usually in historical stages), while social technology claimed that social interventions based on expert knowledge (possessed by a privileged group that acts as a trustee for the common good) are necessary to achieve positive social change. Both roots can be found in 20th century development theory, which is as often a 'description of ongoing self-propelled processes of social change' as it is a 'blueprint for action' (Cooper/Packard 1997: 8). In a more critical vein, Alcalde (1987: 223), concerning the rise of the idea of Third World *development* during the first half of the 20th century, argues that the 'first and broadest function of the idea of development was to give economic activity, particularly foreign economic activity, a positive and essential meaning for the lives of less-developed peoples'.

This critical perspective on *development* is characteristic of the so-called Post-Development school in development theory (see above all Esteva 1987, Sachs 1992, Escobar 1995, Rahnema 1997a, for the debate see Ziai 2004a, 2007). Whereas earlier critiques of development theory and policy were usually focusing on inadequacies and shortcomings which prevented the achievement of development in the South, Post-Development launched a fundamental critique which rejected the entire paradigm and denounced *development* as a 'failed project' (Esteva 1985: 78f) and an 'ideology' (Rahnema 1997b: 379). Already here it becomes visible that in Post-Development, *development* refers on the one hand to the practices of post–World War II aid which aimed at *developing* the *underdeveloped* regions, on the other hand to a certain concept of social change. This article will deal exclusively with the latter, leaving aside the rather controversial call to stop all projects of development aid.

Post-Development has been widely criticised, above all for homogenising *development* and neglecting its positive aspects, for romanticising local communities and legitimising oppressive traditions, and for being just as paternalistic as the chastised development experts (see above all Corbridge 1998, Kiely 1999, Nederveen Pieterse 2000). However, it has been shown that these criticisms are justified only in respect to some Post-Development texts, but not to others, leading to a differentiation between neopopulist and skeptical Post-Development (Ziai 2004b).

Ahorro (2008) identifies a second wave of Post-Development which acknowledges that many criticisms of (neopopulist) Post-Development were exaggerated or flawed but wants to build on some of their insights and provides either more balanced empirical findings or a more nuanced critique of development discourse. The chapter attempts to contribute to the latter group.

But is it really possible to talk about the discourse of development in the singular? Are there not vast differences between approaches inspired by modernisation theory or by dependency writers, proponents of balanced or unbalanced growth, export orientation or import substitution, capitalist or socialist development? Of course there are. But there are a number of assumptions and discursive regularities shared by very different perspectives on development theory and policy. Four of them can be termed core assumptions, for they form the basis of nearly everything that is written and spoken on the topic. These are:

1)   The existential assumption: There is such a thing as *development*, i.e. *development* functions as an organising and conceptual frame. An organising frame, because the term allows the linking of diverse social, economic, political and cultural phenomena to a single process of *development*. In the words of Foucault, it allows 'to group a succession of dispersed events, to link them to one and the same organising principle, to subject them to the exemplary power of life . . . to discover, already at work in each beginning, a principle of coherence and the outline of a future unity' (Foucault 1972: 22). A conceptual frame, because the term allows us to make sense of diverse social, economic, political and cultural phenomena, to interpret them as manifestations of *development* and *underdevelopment*. The concept makes the 'images of the ragged poor of Asia [or other continents] . . . legible as markers of a stage of development. . . . Within this problematic, it appears self-evident that debtor Third World nation-states and starving peasants share a common "problem", that both lack a single "thing": "development"' (Ferguson 1994: xiii). In fact, the continuing debt crisis of many states in the South and the chronic hunger prevalent in many rural areas in the South

may both be somehow linked to relations of power in the global political economy, but on a concrete level have quite different causes.

2) The normative assumption: *development* is a good thing. Although rarely made explicit, the assumption is ubiquitous in development policy. *Development* denotes the state of a good society or the process leading to it, which is why Chambers (1997) rephrased it as 'good change'. As a consequence, stagnation is seen as bad, a good society can be achieved only through change and progress.

3) The practical assumption: *development* can be achieved. Not only that *development should* be realised all over the world, it is assumed that it is *possible* to realise it all over the world. The normative and the practical assumption together constitute the foundation of the entire development industry – institutions, experts, projects, etc.

4) The methodological assumption: units can be compared according to their *development*. Units of analysis are usually geographically and politically separated entities: states (sometimes also continents or regions). The possibility of comparison implies that there is a universal scale on which *development* can be measured, leading to the identification of *developed* and *less developed* (or *underdeveloped* or *developing*) units.

These assumptions are, however, quite abstract. They determine that there are *developed* and *less developed* countries, but not which ones. They determine that *development* should be achieved, but not what it looks like and how this can be done. Additional assumptions were necessary, and they are to be found in the classical paradigm of development which was dominant from the 1950s to the 1970s and still is very influential. The most prominent of these concrete assumptions are:

1) The specification of the goal: the industrialised countries of North America and Europe are *developed*. Other countries, specifically those of Asia, Africa and Latin America, are *less developed*. These countries of the global South *need development*.

2) The specification of the process: the countries of the global South need economic growth, industrialisation and modernisation in order to become *developed*. Therefore, specific interventions (also interventions in the market mechanism) are necessary to help them, which usually consist in the transfer of capital, technology and knowledge from the North.

3) The legitimation of the process: These interventions (development projects and programmes) are based on expert knowledge on how to further *development*, how to attain a good society and improve the lives of the people. Therefore, they are legitimate.

Other assumptions contain further specifications and details, e.g. that *development* can be measured by the gross national product or per capita income (an assumption that has been challenged by the Human Development Index since the 1990s) or the philosophical foundations of *Homo oeconomicus*, Cartesian rationality and a Baconian view on nature (see Ziai 2004a).

Why we should abandon the concept

In the first section of this chapter we saw that discourses provide a contingent way of constructing reality; in the second, we dealt with the assumptions of development discourse. This section aims to provide arguments why development researchers should rethink or even dismiss the concept of *development*. It argues that the assumptions outlined in the previous section have Eurocentric, depoliticising and authoritarian implications.

Eurocentric implications

The concept of *development* has Eurocentric implications, because it assumes European societies (including the European settler colonies in North America) as ideal models: they are referred to as *developed*, i.e. as mature and complete in contrast to other societies which are deviations from this norm: the *less developed* or *developing* ones. These are framed linguistically as lacking, backward and inferior. This means that through this denomination other societies are not accepted on their own terms, but merely as inferior versions of one's own society, because the standards of a good society are assumed to be both universal and identical with particular European standards: There is a universal scale of *development* at the top of which we find the US and Western Europe, while poorer societies are deemed traditional and thus have to become modern (i.e. Western). The idea that non-Western societies are historically backward and can be compared to earlier periods of European history has been described as the 'transformation of geo-cultural differences into historical stages' (Nandy 1992: 146), as the 'chronification of spatial co-existence' (Melber 1992: 32) or simply as the 'colonizer's model of the world' (Blaut 1993) because it justified the colonial expansion of the most advanced states. The historical processes that these *developed* societies underwent in the past centuries are thus not seen as contingent (dependent on certain capitalist relations of production, a colonial division of labour and certain – patriarchal – productivist values), but as universal progress of humanity. Here, the evolutionist heritage of the concept of *development* is visible.

In this context, the methodological assumption of discrete development units fails to realise that these historical processes cannot simply be reproduced by other countries in completely different historical (economic, political, social) global environments. And the normative assumption that these processes have led to better, *developed* societies neglects the downside of the historical processes of colonial industrial capitalism as well as the possibility that some cultures or some people in general might object to the assumption that highly individualised consumer societies based on competition, infinite human needs and unimpaired exploitation of nature constitute the best of all possible worlds.

Thus, from the perspective of the West, our own society serves as the standard by which the inferiority of the (*less developed*) Other is identified. The diagnosis implies the therapy: they have to become more like us: more modern, more productive, more secular, more democratic, etc. Not only historically, but also conceptually the project of *developing* the *underdeveloped* continued the older one of civilising the uncivilised. While the Other is constructed as an inferior version of the Self in order to constitute the latter's identity as enlightened and superior (Hall 1992), the attempts to reform the Other in the image of the Self will never succeed entirely – the copy will never achieve the status of the original, at least 'not quite' (Bhabha 1994: 85–92). The concept is tainted with the colonial notion of European superiority.

Now few would contest that for many people in the world, a middle-class existence in the US and the democratic values of the Enlightenment often associated with the West do seem vastly more attractive than their current situation. Does this not prove the superiority of these societies, at least in the eyes of the majority? And here, critics of Post-Development have added, it appears paternalistic and cynical for intellectuals in the North to dismiss the attempts to ameliorate global inequality as Eurocentric and authoritarian. Which right do the rich have to tell the poor that they should not follow their example? As the author is also situated in the North and enjoys a middle-class existence, the question is even more pressing. While the traditional answer of the development expert was that the rich have no right to do so because all people have a claim to the superior way of life, neopopulist Post-Development would answer that this way of life is not superior but destructive (and, implicitly, that it is therefore legitimate to tell the poor not to follow the example of the rich). Skeptical Post-Development would reject both positions and argue that '[t]here are numerous ways of living a "good life", and it is up to each society to invent its own' (Rist 1997: 241).

Still, the attractiveness of North America and Western Europe does not prove the superiority of these societies. Such a conclusion would be premature for several reasons. It leaves out the realisation that many aspects of these *developed* societies, e.g. racism against immigrants, seem not attractive at all to the majority. Migrants are often dissatisfied with their economic and political situation in their country of origin, not with their country or culture in general. It also leaves out the relation between affluence in one and misery in another part of the world and the question of non-universalisable, oligarchic models of society, which can be maintained only because the production of other societies is geared to the demands of the oligarchic society or because their level of pollution does not reach the level of the oligarchic one. And it neglects that although the terms democracy and human rights are sometimes claimed to be European inventions, the underlying concepts of political self-determination, moral standards and individual rights are definitely not, as many tribal societies with consensual democratic decision-making procedures have proven (Sigrist 2005).

Depoliticising implications

The concept of *development* has depoliticising implications, because it obscures inequalities and conflicts on the national and international level. The World Development Reports up until very recently still constructed a scale along which the development units are placed according to their per capita income. Although they also include statistics on Gini-coefficients, this still suggests that the average income denotes a certain level of *development* of the population. This ranking neglects social inequality and the tremendous differences between living standards in the favelas and the residential estates. Not only here, but in general *development* appears as something which refers to the situation of a group of people living in one country and which improves the life of all members of this group (see the methodological and normative assumptions in the second section of this chapter).

Correspondingly, the classical paradigm of development constructs social problems (whose existence is not called into question) in peripheral countries as *development* problems, as problems linked to a lack of capital, knowledge, technology, productivity, institutions, etc., which can be solved by projects or programmes of development which deal with these shortcomings. These development interventions are therefore serving the common good and benefiting all members of society – at least if they are successful. First of all, this perspective again neglects the differences between the supposed beneficiaries, between, say, farmers and landless labourers, small farmers and *latifundistas*, rural and urban poor, men and women, wage labourers and company owners, ruling elites and marginalised groups. Second, this perspective assumes that social problems can be solved with technocratic solutions – with solutions unconcerned with politics, relations of power and conflicts of interest, solutions that are rational and that no one can object to. However, problems of social inequality can only rarely be dealt with successfully in this manner, which is why James Ferguson argues: 'By uncompromisingly reducing poverty to a technical problem, and by promising technical solutions to the sufferings of powerless and oppressed people, the hegemonic problematic of "development" is the principal means through which the question of poverty is de-politicized in the world today' (1994: 256).

In his study of a large integrated rural development programme in Lesotho, Ferguson (1994) not only illustrates that in the name of *development* the massive transfer of resources to the government enabled the ruling party to extend its administrative control in an oppositional province through financial support of its followers and infrastructure projects.[2] He also points out that this technocratic bias in development discourse is reproduced by the institutional interests of development organisations:

> An academic analysis is of no use to a 'development' agency unless it provides a place for the agency to plug itself in, unless it provides a charter for the sort of intervention that the agency is set up to do. An analysis which suggests that the causes of poverty in Lesotho are political and structural (not technical and geographical), that the national government is part of the problem (not a neutral instrument for its solution), and that meaningful change can only come through revolutionary social transformation in South Africa has no place in 'development' discourse simply because 'development' agencies are not in the business of promoting political realignments or supporting revolutionary struggles. . . . For an analysis to meet the needs of 'development' institutions, it must do what academic discourse inevitably

fails to do; it must make Lesotho out to be an enormously promising candidate for the only sort of intervention a 'development' agency is capable of launching: the apolitical, technical 'development' intervention.

(1994: 68f)

In other words: development organisations are designed (and allowed) to launch technocratic projects in the common interest, not to take sides with the less privileged parts of the population in conflicts on the national or international level. So in combating poverty while avoiding political conflict, these organisations try to ameliorate the results of asymmetrical relations of power while not openly questioning or attacking these relations.

Although some NGOs adopt a more political and conflictive stance towards these issues, the large majority of development organisations and consultants knows very well and adheres to the limits of what can be said and written in terms of project proposals and reports without endangering the flow of money in the development industry. It is far easier to obtain funding for improved irrigation systems in agriculture (*development*) than for supporting the struggle of indigenous groups or landless labourers for fundamental social change (politics). And a relatively recent study by Li (2007) illustrates that the depoliticising implications of development discourse are still very influential, even when sustainability and participation are project priorities.

Authoritarian implications

The concept of *development* has authoritarian implications because it prescribes interventions in people's lives that these people themselves may disapprove of. Knowledge about development is knowledge about what a good society looks like and how it can be realised. In so far as there are competing conceptions about this goal and the ways to get there, it invariably contains an authoritarian element because it is based on one particular conception which is then assumed to be universal while other conceptions are ignored or subordinated. Development interventions based on expert knowledge are in the classical paradigm not in need of legitimation by the people affected by these interventions, because they are – as rational measures in the common interest – legitimated through expertise and through their results (output legitimacy, as the political scientists say). Here, the heritage of social technology and the principle of trusteeship are obvious. The experts know better what the people need than they themselves.

This holds true even after the trusteeship has been transferred to national elites after decolonisation, as is demonstrated by laws sanctioning nonparticipation in development projects with corporeal punishment in Tanzania in the 1960s (Potter 2000: 287) by the violence accompanying the campaign to wipe out smallpox in India (Apffel-Marglin 1990), or by the Regional President of Southern Sudan announcing 'If we have to drive our people to paradise with sticks, we will do so for their own good' (Alvares 1992: 108). But of course Western experts still play an important role in the business; one of them self-critically remarks that *development* 'is an empty word which can be filled by any user to conceal any hidden intention, a Trojan horse of a word. It implies that what is done to people by those more powerful than themselves is their fate, their potential, their fault' (Frank 1997: 263).

Still, one might argue that if these interventions have positive results for the people concerned, this might make up for the lack of democratic participation and input legitimacy. This may well be the case, but a look at the history of development policy reveals a long list of White Elephants, failed projects and disastrous consequences of development projects. Probably the most obvious cases are large infrastructure projects like dams. According to the (rather conservative) estimates of the World Dam Commission, 40–80 million people have lost their homes as a result of dam projects in the name of *development* (WCD 2000: xxx). Usually, these people are counted as environmental refugees. It might be more appropriate to refer to them as development refugees.

These interventions are more often than not designed or evaluated for funding by experts who are not locals nor speak the local languages, but who possess universally applicable knowledge on the process of *development*. As the process is assumed to take place in all societies roughly in the same manner, the experts can be sent to any country, even without having been there before. They did not grow up or live in this society, but still they know how it is supposed to change.

Thus it can be argued that the authoritarian implementation of what has been defined as the common good is a structural feature of *development* – despite the attempts to introduce the principles of participation, ownership and empowerment in development policy since the 1980s. While rigidly following these principles would be a powerful antidote against these authoritarian features, the practice shows that participation is in most cases closely confined due to the institutional constraints of the development industry (Cooke/Kothari 2001). As long as there are donors who spend taxpayers' money on *development*, they will be reluctant to give up control, even if only out of responsibility towards their constituency – after all, they are supposed to represent their national interest. Thus orthodox conceptions of politics and identity play an important role in maintaining these relations of power as well.

Because of these Eurocentric, depoliticising and authoritarian implications of the concept it should be abandoned. From the point of view of poststructuralism, these implications have dangerous effects and 'changing the order of the discourse' is no mere linguistic endeavour but 'a political question' (Escobar 1995: 216).

On the difficulty of redefining 'development'

Now one could certainly argue that within the academic debate in development theory, there has been an awareness of some of these criticisms for a considerable time, and that there have been numerous attempts to redefine *development* in a more critical manner. Beyond economic growth, *development* was in the course of its career to include unemployment, basic needs, redistribution, self-reliance, school education, life expectancy, gender equality, empowerment, democracy and human rights or simply freedom. It was redefined as endogenous, participatory, alternative, sustainable and human development. So the response to the criticisms raised above would be that development theory has learned and progressed as a reaction to the criticisms. A similar response, often from the Marxist camp, would be that the criticisms only apply to normative conceptions of *development* (as used in development policy), but not to those that are merely descriptive or analytical and talk about the *development* of capitalism. Within the poststructuralist framework, both could argue that the signifier *development* can be and has been linked to other signifieds than was the case in the classical paradigm, and that a critical redefinition of the concept would therefore be rid of its supposedly nasty implications.

In this context, careful critics have questioned the theoretical coherence of the poststructuralist criticism of development discourse: If it is acknowledged that the meaning of *development* has changed regularly in the history of development policy and is context-specific, up to the point where it was condemned as an 'amoeba-like concept' (Esteva 1985: 79), how can one reject the entire concept irrespective of its content? Crush, commenting on one of the Post-Development proponents (1995: 3), rightly argues: 'in the very call for banishment, Sachs implicitly suggests that it is possible to arrive at an unequivocal definition'.

The answer that can be given to these objections is twofold. For one, most of the redefinitions and alternative concepts of *development* still share most of the core assumptions of development discourse and often even the tenets of the classical paradigm: 'our' society is *developed*, 'theirs' is not, therefore investments and technology and experts from the North are necessary to improve their lives. This holds true even for many of the allegedly descriptive and analytical versions. And even differing concepts of *development* may have a similar function in that irrespective of their content they legitimate interventions based on expert knowledge and carried out under the principle of trusteeship in the name of the common good.

Second, even if the assumptions discussed are questioned by the redefined concept, and this is the case when sustainability leads to rejecting the model of the industrialised countries or when participation and empowerment lead to a rejection of expert knowledge and trusteeship, linking the signifier to a new signified it not as easy as it might seem in the first place:

> *Development cannot delink itself from the words with which it was formed – growth, evolution, maturation. Just the same, those who now use the word cannot free themselves from a web of meanings that impart a specific blindness to their language, thought, and action. No matter the context in which it is used, or the precise connotation that the person using the word wants to give it, the expression becomes qualified and coloured by meanings perhaps unwanted. The word always implies a favourable change, a step from the simple to the complex, from the inferior to the superior, from worse to better. The word indicates that one is doing well because one is advancing in the sense of a necessary, ineluctable, universal law and towards*

*a desirable goal. . . . for two-thirds of the people on earth, this positive meaning of
the word 'development'. . . is a reminder of what they are not. It is a reminder of
an undesirable, undignified condition.*

(Esteva 1992: 19, emphasis in the original)

The web of meanings tied around the concept during six decades of development policy cannot be unmade simply by adopting a progressive definition. The –
perhaps unwanted – implications are still there, even if we try to give the term
a different meaning. Of course, from a poststructuralist point of view, there is
no guarantee that any new alternative concept will not be instrumentalised and
linked to similarly negative images and connotations. However, this possibility
cannot be evaded, there are no pure or essentially critical signifiers, meaning is
always contested and there are always discursive struggles. Regarding the concept
of *development* and its implications, attempts to redefine it in a progressive manner
seem to be but a losing battle, or at least one that faces extremely long odds and
may take decades. A simpler alternative is to drop the concept and find a new one.

On misunderstandings and their productivity

Even if one does not share the analysis presented here regarding the negative
implications of the concept of *development*, I argue there is still a case to abandon
the concept simply because it causes so many misunderstandings and through
this obstructs the academic and political debate. Misunderstandings results from
the fact that the same signifier is linked with different signifieds in the systems
of representation of different actors. Whereas one assumes *development* to denote
a higher income for the rural population, a second links it with a better investment climate for multinational companies leading to employment and economic
growth, a third with sustainable resource use, a fourth with better health care for
mothers and infants, a fifth with economic and cultural imperialism, and a sixth
with an opportunity to make a living in the aid business. *Development* means different things to different people. The productivity of these differences in definition lies in the fact that they allow these people to cooperate without having to
engage in conflict about their different assumptions and world views.

Even a cursory glance reveals that within development projects and programmes the term refers to, e.g. road building, hydroenergy and irrigation,
resettlement, birth control, biodiversity conversation, introduction of more productive agricultural techniques, food-for-work programmes, counterinsurgency
measures, microcredit provision and small enterprise promotion, fighting corruption and improvement in electoral participation (see chapter 10). We simply
have to acknowledge that although these measures may have all been carried out
under the banner of improving living standards and pursuing the common good,
we are dealing with extremely heterogeneous interventions that may affect the
lives of different groups in positive or negative ways.

However, especially the latter aspect is obscured by the normative assumption
that *development* is something good – and by the assumption that development

organisations produce *development*. There are plenty of examples that the work of development organisations has not benefited but sometimes even harmed the poor. But again we are caught up in misunderstandings: a project may be successful in promoting *development* in the sense of improving agricultural productivity yet fail in achieving *development* in the sense of reducing poverty because only well-off farmers can afford the new technology. Often, two meanings of *development* are conflated: on the one hand a 'process of transition or transformation toward a modern, capitalist, industrial economy' and on the other the 'reduction or amelioration of material want' (Ferguson 1994: 15). Criticisms raised against negative consequences of development policies are usually countered with references to the latter meaning, which subsequently often serve to legitimate interventions which are closer to the former meaning. But even if this is not the case, misunderstandings abound.

It should not be ignored that these misunderstandings can be beneficial to progressive NGOs as well. There are some NGOs whose understanding of *development* comes close to 'supporting marginalised groups in the South in their political struggles'. Because their interventions and projects are designated as *development*, there is a chance that they will obtain funding by development institutions which have a rather different – often a slightly more conservative – understanding of the concept.

Often, however, the productivity of misunderstandings related to the concept is less benign: it allows countless interventions with often highly dubious aims and effects to be launched in the name of the common good while being supported or even conducted by people who would otherwise not subscribe to these aims and effects. And it allows institutions like the World Bank to co-opt critical approaches and initiatives by claiming that they are pursuing the same goal as the institution itself – *development*.

Alternative concepts

For these reasons, I propose that we as development researchers should be more careful and more precise in our language – and maybe in our practices of producing knowledge and legitimating policy. If we are examining strategies of farmers to cope with climate change or looking for factors contributing to economic marginality or analysing conflicts about irrigation or land distribution, there is nothing wrong with it. But why should we call all this development research and thereby blur what we are actually doing by subsuming it under this all-too-vague concept with dubious implications?

Some people argue, we should do so for lack of a better concept. But do we really need such a general concept which covers change and improvement at the same time? If we are for example referring to rural-urban migration or processes of de-industrialisation, we do not have to talk about processes of *development*, we can use the concept of social change in general or we can use these more specific descriptions. If we are referring to processes of redistribution on an international scale through bilateral and multilateral agencies, there is no need to call this development aid – we could designate this as global social policy. If we are striving for a world different from the present one in which tens of thousands of people are dying each single day for lack of food, clean water or affordable medicine while others live in affluence, we should admit that we are guided by the ideals of justice and solidarity or the concept of human rights – instead of using the vague and problematic notion of *development*. After all, what development theory and policy are concerned with can in a more precise way be described as the explanation and amelioration of global social inequality. Analysing change and improving livelihoods could thus be the future objectives of what is until now called development theory and policy.

If we want to measure the qualities of different ways of living and compare them, we can include incidences of suicide and violent crime, racism and sexism, the propensity to conduct wars, the relation to nature and other societies and therefore the pressing question to what extent a certain way of living depends on the subordination of other economies and ecologies (their resources, their labour power) for its consumption patterns or on the production of exclusion and inequality. What would such a reorientation mean for those conducting research and guiding policy on the political, economic, social, cultural and ecological systems of this world, and their interconnections? Let us find out.

There is an increasing awareness of indigenous concepts which could replace the now dominant notion, concepts like *buen vivir* (*sumak kawsay* in Kichwa) (Gudynas 2011), *ubuntu* (Andreasson 2007) or *haq* (Madhok 2009). In the words of Rahnema (1997b: 391): 'The end of development should not be seen as an end to the search for new possibilities of change.' It should be seen as the beginning of less Eurocentric and vague notions of change.[3]

Notes

1   For the problems of postpositivist empirical research, see Ziai 2010.
2   His field research was conducted in the early 1980s and therefore does not reflect the neoliberal turn in development policy.
3   Needless to say, alternative concepts of social change and improvement also need to be questioned concerning their implications or their instrumentalisation.

Bibliography

Ahorro, Joseph 2008: *The Waves of Post-Development Theory and a Consideration of the Philippines*. Presentation at the Canadian Political Science Association 2008 Conference. Online http://www.cpsa-acsp.ca/papers-2008/Ahorro.pdf (April 20, 2012).

Alcalde, Javier Gonzalo 1987: *The Idea of Third World Development: Emerging Perspectives in the United States and Britain, 1900–1950*. Lanham, MD: University Press of America.

Alvares, Claude 1992: *Science, Development and Violence: The Revolt Against Modernity*. Delhi: Oxford University Press.

Andreasson, Stefan 2007: *Thinking Beyond Development: The Future of Post-development Theory in Southern Africa*. Presentation on the British International Studies Association Conference 2007.

68   *Archaeology*

Apffel-Marglin, Frédérique 1990: Smallpox in Two Systems of Knowledge. In: Apffel-Marglin, Frédérique/Marglin, Stephen (eds.) *Dominating Knowledge: Development, Culture and Resistance*. Oxford: Clarendon, 102–144.

Belsey, Catherine 2002: *Poststructuralism: A Very Short Introduction*. Oxford: Oxford University Press.

Bhabha, Homi 1994: *The Location of Culture*. London: Routledge.

Blaut, James Morris 1993: *The Colonizer's Model of the Earth: Geographical Diffusionism and Eurocentric History*. New York: Guilford.

Chambers, Robert 1997: *Whose Reality Counts? Putting the First Last*. London: ITDG.

Chang, Ha-Joon 2003: *Kicking Away the Ladder: Development Strategy in Historical Perspective*. New York: Anthem.

Cooke, Bill/Kothari, Uma (eds.) 2001: *Participation: The New Tyranny?* London: Zed.

Cooper, Frederick/Packard, Randall 1997: Introduction. In: Cooper, Frederick/Packard, Randall (ed.) *International Development and the Social Sciences: Essays on the History and Politics of Knowledge*. Berkeley: University of California Press, 1–41.

Corbridge, Stuart 1998: 'Beneath the Pavement Only Soil': The Poverty of Post-development. *Journal of Development Studies* 6, 138–148.

Cowen, Michael P./Shenton, Robert W. 1996: *Doctrines of Development*. London: Routledge.

Crush, Jonathan (ed.) 1995: *Power of Development*. London: Routledge.

Diaz-Bone, Rainer/Bührmann, Andrea/Gutierrez Rodriguez, Encarnacion/Schneider, Werner/Kendall, Gavin/Tirado, Francisco 2007: The Field of Foucaultian Discourse Analysis: Structures, Developments and Perspectives. *Forum: Qualitative Social Research* 8(2), Art. 30.

Escobar, Arturo 1995: *Encountering Development: The Making and Unmaking of the Third World*. Princeton, NJ: Princeton University Press.

Esteva, Gustavo 1985: Development: Metaphor, Myth, Threat. *Development: Seeds of Change* 3, 78–79.

Esteva, Gustavo 1987: Regenerating People's Space. *Alternatives* 12, 125–152.

Esteva, Gustavo 1992: Development. In: Sachs, Wolfgang (ed.) *The Development Dictionary: A Guide to Knowledge as Power*. London: Zed, 6–25.

Ferguson, James 1994: *The Anti-Politics Machine: 'Development', Depoliticization and Bureaucratic Power in Lesotho*. Minneapolis: University of Minnesota Press.

Foucault, Michel 1972 (1969): *The Archaeology of Knowledge & The Discourse on Language*. New York: Pantheon Books.

Foucault, Michel 1980: *Power/Knowledge: Selected Interviews & Other Writings 1972–1977*. New York: Pantheon.

Frank, Leonard 1997: The Development Game. In: Rahnema, Majid, *The Post-Development Reader*. London: Zed, 263–268.

Gudynas, Eduardo (2011): *Buen Vivir*: Today's Tomorrow. *Development* 54(4), 441–447.

Hall, Stuart 1992: The West and the Rest: Discourse and Power. In: Hall, Stuart/Gieben, Bram (eds.) *Formations of Modernity*. London: Polity Press, 276–320.

Keller, Rainer 2005: Analysing Discourse: An Approach from the Sociology of Knowledge. *Forum: Qualitative Social Research* 6(3), Art. 30.

Kiely, Ray 1999: The Last Refuge of the Noble Savage? A Critical Assessment of Post-development Theory. *European Journal of Development Research* 11(1), 30–55.

Kößler, Reinhart 1998: *Entwicklung*. Münster: Westfälisches Dampfboot.

Madhok, Sumi 2009: *Rethinking Agency: Developmentalism, Gender and Rights*. London: Routledge.

Martinussen, John 1997: *Society, State and Market: A Guide to Competing Theories of Development*. London: Zed.

Melber, Henning 1992: *Der Weißheit letzter Schluß. Rassismus und kolonialer Blick*. Frankfurt: Brandes & Apsel.

Münker, Stefan/Roesler, Alexander 2000: *Poststrukturalismus*. Stuttgart: Metzler.

Nandy, Ashis 1992: *Traditions, Tyranny, and Utopias: Essays in the Politics of Awareness*. Delhi: Oxford University Press.

Nederveen Pieterse, Jan 2000: After Post-development. *Third World Quarterly* 20(1), 175–191.

Nisbet, Robert 1969: *Social Change and History: Aspects of the Western Theory of Development*. Oxford: Oxford University Press.

Potter, David 2000: The Power of Colonial States. In: Allen, Tim & Thomas, Alan (eds.) *Poverty and Development Into the 21st Century*. Oxford: Open University Press, 271–287.

Rahnema, Majid (ed.) 1997a: *The Post-Development Reader*. London: Zed.

Rahnema, Majid 1997b: Towards Post-Development: Searching for Signposts, a New Language and New Paradigms. In: Rahnema, Majid (ed.), *The Post-Development Reader*. London: Zed, 377–403.

Rist, Gilbert 1997: *The History of Development: From Western Origins to Global Faith*. London: Zed Books.

Sachs, Wolfgang (ed.) 1992: *The Development Dictionary: A Guide to Knowledge as Power*. London: Zed.

Sigrist, Christian 2005: *Regulierte Anarchie: Untersuchungen zum Fehlen und zur Entstehung politischer Herrschaft in segmentären Gesellschaften Afrikas*. Münster: Lit.

Smith, Steve 1996: Positivism and Beyond. In: Smith, Steve/Booth, Ken/Zalewski, Marysia (eds.) *International Theory: Positivism and Beyond*. Cambridge: Cambridge University Press, 11–44.

Wodak, Ruth/Meyer, Michael 2009: Critical Discourse Analysis: History, Agenda, Theory. In: Wodak, Ruth/Meyer, Michael (eds.) *Methods of Critical Discourse Analysis*. London: Sage, 1–33.

World Commission on Dams 2000: *Dams and Development: A New Framework for Decision-Making*. London: Earthscan.

Ziai, Aram 2004a: *Entwicklung als Ideologie? Das klassische Entwicklungsparadigma und die Post-Development Kritik*. Hamburg: Deutsches Übersee-Institut.

Ziai, Aram 2004b: The Ambivalence of Post-development: Between Reactionary Populism and Radical Democracy. *Third World Quarterly* 25(6), 1045–1060.

Ziai, Aram (ed.) 2007: *Exploring Post-Development: Theory and Practice, Problems and Perspectives*. London: Routledge.

Ziai, Aram 2010: Post-positivist Metatheory and Research in International Relations: A Comparison of Neo-gramscian, Feminist and Post-structuralist Approaches. *Hamburg Review of Social Sciences* 5(1/2), 31–60.

6 Development discourse
Appropriation and tactical polyvalence

Let us start by examining the following quotes, which depict the asymmetrical relations between the global North and the global South at different points in time in the 20th century. In 1901, President Theodore Roosevelt portrayed the relation of the US to the rest of the world as follows: 'this nation most earnestly desires sincere and cordial friendship with others. . . . Wars with barbarous or semi-barbarous peoples come in an entirely different category, being merely a most regrettable but necessary international police duty which must be performed for the sake of mankind' (cited in Alcalde 1987: 4). There could be no doubt that the barbarous peoples he referred to were people of colour who lived outside of Europe and North America. Half a century later his successor Harry Truman struck a different note when envisioning future US foreign policy: 'More than half the people of the world are living in conditions approaching misery. . . . I believe that we should make available to peace-loving peoples the benefits of our store of technical knowledge in order to help them realise their aspirations for a better life' (cited in Rist 2008: 71). And the economist Paul Rosenstein-Rodan in 1944 anticipated Truman's 'program of development', when he demanded: 'we have to provide for some international action to improve the living conditions of those people who missed the industrialisation "bus" in the nineteenth century' (cited in Alcalde 1987: 154).

Comparing the above quotes, one cannot but wonder about the shift in the way the relation between the North and the South, or more precisely: the US and certain peoples in Africa, Asia and Latin America, has been conceived. Whereas in the beginning of the 20th century people in the non-Western world were seen by politicians in North America and Western Europe as racially inferior and could be killed with impunity, so that the relation between the North and the South was primarily framed in terms of security, since the middle of the 20th century the aim of politics seems to be to help these people and improve their living conditions through a programme of development. Thus between 1900 and 1950, the dominant way of speaking and writing about the South from the perspective of the North underwent a significant change, a change which can be depicted as one from a discourse of colonialism to a discourse of development, implying the norm of helping certain peoples in the sense of improving their material condition. This chapter is concerned with the constitution, appropriation and contestation of this new discourse and its corresponding norms.

On the theoretical level, the article is inspired by the Post-Development school (Sachs 1992, Escobar 1995, Rahnema 1997a), as well as different strands of post-colonial analysis. In contrast to the first wave of Post-Development theory, the emphasis here is not merely to focus on the power of Western discourses in constructing the reality of the Other outside the West, a strategy of analysis linked to Said's (1978) analysis of *Orientalism*, but also to examine the ways in which these discourses were modified, appropriated and transformed by non-Western subjects and thus produced unintended effects, understood in terms of Bhabha's (1994) concept of hybridisation.

The constitution of 'development'

In the literature, there is disagreement as to when the discourse of development emerged. Gustavo Esteva (1992) claims it was in Truman's inaugural address in 1949, other researchers situate the discourse in late colonialism:[1] Robert Nisbet (1969) points to 19th-century evolutionism (for example of Spencer and Marx), while Michael Cowen and Robert Shenton (1996) attribute responsibility to the Saint-Simonian doctrines (also of the 19th century). Reinhart Kößler (1998) and Philipp Lepenies (2014) point to its origins in Enlightenment philosophy.

In this article, discourse shall be briefly defined as a system of statements, which are produced according to certain rules of formation, certain regularities concerning their objects, concepts and subject positions (Foucault 1972: 31–76, Diaz-Bone et al. 2007). This discourse allows for (and is influenced by) certain nondiscursive[2] practices, merging with them to a strategic dispositive (Foucault 1980: 119–23).

Regarding the idea of *development*, it is useful to distinguish between concepts of evolutionary social change (usually brought about by capitalist modes of production) and concepts designed to ameliorate negative effects of this change. Cowen and Shenton (1996: 3–5) refer to the first as 'immanent development', to the second as 'intentional development'. The idea of a general pattern of social change in which some societies (in Western Europe and North America) are at a more advanced and others at a backward stage (what could be called the evolutionist legacy of development) was present already in 18th- and 19th-century thinking in social philosophy and political economy. And policies (based on expert knowledge and trustees) to reform societies and improve the lot of the poor to maintain social order (the trusteeship legacy) were applied in the 19th century as well – but predominantly in Europe (Cowen/Shenton 1996: 12). In the colonies, however, Europeans saw their task not merely as exploiting these areas, but also as uplifting and civilising the barbarians and savages (what Rudyard Kipling described as the 'White Man's Burden'), so at least in part they did perceive themselves as being entrusted and responsible for the native population. But this responsibility was usually understood in terms of civilising and Christianising and not in terms of raising their standard of living. The *development* of these areas (as in the British Colonial Development Act of 1929) referred to the natural resources and the infrastructure, not to improving the material conditions of their inhabitants.

Thus the discourse of development as we know it, a concept of international policies linked with practices aiming at the improvement of the material conditions of people living in Africa, Asia and Latin America, was in fact gradually constituted in the first half of the 20th century. After World War I, in the Versailles Treaty and the League of Nations Covenant of 1919, the *development* of the colonised populations was already an issue, but they were still treated as inferior:

> *To those colonies and territories which as a consequence of the late war have ceased to be under the sovereignty of the States which formerly governed them and which are inhabited by peoples not yet able to stand by themselves under the strenuous conditions of the modern world, there should be applied the principle that the well-being and development of such peoples form a sacred trust of civilisation and that securities for the performance of this trust should be embodied in this Covenant. The best method of giving practical effect to this principle is that the tutelage of such peoples should be entrusted to advanced nations who by reason of their resources, their experience or their geographical position can best undertake this responsibility, and who are willing to accept it, and that this tutelage should be exercised by them as Mandatories on behalf of the League.*
>
> (League of Nations Covenant, Art. 22, italics added)

A careful reading of Truman's inaugural address reveals that the Western claim to superiority has markedly diminished between 1919 and 1949: it is predominantly confined to the level of technical knowledge and material wealth, and the commonplace assumption that people in the South were unable to govern themselves (which made the benign tutelage of the West necessary) has disappeared. The old imperialism based on this premise was rejected and instead a 'program of development' was announced to relieve the misery of the formerly colonised, albeit one 'based on democratic fair-dealing', namely, on a relationship which bears semblance to one between equal subjects (Truman 1949 cited in Rist 2008: 71).

The work of Javier Gonzalo Alcalde (1987) examines the factors that played an important role in the constitution of these discourses. To summarise briefly: as a consequence of World War I Britain had to initiate a new focus on the *development* of the colonial economies. The war had led to a wave of nationalism in the colonies sought to appease by Britain with promises of material well-being. After the war, the League of Nations occasioned the first reflections on the relation between economic development and popular welfare, manifest later in the Colonial Development Act of 1929 and its replacement with the Colonial Development and Welfare Act of 1939/40. The Great Depression of 1929 had impoverishing effects which led to the first international comparisons of living standards and proposals of basic needs standards and gave rise to the New Deal whose reliance on government planning and welfare programs had international repercussions: it triggered plans to draw the advanced economies out of the recession through a world development program based on capital investment in the South. World War II resulted in an end of US isolationism and saw first successful attempts to employ development assistance as a policy instrument, which persuaded governments of both industrialised and nonindustrialised countries to rally behind the call for *development* of the global South. Last but certainly not the least, anti-colonial struggles and the Russian Revolution (1917–1918) compelled the West to promise the colonised peoples economic progress and technological advancement and to demonstrate that capitalism could bring welfare to the poor as well. The strategic concerns of the Cold War restored development assistance after a brief postwar interval, trying to secure prosperity by fighting poverty (or at least appearing to do so). By 1950, social and economic progress was merged in the idea of *development* whose 'first and broadest function', according to Alcalde, was 'to give economic activity, particularly foreign economic activity, a positive and essential meaning for the lives of less-developed peoples' (1987: 223).

However, one factor underestimated by Alcalde should be mentioned: one of the most, if not *the* central difference between the framing of North-South Relations in 1919 and in 1949 was the disappearance of the racist claim that certain people were not capable of self-government. Several studies from the 1950s (e.g., Césaire 1972 [1955] and Adorno et al. 1993 [1951]) reveal that racist discourses were still very much prevalent in the US and Europe at this time, but the horrors of the Holocaust had started to discredit this type of thinking – or at least its unadorned exposure in international relations. After the Universal Declaration of Human Rights, racist ideas of white supremacy were increasingly frowned upon on the international stage, and this is reflected in the shift from colonial to development discourse.

Andreas Eckert (2012: 20) also points out that the massive strikes in Africa, strong nationalist movements in many colonies and the Second World War led to a shift in perception among the colonisers during the 1940s: the backwardness of the colonised was seen no longer as a permanent racial quality, but as a cultural feature subject to change, so that colonial rule could thus be legitimised as progressive and that development aid could continue the civilising mission under a new guise.

Both discourses describe the Other as deficient in relation to the Self (civilised vs. uncivilised, *developed* vs. *underdeveloped*) and operate through similar dichotomies between superior and inferior (modern vs. traditional, advanced technology vs. manual labour, prosperity vs. misery, assisting vs. assisted, etc.). Yet some marked differences can be observed. The objects of the discourse are now geographical regions, not (or hardly) any longer people: a shift from biology to economic geography. And although two different types of objects exist (*developed* and *underdeveloped* countries), the difference is not qualitative and insurmountable any longer, but the latter can become like the former at some point in the future.[3] Thus the trusteeship for the *development* of the country, which can no longer be justified by theories of race, passes with independence from the colonial masters to the postcolonial elites who run these countries. As there still is an assumption of cultural inferiority, this trusteeship is often linked to expert knowledge from the West (Western university degrees, Western theories, etc.).

The appropriation of 'development'

Majid Rahnema (1997b: ix) points out that the new discourse on development was widely adopted by different groups for different reasons: by leaders of independence movements hoping to 'transform their devastated countries into modern nation-states' (ibid.), by the masses in the ex-colonies hoping for an end to subjugation and a better life, and by the former colonial masters seeking a new system of domination which allowed them to maintain their presence in these regions 'to exploit their natural resources, . . . use them as markets for their expanding economies or as bases for their geopolitical ambitions' (ibid.). Rahnema describes this adoption of the discourses of development and its corresponding values as a virus which invaded and colonised Third World subjects from within: 'The "power" of development, like that of the AIDS virus, lies in its internalisation by the host' (Rahnema 1997c: 119).[4] While he stresses the ideological aspirations of the discourse, he entirely neglects its progressive aspects and processes of appropriation – and thus portrays the infected subjects as helpless victims of this power. By appropriation I mean the practice of adopting and (possibly) simultaneously transforming a discourse to one's own ends – in contrast to denouncing the discourse as alien, colonial or Western and rejecting it, which is the only alternative that Rahnema envisions.

Frederick Cooper has examined such processes of appropriation and concludes:

> Development ideology was originally supposed to sustain empire, not facilitate the transfer of power. Yet developmentalist arguments – about labor policy as much as economic planning – were something trade union and political leaders could engage with, appropriate, and turn back. This framework allowed them to pose demands in forms that could be understood in London or Paris, that could not be dismissed as 'primitive'. . . . Much as one can read the universalism of development discourse as a form of European particularism imposed abroad, it could also be read . . . as a rejection of the fundamental premises of colonial rule, a firm assertion of people of all races to participate in global politics and lay claim to a globally defined standard of living.
>
> (Cooper 1997: 84)

Taking into account Cooper's arguments allows us to conceive the adoption of development discourse by actors in the South not in Rahnema's terms as manipulation and infection, but as a strategical appropriation.

One of the reasons for the success of development discourse in the second half of the 20th century is that the identity offered by this discourse (being *less developed*) proved to be far more attractive to the formerly colonised in comparison to the one provided by racist colonial discourses (being uncivilised). The other reason lies in the appropriation of the discourses – primarily – by the postcolonial elites in myriad ways. I would like to particularly focus on two significant aspects: the appropriation at the national level of the programs of National

Development and the appropriation at the international level of the UN declarations of Development. Both processes shall be briefly sketched here, especially
with respect to one crucial element of the discourse: trusteeship.

In the case of India, the appropriation of the discourse already began in 1938,
when the Congress party set up a National Planning Committee (headed by
Jawaharlal Nehru) whose task was to devise a program of national development
(Bose 1997: 38). After independence, *development* became for the Indian state 'a
primary source of its own self-justification' (ibid., 53), even as the accumulation
of capital and processes of industrialisation were prioritised over improvement
in the quality of life of the poor in concrete projects and programs. This was
apparent in the building of massive dams, which were lauded by Nehru as 'tem-
ples of modern India' (cited in Roy 1999). Since independence 3,300 large dams
have been built in India, displacing an estimated thirty to 40 million people, the
majority of them tribal and other marginalised communities (Roy 1999). Nehru
said to the villagers displaced by the Hirakud dam in 1948: 'If you are to suffer,
you are to suffer in the interest of the country' (cited in Roy 1999). He might just
as well have said: in the name of national development, because this is how the
dams were usually justified.[5]

This sheds light on the fact that the trusteeship over the presumably ignorant people, the ability to know what was good for them even if they themselves
apparently did not (Cowen/Shenton 1996: 25–27), was taken over by the postcolonial elites from the former colonial masters without any qualms. In the case
of the Sardar Sarovar dam, the World Bank had to withdraw its support after
massive protest campaigns by civil society groups in national as well as international arenas – but the Indian state carried forward the project nevertheless.
This trusteeship arrogated itself the right to exert violence if the people were
obstinate enough to resist the well-meaning policies of those who knew better.
Apffel-Marglin (1990: 118–120) documents how in the course of the Indian
state's smallpox eradication campaign, vaccination squads raided villages and
forcefully vaccinated unwilling villagers (who employed traditional, culturally
embedded and in terms of disease prevention slightly less effective methods of
inoculation) – all in the name of *development* and based on scientific knowledge.[6] Although this may seem an extreme case, similar instances can be found
in other countries, too. In some regions in Tanzania in the 1960s, participation
in development projects was mandatory, and refusal could be punished by six
strokes (Potter 2000: 287). The list of violence exerted in the name of national
development is long and the connection between violence and *development* is
no coincidence (see Nandy 1995 and 2004). Thus we can conclude that at the
national level, the principle of trusteeship has been reaffirmed through appropriation by national elites.

Looking at the appropriation of the norm at the international level, it is
instructive to examine the UN declarations on *development* and the corresponding policies. The representatives of the increasing number of former colonies,
which had become independent states, have used the UN as a forum to articulate demands for financial transfers and special treatment in multilateral trade

agreements – mobilising their constituted identities as *underdeveloped* coun-tries. Moreover, they have vigorously rejected any international tutelage, often denouncing the policies of the International Financial Institutions.

While the Expanded Programme of Technical Assistance, inaugurated under the auspices of the UN in 1950, was still uncontroversial, in subsequent years the question of development finance led to fierce debates. To meet their par-ticular needs, a report by a group of experts appointed by the Secretary-General on 'Measures for the Economic Development of Under-Developed Countries' published in 1951 proposed an International Development Authority which was to disburse grants (Adams 1993: 55). The idea was taken up and the countries defined as such launched a major campaign in the General Assembly, opposed by the UN and other rich countries not willing to fund such an institution. In 1953, another committee dealing with the issue proposed a Special United Nations Fund for Economic Development (SUNFED) in which control over finance would be equally shared between major contributors and other members (ibid.). The proposal was hotly debated but did not prevail, and instead in 1959, as a con-solation prize, the United Nations Special Fund, came into being – with a budget 10 times smaller than that envisioned for SUNFED (ibid.: 56).

However, these demands for a UN Fund for Economic Development and a UN Economic Development Agency in the early postwar period led also to the estab-lishment of the International Development Association, an offshoot of the World Bank that provided interest-free loans to the *least developed* countries (UNIHP 2010: 2f). Of course, as a daughter to the International Bank for Reconstruction and Development, control over finance remained with the major shareholders in the North. Despite the defeat of a financial institution in which Southern coun-tries would have a decisive influence, the campaign 'is an important example of their early determination to bring their new-found strength to bear on the design of international economic institutions' (Adams 1993: 57) – and an example of how the discourse of development was appropriated to ends not intended by its original proponents. The status as *underdeveloped* countries was used to demand (in a UN resolution of 1951) 'international measures required to mitigate the vulnerability of the economies of underdeveloped countries to fluctuations in international markets, including measures to adjust, establish and maintain appropriate relations between prices of raw materials on the one hand, and essen-tial manufactured goods on the other' (Adams 1993: 59). These measures – price regulations to oppose declining terms of trade – can be seen as political interven-tions in the economy directly based on dependency theorems, launched in the name of *development*.

In 1961, the UN declared the first Development Decade calling upon its member states to pursue economic policies to achieve 'self-sustaining economic development in the less developed countries' (UN 1961). This included pursu-ing stable and remunerative prices for primary commodities, an equitable share of earnings from extraction and marketing of natural resources and greater pri-vate investment on terms satisfactory for both importers and exporters of capital. The declaration was accompanied by resolutions 1522 and 1711, which express the hope that the flow of assistance money to the *less developed* countries should reach 'as soon as possible approximately 1 per cent of the combined incomes of the economically advanced countries' (UN 1960).[7] In the following years, the World Food Program, the UN Research Institute for Social Development, the UN Conference for Trade and Development (UNCTAD) and the UN Industrial Development Organisation (UNIDO) were established. More often than not, the recommendations of these organisations were incongruous with the agenda of the *developed* states during the 1960s and 1970s.

In particular the UNCTAD, the first of which took place in 1964, was convened 'against the clear wishes of the major industrial countries' (Adams 1993: 79) and provided a forum for the *less developed* countries to demand ever more regulations of international trade to further their *development* as well as to negotiate international commodity agreements (ibid.: 95). According to Adams, the 'very principle on which UNCTAD had been founded' was 'the need for special and differential treatment to be accorded to developing countries to allow them to survive and prosper in a world of unequals' (185). It also functioned as a site where a common identity and a united front in the Group of 77 could be forged (80).

In the 1970s, the first declaration was followed by the International Development Strategy for the second UN Development Decade (UN 1970). Here, the heads of state not only claimed that *development* required the 'elimination of colonialism, racial discrimination, apartheid and occupation of territories of any State' (Art. 5), but also 'in the conviction that development is the essential path to peace and justice' reaffirmed in their 'common and unswerving resolve to seek a better and more effective system of international co-operation whereby the prevailing disparities in the world may be banished and prosperity secured for all' (Art. 6). Because if 'undue privileges, extremes of wealth and social injustices persist, then development fails in its essential purpose'. Therefore, 'a global development strategy based on joint and concentrated action by developing and developed countries in all spheres of economic and social life' was required, 'in industry and agriculture, in trade and finance, in employment and education, in health and housing, in science and technology' (Art. 7). Thus, the discourse of development is appropriated by the new majority of Third World heads of state in the UN for three primary reasons: first, to reject international trusteeship (bear in mind that just a few decades earlier the necessity of *development* was employed to legitimise colonialism); second, to demand social justice and equality and denounce prevailing disparities; and third, to devise a comprehensive program of planned intervention which would include the global economy. The Declaration on the Establishment of a New International Economic Order (UN 1974) underlined the latter point unambiguously and could be seen as the concretisation of such a program. Additionally, it claimed the right of states to adopt the economic or social system 'most appropriate for its own development' without being subjected to discrimination (Art. 4d), to nationalise enterprises (Art. 4e) and regulate and supervise transnational corporations (Art. 4g). The declaration was followed by a more detailed programme of action outlining the envisioned regulations of the economy. In his address concerning the NIEO, the Algerian president of the General Assembly stated that the present order 'constitutes the major obstacle standing in the way of any hope of development and progress for all the countries of the Third World' (cited in Adams 1993: 123).

It is obvious that, based on their classification as *less developed*, the leaders of Third World states were using the UN as a platform to launch demands for redistribution, justice and economic intervention in the name of *development*. In other words, they were appropriating the discourse of development in a way that was at odds with the imperialist objectives of the discourse of only a couple of decades earlier. This demonstrates what Foucault (1978: 100) has called the 'tactical polyvalence of discourses': they can be used for different or even opposite political ends. Regarding the principle of trusteeship, one can conclude that while the appropriation of the discourse of development by Third World elites has led to a rejection of the principle on the international level, on the national level the principle has been reaffirmed.

The contestation of 'development'

Taking a closer look at the processes of appropriation reveals that while the discourse of development has been appropriated by Third World leaders in the 1960s and 1970s, it has not been fundamentally contested. Neither has the goal to transform the *underdeveloped* regions into *developed* ones (by means of economic growth, industrialisation and modernisation) been questioned, nor the underlying constructions of identity (*developed* vs. *underdeveloped*) and the central principle of trusteeship. However, since the 1980s, such contestations have occasionally taken place. Two of them will be briefly discussed here: the discourse of participation and ownership and the discourse of Post-Development. Both cases will be supplemented by practical examples from Bolivia, because here the clashes between different discourses can be observed easily.

Although the discourse of participation originates in the 1980s (Chambers 1983, Leal 2010) and ownership became a topic of development policy only in the late 1990s (Buiter 2010), both approaches are in unison in their rejection of top-down development approaches and their emphasis to 'let the people decide what development is for them'.[8] However, if this statement were to be taken seriously, it would spell the end of the principle of trusteeship in development discourse, which assumes that experts are competent to decide for the people. Thus, the discourse of participation and ownership in development policy is fraught with ambiguity and contradictions.

The meaning of participation of course depends on the question who participates in what. Early concepts and techniques of participation (like Participatory Rural Appraisal or Participatory Learning and Action) were linked to the idea of marginalised people taking control over their lives. However, the application of participation in the practice of development organisations was often more concerned with a more efficient implementation of projects. And if participation is restricted (on the level of actors) to male village elders or (on the level of decision-making) to the manner of project implementation, it will hardly lead to empowerment – at least if empowerment is understood in the sense of more self-determination of marginalised people and a change in the relations of power.[9] On the other hand, its emancipatory potential must not be underestimated, as the discourse could be a useful tool for such an empowerment (Hickey/Mohan 2004).

In contrast to the concept of participation, which was directed against top-down decision-making in development projects, the concept of ownership had a similar thrust, but operated more on a macro-level (usually referring to the ownership of countries): it was directed against top-down decision-making in international development policy. Of particular concern was the trusteeship assumed by the International Financial Institutions in the context of the Structural Adjustment Programs (SAP), but representatives of recipient countries complained about donor-driven development policy also in general. Since the late 1990s and especially since the Paris Declaration of 2005, documents and strategies of development policy usually have to be 'owned' by the recipient country, meaning that the latter's government – and not the donor organisations – devised and drafted these papers. However, the case of the World Bank's Poverty Reduction Strategy Papers (PRSPs) demonstrates that more often than not, the donors still exert considerable influence on these strategies (Spanger/Wolff 2003, WDM 2005, Siebold 2008). And even if there is country ownership of a poverty reduction strategy, it often comes down to 'this programme is supported by the people who own the country' (Buiter 2010: 228) – i.e. although officially civil society participation is mandatory in devising PRSPs, this participation is often confined to ruling elites or at best professional NGOs in the capital and usually excludes poorer sections of society.

Thus, while the discourse of participation in its dominant form questions the universal superiority of expert knowledge and suggests participation of project-affected people as a way to achieve more successful development projects, it does not do away with the role of experts and the development industry in general, nor with the fundamental assumptions concerning problems and identities it is based on. This could also be said about the discourse of country ownership, which, at least rhetorically, explicitly rejects the principle of international trusteeship and thus the influence of international or foreign actors like the World Bank, the IMF or Northern donor organisations on national development policy.

Numerous studies demonstrate that the structures of the development industry certainly impose limits on the extent of participation and ownership – after all, experts and donor organisations still want to have a say in development policy and because of privileged speaker positions and financial leverage often exert crucial influence. However, there may also be another dimension, as shown by the development project 'Towards an Inclusive Election Process', launched in 2002 in Bolivia and funded by a number of European development agencies.[10] Its objective was to improve political participation in the election process and the local promoters who had planned the project were organised in the Pro Citizens' Participation Consortium. The project aimed to tackle the problem of lack of participation of a large part of the indigenous population in the election process by explaining to these groups citizens' rights and supporting their claims to an identity card. However, the Bolivian government was convinced that the problem was already dealt with through educational programs and that this was sufficient. The support and resources which the project intended to provide to grassroots organisations mobilising people to vote was perceived as interference in internal political matters and maybe even an infringement on sovereignty. Thus the project was denounced as donor-driven and in violation of the principle of country ownership. This led to the withdrawal of two development agencies from the project, while the other two continued to fund it (Eyben/Ferguson 2004, Eyben/Leon 2005).

What becomes visible here is again the tactical polyvalence of discourses: the discourse of country ownership, which was originally directed against international trusteeship, is used here as an instrument to reaffirm the principle of trusteeship on a national scale and to prevent increased political participation. If the discourse of participation and ownership is seen as a unity, then this discourse is appropriated by Third World elites and turned against First World donors who are reproached with not abiding by their principles and thus faced with a dilemma: either they renounce the principle of country ownership or the objective of increased political participation, but they cannot have both.

While in the case of participation and ownership the objective of transforming the *underdeveloped* countries into *developed* ones and the implicit constructions of superior and inferior identities were not contested and merely the central element of trusteeship was challenged, the discourse of Post-Development (PD) acts as a more fundamental challenge to development discourse. The objective is often regarded as neither feasible nor desirable, and the construction of *developed* and *underdeveloped* countries is rejected as a narrow universalism based on Eurocentric criteria. Furthermore, the authority of the development experts is also contested.

As characteristic elements of PD, Arturo Escobar (1995: 214) identifies the rejection of the entire paradigm of development and its economic reductionism, an interest in local culture and knowledge, a critical stance towards established scientific discourses, and the promotion of pluralistic grassroots movements. A closer look reveals that it is useful to differentiate between two variants of PD: a neopopulist variant which rejects Western modernity and seeks recourse to traditional cultures (e.g. Esteva/Prakash 1998), and a skeptical variant which similarly denounces cultural domination and Eurocentrism but refrains from outlining alternative models of society beyond supporting grassroots initiatives[11] and explicitly recognises the right of local communities in the global South to opt for a Western model (Banuri 1990: 95f, Marglin 1990: 27).

Although at first glance we observe a radical repudiation of the discourse of development, a critical analysis yields that in some PD writings, the central element of trusteeship is brought in again through the backdoor: when Rahnema (1997d: 388f) suggests that the needs of the people should not be ascertained by democratic processes, but by the 'good and authoritative persons' of a community, this is an unambiguous reaffirmation of the principle. Thus PD discourse can serve both radical democratic as well as conservative political ends, and this constitutes its ambivalence (Ziai 2004b).

The concept of *Buen Vivir* which enjoys enormous popularity in Bolivia and Ecuador (and increasingly other countries as well) can be seen as a manifestation of PD discourse. *Buen vivir* (good life) is the Spanish expression for *sumak kawsay* in Kichwa and *suma quamaña* in Aymara (Baéz/Cortez 2012). Even though *buen vivir* may be a plural endeavour and may be used with different meanings, it is generally seen as 'a replacement of the very idea of development' (Gudynas 2011: 445). Other characteristic features are that it is rooted in traditional indigenous world-views and envisions the possibility of a good life only in one's social context and not as an individual good life, on the basis of the dissolution of the dichotomy between society and nature (renouncing the idea that nature should be dominated and controlled by mankind) and as part of a process of (mental) decolonisation (ibid., Fatheuer 2011: 19f).

The ambivalence of PD is also visible in the debate around *buen vivir* in Bolivia: whether and to what extent it ignores processes of cultural transformation and hybridisation, constructing a pure and traditional indigenous identity; whether and to what extent it allows for emancipatory processes of decolonisation and self-assertion, whether and to what extent it is used by national elites as a mobilising ideology to evade class and gender conflicts – these are pertinent questions to be seriously examined (Ascarrunz 2011). And so is the question, whether and to what extent the counterdiscourse of *Buen Vivir* and its related practices negotiate aspirations for a better life not entirely different from those that Third World people have been expressing with the idea of *development*.

It can be observed that even the counterdiscourses to *development* which contest and repudiate the concept, sometimes bear traces and patterns which are somewhat familiar. This, however, must not lead to homogenising their differences, which are worthwhile being pointed out.

Conclusion

Although the discourse of development was constituted in the first half of the 20th century as a transformation of colonial discourse which legitimised the North to maintain economic domination and exert global influence, during the course of the next decades the discourse was appropriated by the newly independent countries of the South in ways not intended by the North, which included demands for financial transfers and even a more regulated global economic order. While these appropriations left the principle of trusteeship, a central component of the discourse, untouched at least on the national level, some of the more recent contestations of the discourse – linked to the concepts of participation and Post-Development – have challenged this principle. However, a closer look reveals that even a rejection of trusteeship can be used to reintroduce the principle through the back door. Politically speaking, there are no safe discourses. This is, and here Foucault seems right, a consequence of the tactical polyvalence of discourses.

Notes

1 See e.g. the research project on 'Colonial Concepts of Development in Africa' at the University of Vienna (http://www.univie.ac.at/colonial-development/seiten/projekt. html).

2 These practices which Foucault refers to as nondiscursive are nonverbal, physical practices, which are, however, mediated through discourses.

3 Of course the civilising mission of colonialism had also included a diminishing of the difference, but its disappearance was inconceivable – the Other could be 'almost the same but not quite' (Bhabha 1994: 122).

4 This analogy is of course highly problematic. Rahnema presents as natural a certain way of life and as unnatural any deviance. He engages in a biologisation of social phenomena which ignores their contingent nature and their political aspects.

5 When protesters in Germany demanded a stay on the construction of the Sardar Saro-var dam in 1999 and rallied behind the slogan 'No human sacrifices for development!', a high ranking official of the Indian embassy replied: 'So you want our country to remain underdeveloped!' (personal experience). Of course, there had also been mass protests in India itself against the dam – which was to submerge the homes of hundreds of thousands of villagers (mostly indigenous peoples) – but they were usually beaten down by the police and the activists often ended up in jail (Mehta 1994, Roy 1999).

6 With Spivak (1999: 82) we can refer to this as an enabling violation. With this term she describes the legacy of colonialism and the ambivalence of violent interventions which may have positive results for at least some of its victims in certain ways. However, this does not legitimate the violence.

7 This figure was lowered to 0.7% but seen as obligatory in the next Development Decade Declaration.

8 This sentence (or variations of it) was the one used most often by development experts of different development policy organisations to describe their views on *development* in interviews I conducted for my PhD thesis (Ziai 2004a). The interviewees linked this attitude to the concepts of participation, ownership and partnership.

9 For these and other criticisms see Rahnema 1990, White 1996, and Cooke/ Kothari 2001.

10 DFID (Great Britain), SIDA (Sweden), DANIDA (Denmark) and NEDA (Netherlands).

11 This lead to the accusation of 'Pontius-Pilate-politics' (Kiely 1999: 45).

Bibliography

Adams, Nassau A. 1993: *Worlds Apart: The North-South Divide and the International System.* London: Zed Books.

Adorno, Theodor W./Frenkel-Brunswik, Else/Levinson, Daniel 1993 (1951): *The Authoritarian Personality: Studies in Prejudice.* New York: W.W. Norton.

Alcalde, Javier Gonzalo 1987: *The Idea of Third World Development: Emerging Perspectives in the United States and Britain, 1900–1950.* Lanham, MD: University Press of America.

Apffel-Marglin, Frédérique 1990: Smallpox in Two Systems of Knowledge. In: Apffel-Marglin Frédérique/Marglin, Stephen (eds.) *Dominating Knowledge: Development, Culture and Resistance.* Oxford: Clarendon, 102–144.

Apffel-Marglin, Frédérique/Marglin, Stephen (eds.) 1990: *Dominating Knowledge: Development, Culture and Resistance.* Oxford: Clarendon.

Ascarrunz, Beatris 2011: Tiefgefrorene Identitäten helfen nicht weiter. Die aktuelle Debatte über das vivir bien in Bolivien. In: *ila (Zeitschrift der Informationsstelle Lateinamerika)* Nr. 348, 12–15.

Báez, Michelle/Cortez, David 2012: Buen Vivir, Sumak Kawsay, Online Dictionary Social and Political Key Terms of the Americas: Politics, Inequalities, and North-South Relations, Version 1.0. Online http://elearning.uni-bielefeld.de/wikifarm/fields/ges_cias/field.php/Main/Unterkapitel11.

Banuri, Tariq 1990: Modernisation and its Discontents: A Critical Perspective on the Theories of Development. In: Apffel-Marglin Frédérique/Marglin, Stephen (eds.) *Dominating Knowledge: Development, Culture and Resistance.* Oxford: Clarendon, 73–101.

Bhabha, Homi K. 1994: *The Location of Culture.* London: Routledge.

Bose, Sugata 1997: Instruments and Idioms of Colonial and National Development: India's Historical Experience in Comparative Perspective. In: Cooper, Frederick/Packard, Randall (eds.) *International Development and the Social Sciences: Essays on the History and Politics of Knowledge.* Berkeley: University of California Press, 45–63.

Buiter, Willem H. 2010: Country Ownership: A Term Whose Time Has Gone. In: Cornwall, Andrea/Eade, Deborah (eds.) 2010: *Deconstructing Development Discourse: Buzzwords and Fuzzwords.* Bourton: Practical Action, 223–230.

Césaire, Aimé 1972 (1955): From Discourse on Colonialism. In: Williams, Patrick/Chrisman, Laura (eds.) 1994: *Colonial Discourse and Post-colonial Theory: A Reader.* New York: Columbia University Press, 172–180.

Chambers, Robert 1983: *Rural Development: Putting the Last First.* Essex: Longman.

Cooke, Bill/Kothari, Uma 2001: *Participation: The New Tyranny.* London: Zed Books.

Cooper, Frederick 1997: Modernising Bureaucrats, Backward Africans, and the Development Concept. In: Cooper, Frederick/Packard, Randall (eds.) *International Development and the Social Sciences: Essays on the History and Politics of Knowledge.* Berkeley: University of California Press, 64–92.

Cooper, Frederick/Packard, Randall (eds.) 1997: *International Development and the Social Sciences: Essays on the History and Politics of Knowledge.* Berkeley: University of California Press.

Cornwall, Andrea/Eade, Deborah (eds.) 2010: *Deconstructing Development Discourse: Buzzwords and Fuzzwords.* Bourton: Practical Action.

Cowen, Michael P./Shenton, Robert W. 1996: *Doctrines of Development.* London: Routledge.

Diaz-Bone/Bührmann, Andrea/Gutiérrez Rodríguez, Encarnacíon/Schneider, Werner/Kendall, Gavin/Tirado, Francisco 2007: The Field of Foucaultian Discourse Analysis: Structures, Developments and Perspectives. *Forum Qualitative Social Research* 8(2), Art. 30. Online http://www.qualitative-research.net/index.php/fqs/article/view/234/518 (December 23, 2013).

Eckert, Andreas 2012: Rechtfertigung und Legitimation von Kolonialismus. *Aus Politik und Zeitgeschichte* 44–45, 17–22.

Escobar, Arturo 1995: Encountering Development: The Making and Unmaking of the Third World. Princeton, NJ: Princeton University Press.

Esteva, Gustavo 1992: Development. In: Sachs, Wolfgang (ed.) *The Development Dictionary: A Guide to Knowledge as Power.* London: Zed Books, 6–25.

Esteva, Gustavo/Prakash, Madhu Suri 1998: *Grassroots Post-Modernism: Remaking the Soil of Cultures.* London: Zed Books.

Eyben, Rosalind/Ferguson, Clare 2004: How Can Donors Become More Accountable to Poor People. In: Groves, Leslie/Hinton, Rachel (eds.) *Inclusive Aid: Changing Power and Relationships in International Development.* London: Earthscan, 163–180.

Eyben, Rosalind/ Leon, Rosario 2005: Whose Aid? The Case of the Bolivian Elections Project. In: Mosse, David/Lewis, David (eds.) *The Aid Effect: Giving and Governing in International Development*. London: Pluto Press, 106–125.

Fatheuer, Thomas 2011: *Buen Vivir: A Brief Introduction to Latin America's New Concepts for the Good Life and the Rights of Nature*. Berlin: Heinrich Böll Stiftung, Ecology Publication Series Vol. 17.

Foucault, Michel 1972 (1969): *The Archaeology of Knowledge & The Discourse on Language*. New York: Pantheon Books.

Foucault, Michel 1978 (1976): *The History of Sexuality. Volume 1: An Introduction*. New York: Random House.

Foucault, Michel 1980: *Power/Knowledge: Selected Interviews & Other Writings 1972–1977*. New York: Random House.

Gudynas, Eduardo 2011: Buen Vivir: Today's Tomorrow. *Development* 54(4), 441–447.

Hickey, Samuel/Mohan, Giles (eds.) 2004: *Participation: From Tyranny to Transformation? Exploring New Approaches to Participation in Development*. London: Zed Books.

Kiely, Ray 1999: The Last Refuge of the Noble Savage? A Critical Assessment of Post-Development Theory. *European Journal of Development Research* 11(1), 30–55.

Kößler, Reinhart 1998: *Entwicklung*. Münster, Westfälisches Dampfboot.

Leal, Pablo Alejandro 2010: Participation: The Ascendancy of a Buzzword in the Neo-liberal Era. In: Cornwall, Andrea/Eade, Deborah (eds.) *Deconstructing Development Discourse: Buzzwords and Fuzzwords*. Bourton: Practical Action, 89–100.

Lepenies, Philipp 2014: La rage de vouloir conclure: Wissensvermittlung als Entwicklungsengpass oder warum Experten so arbeiten, wie sie es tun. In: Ziai, Aram (ed.) *Im Westen nichts Neues? Stand und Perspektiven der Entwicklungstheorie*. Baden-Baden: Nomos, 213–234.

Marglin, Stephen A. 1990: Towards the Decolonisation of the Mind. In: Apffel-Marglin Frédérique/Marglin, Stephen (eds.) Dominating Knowledge: Development, Culture and Resistance. Oxford: Clarendon, 1–28.

Mehta, Pradeep S. 1994: Fury Over a River. In: Danaher, Kevin (ed.): *50 Years is Enough: The Case Against the World Bank and the International Monetary Fund*. Boston, MA: South End Press, 117–120.

Nandy, Ashis 1995: *Development and Violence*. Trier: Zentrum für europäische Studien.

Nandy, Ashis 2004: Revisiting the Violence of Development: An Interview with Ashis Nandy. *Development* 47(1), 8–14.

Nisbet, Robert 1969: *Social Change and History: Aspects of the Western Theory of Development*. Oxford: Oxford University Press.

Potter, David 2000: The Power of Colonial States. In: Allen, Tim/Thomas, Alan (eds.) *Poverty and Development into the 21st Century*. Oxford: Oxford University Press/Open University, 271–288.

Rahnema, Majid 1990: Participatory Action Research: The 'Last Temptation of Saint' Development. *Alternatives* 15(2), 199–226.

Rahnema, Majid (ed.) 1997a: *The Post-development Reader*. London: Zed.

Rahnema, Majid 1997b: Introduction. In: Rahnema, Majid (ed.) *The Post-development Reader*. London: Zed, ix–xix.

Rahnema, Majid 1997c: Development and the People's Immune System: The Story of Another Variety of AIDS. In: Rahnema, Majid (ed.) *The Post-development Reader*. London: Zed, 111–129.

Rahnema, Majid 1997d: Towards Post-development: Searching for Signposts, a New Language and New Paradigms. In: Rahnema, Majid (ed.) *The Post-development Reader*. London: Zed, 377–403.

Rist, Gilbert 2008: The History of Development. In: *Western Origins to Global Faith*, 3rd ed. London: Zed Books.

Roy, Arundhati 1999: The Greater Common Good. Online http://www.narmada.org/gcg/gcg.html (January 1, 2013).

Sachs, Wolfgang (ed.) 1992: *The Development Dictionary: A Guide to Knowledge as Power.* London: Zed Books.

Said, Edward 1978: *Orientalism.* New York: Vintage.

Siebold, Thomas 2008: *Armutsorientierte Entwicklung mithilfe von PRSPs? Eine Zwischenbilanz für Subsahara-Afrika. INEF-Report* 95. Duisburg: Institut für Entwicklung und Frieden.

Spanger, Hans-Joachim/Wolff, Jonas 2003: *Armutsreduzierung durch Demokratisierung? PRSP: Chancen und Widersprüche einer neuen entwicklungspolitischen Strategie. HSFK-Report* 6. Frankfurt: Hessische Stiftung Friedens- und Konfliktforschung.

Spivak, Gayatri Chakravorty 1999: *A Critique of Postcolonial Reason: Toward a History of the Vanishing Present.* Cambridge, MA: Harvard University Press.

UN 1960: Resolution 1522. *Accelerated Flow of Capital and Technical Assistance to the Developing Countries.*

UN 1961: Resolution 1710. *United Nations Development Decade: A Programme for International Economic Co-operation.*

UN 1970: Resolution 2626. *International Development Strategy for the Second United Nations Development Decade.*

UN 1974: Resolution 3201. *Declaration on the Establishment of a New International Economic Order.*

UN Intellectual History Project 2010: *The UN and Development Policies.* Briefing Note Number 7.

WDM 2005: *One Size for All: A Study of IMF and World Bank Poverty Reduction Strategies.* London: World Development Movement.

White, Sarah 1996: Depoliticising Development: The Uses and Abuses of Participation. *Development in Practice* 6(1), 6–15.

Ziai, Aram 2004a: *Entwicklung als Ideologie? Das klassische Entwicklungsparadigma und die Post-Development Kritik.* Hamburg: DÜI.

Ziai, Aram 2004b: The ambivalence of Post-Development: between reactionary populism and radical democracy. *Third World Quarterly* 25(6), 1045–1061.

Part III
Genealogy

7 The transformation of development discourse

Participation, sustainability, heterogeneity

Following or criticising the Post-Development approach in development theory (see above all Sachs 1992a), many studies have been analysing the discourse of development in the past two decades (Ferguson 1994, Crush 1995, Moore/ Schmitz 1995, Cowen/Shenton 1996, Cooper/Packard 1997, Grillo/Stirrat 1997, Rahnema 1997, Eriksson Baaz 2005, Groves/Hinton 2005, Mosse/Lewis 2005, Cornwall/Eade 2010, Ziai 2013). Although these – often interesting and insightful – studies and this line of inquiry in general have often been associated with the work of Michel Foucault (e.g., Storey 2000: 40), most of them have more or less traced the link between knowledge and power and few of them have seriously engaged in applying Foucaultian concepts (these notable exceptions are, e.g., Escobar 1988 and 1995, Brigg 2002, Rossi 2004, Li 2007). However, none of these have actually implemented the methodology for discourse analysis outlined in Foucault's *Archaeology of Knowledge* (1972). The article undertakes a first attempt to do so.[1]

The methodological approach of archaeological discourse analysis is able to illuminate discursive structures and thus aspects of development policy hitherto unnoticed. The way the objects of development policy are discursively constructed and the rules according to which this is done are certainly relevant to scholars of development studies. Applying the approach outlined in chapter 4, this chapter will deal with the transformations in development discourse which occurred as a reaction to the 'crisis of development theory' in the 1980s and the corresponding rise of new concepts in development policy. Three of these discursive transformations, the rise of concepts like civil society participation, ownership and empowerment, the awareness of ecological questions and the commitment to sustainable development, and the rejection of one-size-fits-all solutions in development policy, are examined more thoroughly in the context of an empirical study of development institutions in the beginning of the 21st century. This examination reveals that these transformations resulted in incoherences and contradictions regarding the discourse of development. It is argued that these incoherences and contradictions arise inevitably because some of the new concepts like participation and sustainability have implications which are incompatible with the rules of development discourse which have been formed in the post–World War II period.

The transformation of development discourse

Although the classical development discourse described in chapter 4 was not a rigid, stable system, its rules of formation remained in operation as mostly unquestioned discursive structures from the 1950s to the 1970s. Things have changed since then. Especially since the crisis of development theory in the 1980s and some corresponding historical experiences in development policy the discourse has undergone a number of modifications and processes of change. New concepts have appeared and become influential in development policy, the most prominent of which are sustainable development, good governance, globalisation, global governance, participation, civil society and ownership.[2] The way we talk about *development* has changed, a transformation of development discourse can be observed. The question is, whether the rules of formation of development discourse have been affected by this transformation as well. Even the most sharp-sighted critiques of development discourse such as Escobar (1995) and Ferguson (1994) have not sufficiently explored this transformation and, above all, its implications for the structure of the discourse. It is here that the approach of archaeological discourse analysis can contribute to further our understanding.

Development discourse in the 21st century can be conceptualised as a network of interrelated and partly competing (sub)discourses. Its transformation since the 1980s and the factors leading to the rise of these new discourses can, in a slightly simplified manner, be sketched as follows:

The perception of an impasse in (above all Marxist and structuralist) development theory and its universalist and determinist assumptions (Booth 1985) allowed the neoliberal 'counter-revolution in development theory and policy' (Toye 1987). It also led to a focus on less ambitious and more specific 'middle-range theories' rejecting the universalist one-size-fits-all approaches in development theory and policy and an intensified debate on sociocultural factors in *development*. The perception of failures in development policy led to widely diverging interpretations. In some circles, the market – as opposed to inefficient and corrupt state apparatuses – was discovered as a universal remedy, in others the lack of civil society participation was blamed for the failures. Still others gave up on the entire promise of *development* and suggested confining the efforts to 'relief instead of development aid' (Myrdal 1981) – thoughts which were taken up in later debates about crisis prevention, failed states and trusteeship. A different conclusion of the same diagnosis was drawn by the Post-Development school: turn away from the development industry and look for grassroots 'alternatives to development' (Sachs 1992a, Escobar 1995).

The experience of successful industrialisation in South-East Asia was also interpreted in different ways: while some saw it as proof for the neoliberal hypotheses of the Washington Consensus, the inevitability of world market integration and the beneficial effects of economic globalisation (World Bank 1993), others stressed the significance of institutions for economic policies, advocating a new role of the state – though often without fundamentally challenging neoclassical economics. The end of the Cold War was even more influential: it intensified the neoliberal discourse surrounding market solutions and globalisations (there was no need to prove the superiority of the capitalist system through regulatory social policies) as well as the discourse of abandoning the promise of *development* (fear of former colonies joining the communist bloc had been one if not the major motive for development aid in the first decades) and it made demands for good governance in the South possible (World Bank 1992) (while anti-communist dictatorships were rarely confronted with their shortcomings in the areas of democracy and human rights beforehand). On the other hand, the end of the Cold War also made possible the discourses of One World and Global Governance, in which the world's governments cooperate to solve the world's problems (Commission on Global Governance 1995).

The latter point is also closely related to the perception of global ecological problems which do not stop at the border of nation-states and which endanger the lives of future generations. The concept of sustainable development was promoted by the Brundtland report (World Commission on Environment and Development 1987) and increased in momentum after the Earth Summit in Rio 1992. The concept contributed to the abandoning of the promise of *development* and to the Global Governance discourse. A factor which enabled the rise of the concept of sustainable development was the critique from civil society since the late 1960s. Similar critiques led to the inclusion of the discourses of empowerment, participation and ownership on the one and women (WID) and gender (GAD) on the other hand into development discourse, as well as to the concept of human development put forward by the UNDP. Finally, the politics of structural adjustment was also involved in the rise of the good governance agenda (political factors were made responsible for the disappointing economic results) (Abrahamsen 2000), while the confined capacity of states for certain types of policies in the context of neoliberal globalisation contributed to the perception that globalisation has to be regulated through global governance.

While this cursory description of the transformation of development discourse is based on primary and secondary literature in development theory and policy, my own empirical research for my PhD thesis led to some interesting specifications. In 20 qualitative interviews conducted with staff of different development organisations (the World Bank, the German ministry of development BMZ and two German NGOs, Misereor and medico international),[3] the transformation of development discourse and the prominence of the new concepts were clearly visible. But what could also be discerned were some incoherences and contradictions which – this is my central argument here – arise because some of the more progressive concepts and arguments adopted in this transformation are incompatible with the rules of formation of development discourse outlined in the second section. Nevertheless, these rules are still partly adhered to because they are closely linked to questions of identity and institutional interests. In the following, interview sections centering on three of these new concepts – participation, sustainability and the rejection of universal models – will be drawn on to elaborate my argument.

Participation vs. expert knowledge

Despite ideological differences between the different organisations (and individuals), the sentence which occurred in one form or another in almost all the interviews was 'the people have to decide themselves what development is for them' (Int 8, 9, 12). Variants of this statement were, e.g., 'we are neither legitimised nor competent to define development for others' (Int 16); 'development . . . does not mean that we decide about concrete goals because actually it is the partner who should decide' (Int 2); 'The developing country must be the one who decides about development goals' (Int 6); and 'It is not our task to define for Burkina Faso or indigenous people in Brazil's rainforest how their development should look like. . . . We must not define for others. This is virtually the categorical imperative' (Int 18). This attitude was justified and linked with concepts of 'participation' (Int 3), 'partnership' or 'partner-driven development' (Int 11, 1) and 'ownership' (Int 6, 16).

These statements can be seen as a reaction to the critique of development policy as a top-down, authoritarian enterprise and an endorsement of the view of those critics promoting participation or empowerment since the 1980s (Friedmann 1992, Chambers 1997): that the persons affected by development projects should decide for themselves what kind of social change they desire and what constitutes a good society for them. Here, the transformation of development discourse according to the new concepts of participation, empowerment and ownership manifests itself. Strictly speaking, the transfer of the ability to decide what *development* means for them deprives the experts of their superior competence to do so and eliminates the element of trusteeship – which is revealed as a mechanism for nondemocratic decision-making on social values and priorities.

However, the same persons who emphatically stated this view also had different definitions of *development*, i.e. certain conceptions of how a good society in the South looks like and how it can be realised. These definitions could be the 'satisfaction of basic needs' (Int 6), the 'enlargement of choices' (Int 16), 'justice, peace and the preservation of the creation' (Int 12) or even 'overcoming the health-impairing condition of capitalism' (Int 9) in another case. The same experts who vehemently opposed giving prescriptions for *development* prescribed measures like 'investing in people, empowerment, good investment climate' (Int 16) or 'transfer of capital, education and access to markets' (Int 15) as remedies.

Yet this inevitably leads to a tension in the cooperation with Third World partners: On the one hand the development workers have certain conceptions of *development* and are willing to implement them, on the other hand they are unwilling to force their ideas on others. The tension becomes a contradiction when the development organisations preach participation, partnership, ownership or empowerment while their politics remain framed by conditionality and good governance. Even if the conception of *development* is seen as an offer the people can decline the promise of resource transfers does lead to an adaptation (at least in rhetoric) of the donor's demands on the part of the recipients.[4]

The transfer of the right to define *development* to the partner in the South becomes farcical when the other partner determines the conditions, sets the agenda or decides what sound economic policies look like. Despite the commitment to ideals of participation and partnership, there are some structural elements in the donor-recipient relationship which prevent a symmetrical participation of all actors in the decision-making process. One is that the donors want to maintain control over their resources for reasons of national interest or out of accountability towards the taxpayers. Another is that the expert knowledge questioned by these ideals is closely linked to the identity of those working in the development industry.

Looking at the level of discourse, in order to 'speak development', one has to say what a good society looks like and how it can be attained. This is what development experts are hired to do and this is the place assigned to them in discourse, by the rule of formation of enunciative modalities. The discourse constructs the subject position of a knowing and prescribing expert. The expert is defined by his or her expert knowledge on the process of *development*, the ability to generate, articulate and apply this knowledge is constitutive of his or her identity. A development expert who takes seriously the claims of empowerment discourse and denounces the superior competence in outlining progressive social change would be confronted with the question what the use of experts is if they have no expertise.

To be precise: while statements on historical social change are still possible for experts who refuse to formulate goals for people in the South, any statement which would include normative and political elements like desirable social conditions or preferences concerning the manner in which future social change is envisioned appears illegitimate unless it is based on a clear (and ideally consensual) articulation of the people concerned. In such a scenario, the researchers would be confined to the role of assistants to social movements and communities. This is rather at odds with the traditional role of experts in development discourse.

Of course, the concepts of participation, partnership and empowerment have been adopted in development institutions often only in a selective and depoliticised manner which did hardly question existing relations of power, as has been amply illustrated by the critical literature on the topic (Rahnema 1990, 1992, Macdonald 1995, White 1996, Mohan/Stokke 2000, Cooke/Kothari 2001, Abrahamsen 2004, Cornwall/Brock 2005, Batliwala 2011, Leal 2011). However, my research suggests that even in the supposedly co-opted versions of the concepts which have lost their critical edge they exert enough influence to disturb the order of development discourse and cause incoherences and contradictions, thus highlighting the nonparticipatory and authoritarian rules of the discourse. So even a depoliticised version of participation leads to contradictions in development policy, to unpleasant questions and incoherent practices, which in turn can be used as tools in political change. Thus there may be a potential for a repoliticisation of participation (Hickey/Mohan 2004, Williams 2004).

Sustainability vs. *developed* north

A similar observation can be made regarding the concept of sustainability in development discourse. The concept defines sustainable development as 'development which meets the needs of the present without compromising the ability of future generations to meet their needs' (World Commission on Environment and Development 1987). This has a particular consequence for the role of industrialised countries in the discourse. As one interviewee correctly pointed out: 'If we adopt the concept of sustainability, the industrialised countries are developing countries' (Int 15, a similar phrase appeared in Int 6), because the resource use and environmental pollution caused by these countries indicate that this model of society cannot be universalised. It can be maintained only as long as it is confined to a privileged minority – one could say it is an oligarchic model of society.

Again, telling incoherences and contradictions can be encountered. On the one hand, the concept of sustainability is heralded as the new and only way forward in the interviews. One interviewee emphasised: 'We rigorously promote the concept of sustainable development' (Int 1), another asserted: 'Concerning the concept of development, we adhere to the concept of sustainable development as defined in Rio 1992' (Int 5). Less explicit, but similar commitments could be found in many other interviews (Int 2, 6, 7, 11, 13, 15).

On the other hand the industrialised countries are still constantly referred to as the *developed* societies – which implies that *less developed* or *underdeveloped* societies should become like them, and development policy should help assist them in this process. Although taking the concept of sustainable development and its often quoted definition seriously would render this traditional identification of *developed* and industrialised countries impossible, such an equivalence is exactly what can be found in many interviews. The *developed* countries are specified as the 'OECD member states' (Int 1.4), the 'Western world' (Int 3), or, straightforwardly, as the 'industrialised countries' (Int 6, 18). This is where the incoherence becomes manifest: either the industrialised North provides a model to be copied or its lifestyle is entirely unsustainable. The two perspectives are not compatible.

While the development experts do pay at least lip service to the new influential concept of sustainable development, they still refer to Northern countries as *developed* and thus adhere to the rule of formation of strategies which dates back to the postwar era and identifies the industrialised North as a model for all other societies. According to this rule, the statement 'the USA is an underdeveloped society' does not make any sense, because what is understood as a *developed* society is intimately linked to the US through a chain of equivalence between the signifiers (Laclau/Mouffe 1985: 127ff). That statements like these appear today provides another example of the disturbing effects that an originally critical but supposedly co-opted and mainstreamed concept can unfold in development institutions. Many studies have convincingly argued that sustainable development has been reinterpreted as 'sustainable growth' (World Bank 1989) and instrumentalised as yet another concept reinforcing technocratic constructions of social problems and the competence and duty of the North to manage the planet because of its superior technology (Sachs 1992b, Adams 1995, Sachs 1995, Sachs

1999, Scoones 2011). The argument here does not disprove the criticism raised against this process of co-optation, but puts it into perspective: it is less encompassing as its critics fear.

Heterogeneity vs. one-size-fits-all

A third area where incoherences and contradictions are visible is not as closely related to the rise of a new concept as the first two. However, a significant realisation which became prominent during the crisis of development theory of the 1980s was that the countries of the South were more heterogeneous than had hitherto been assumed. The perception of a growing process of differentiation within this group of countries – into successful industrialisers, rich oil-exporters and an increasingly impoverished rest – (together with the demise of the Soviet bloc) led to the catchphrase 'the end of the Third World' (Harris 1987, Menzel 1992, Berger 1994). The corresponding criticism implied that development theory had been wrong in lumping together a group of countries with widely diverging economic and political conditions and social and cultural backgrounds and in assuming a single bundle of problems and corresponding solutions, a single pattern of social change, a single process of *development* in all of them, a single size for all.

This transformation of discourse can be observed throughout the interviews. The heterogeneity of conditions and factors influencing social change in different societies is readily acknowledged, and we find statements that 'There is not one solution' for the problems of the 'less developed' countries (Int 3), that 'The conditions for development are different in each country. Patterns of development, like the industrialisation of Germany, cannot be transferred to developing countries' (Int 4), and that 'There are no blueprints for development. There are different cultural conditions in each country, different economic, geographical conditions' (Int 5). The interviewees insist that '[e]ach country has to find its own way' (Int 15, 16), 'individual solutions for each country' (Int 6) and a 'tailor-made approach' (Int 16) were needed, and a one-size-fits-all or a cookie-cutter approach are vehemently rejected (Int 16, 18). What this implies is that there is not *one* process of social change which takes place in all societies sooner or later, but that there are different historical *developments*.

Despite this insight, there are numerous references to be found to 'the process of development' (Int 6, 7, 9, 12) which suggest that there is a universal process and thus a single model. Sometimes, the experts were even more explicit and argued that the process of *development* in Europe 'surely is a model' for the *developing* countries (Int 4), maintained that 'if you try to find Somalia's level of development in European history, you have to go back a few hundred years' (Int 18) and stated that 'Development is actually a process, human development simply progresses and there are few cultures who want to live as they did a thousand years ago' (Int 3). In other words: there is a pattern of social change which occurs in all societies irrespective of their different conditions and backgrounds and it has taken place in Europe and North America earlier than in other societies which is why they are at the top of the universal scale of *development*. Modernisation theory is not dead yet. Or rather, the rules of development discourse, specifically the norms guiding the formation of objects and concepts, are still present even after a discursive transformation has asserted the contingency and historicity of processes of social change and the heterogeneity of conditions and factors influencing them in different places of the world. Again, a coherent progress in development policy is prevented by the order of development discourse which assumes that there is universal knowledge on social change irrespective of regional circumstances.

In this context, it is worth while noting that development institutions are based on the assumption of such knowledge. How else could they justify that their experts are able to analyse and design social change in societies where they have not lived for more than a few months or even weeks? That their competence in doing so is superior to those who have lived there all their lives? Only because they possess knowledge on social change which is universal in character and therefore applicable all over the world.

Conclusion

The method of archaeological discourse analysis employed here (building on earlier critiques) has yielded some interesting insights. The objects of development discourse are sociogeographical units categorised as deficient in relation to the norm of the Western society and thus classified as *underdeveloped*. Correspondingly, the concepts of the discourse are always concerned with some lack or deficiency (e.g. failed states), which, however already imply a cure or positive strategy (e.g. state-building). Usually, the problems of these units are constructed as lack of capital, knowledge or technology and in general as problems amenable to nonpolitical, technocratic solutions offered by development institutions and organisations. The diagnosis of deficiency is articulated from the subject position of the knowing, prescribing expert which has to be assumed by anyone performing (speaking in) the discourse. In the history of development policy, several diagnostic cycles can be identified: e.g. in the 1960s the particular aspects of the objects of discourse which gained new visibility in economic modernisation theories were the rates of savings and economic growth. They were seen as keys to *development*. After sustained economic growth during the 1960s had not led to substantial reductions in poverty, *development* was redefined to explicitly include poverty and a new focus on the rural poor and their basic needs emerged, coupled with a new promise given by the development industry. Further cycles put forward a focus on women, the environment, markets, and institutions/governance. Each diagnostic cycle linked the explanation of earlier failures with a new aspect, a new prescription, and a new promise.

Yet some of the concepts adopted in development discourse since the crisis of the 1980s led to significant discursive transformations. In this article, we examined the concepts of participation/ownership/empowerment, sustainable development and the rejection of one size fits all solutions. In all three areas, we see that due to external criticisms and internal learning processes, the discourse of development institutions has taken aboard concepts which appear as progressive in comparison to the older conceptions tending towards top-down measures, universal blueprints and neglect of environmental consequences. However, these progressive changes lead to incoherences in development discourse because some elements of these new ideas are incompatible with the rules of formation of development discourse. The willingness to adopt these new concepts combined with an unwillingness to abandon the discursive rules of *development* produces the contradictions we have encountered in the interviews. The practice of development institutions to include and co-opt formerly oppositional concepts which have (supposedly) been robbed of their critical content thus has unintended effects. On the other hand, progressive transformations in development policy are confronted with certain limits which are constituted not only by the structures of the development industry, but also by the structures of development discourse. Overcoming these limits presupposes not only political will but first of all an awareness of these structures.

Notes

1   The argument of this paper has been presented at the 6th Interpretive Policy Analysis Conference in Cardiff/UK in 2011. I would like to thank the panel conveners Elena Heßelmann and Franziska Müller for useful comments.
2   Neoliberalism does not appear in this list because it is debatable whether it still belongs to development discourse, as it rejects some of its principles (see chapter 8).
3   The interviewees were predominantly from the middle management level and from different departments (not from PR) of the organisations, so as to render the sample at least moderately representative. The interviews were semi-structured and based on questions concerning the conception of *development* and the role of development experts.
4   The experience of the substitution of structural adjustment programs by PRSPs is a vivid illustration of this case. Officially, the government of the recipient country should prepare a poverty reduction strategy based on participation of the civil society – ownership and participation are heralded as the guiding principles of the process (World Bank 2002). But as the World Bank and the IMF decide whether or not this strategy is worth supporting through loans, the recipient governments often confine participation to social policy and adhere to the macroeconomic conceptions of the Washington consensus in order to gain approval of the donors. 'We give them what they want before they start lecturing us', commented an African minister of finance (World Development Movement 2001: 7).

Bibliography

Abrahamsen, Rita 2000: *Disciplining Democracy: Development Discourse and Good Governance in Africa*. London: Zed Books.
Abrahamsen, Rita 2004: The Power of Partnerships in Global Governance. *Third World Quarterly* 25(8), 1453–1467.
Adams, W. M. 1995: Green Development Theory? Environmentalism and Sustainable Development. In: Crush, Jonathan (ed.) *Power of Development*. London: Routledge, 87–99.
Batliwala, Srilatha 2010: Taking the power out of empowerment – an experiential account. In: Cornwall, Andrea/Eade, Deborah (eds.) *Deconstructing Development Discourse: Buzzwords and Fuzzwords*. Bourton: Practical Action, 111–122.

Berger, Mark T. 1994: The End of the 'Third World'? *Third World Quarterly* 15(2), 257–275.

Booth, David 1985: Marxism and Development Sociology: Interpreting the Impasse. *World Development* 13(7), 761–787.

Brigg, M. 2002: Post-Development, Foucault, and the Colonisation Metaphor. *Third World Quarterly* 23(3), 421–436.

Chambers, Robert 1997: *Whose Reality Counts? Putting the First Last.* London: ITDG.

Commission on Global Governance 1995: *Our Global Neighbourhood.* Oxford: Oxford University Press.

Cooke, Bill/Kothari, Uma (eds.) 2001: *Participation: The New Tyranny?* London: Zed.

Cooper, Frederick/Packard, Randall (eds.) 1997: *International Development and the Social Sciences: Essays on the History and Politics of Knowledge.* Berkeley: University of California Press.

Cornwall, Andrea/Brock, Karen 2005: What do Buzzwords do for Development Policy? A critical look at 'participation', 'empowerment' and 'poverty reduction'. *Third World Quarterly* 26(7), 1043–1060.

Cornwall, Andrea/Eade, Deborah (eds.) 2010: *Deconstructing Development Discourse: Buzzwords and Fuzzwords.* Bourton: Practical Action.

Cowen, Michael P./Shenton, Robert W. 1996: *Doctrines of Development.* London: Routledge.

Crush, Jonathan (ed.) 1995: *Power of Development.* London: Routledge.

Eriksson Baaz, Maria 2005: *The Paternalism of Partnership: A Postcolonial Reading of Identity in Development Aid.* London: Zed Books.

Escobar, A. 1988: Power and Visibility: Development and the Invention and Management of the Third World. *Cultural Anthropology* 3(4), 428–443.

Escobar, Arturo 1995: *Encountering Development: The Making and Unmaking of the Third World.* Princeton, NJ: Princeton University Press.

Ferguson, James 1994 (1990): *The Anti-politics Machine: Development, Depoliticization and Bureaucratic Power in Lesotho.* Minneapolis: University of Minnesota Press.

Foucault, Michel 1972 (1969): *The Archaeology of Knowledge & the Discourse on Language.* New York: Pantheon Books.

Friedmann, John 1992: *Empowerment: The Politics of Alternative Development.* Oxford: Blackwell.

Grillo, R. D./Stirrat, R. L. (eds.) 1997: *Discourses of Development: Anthropological Perspectives.* Oxford: Berg.

Groves, Leslie/Hinton, Rachel (eds.) 2005: *Inclusive Aid: Changing Power and Relationships in International Development.* London: Earthscan.

Harris, Nigel 1987: *The End of the Third World: Newly Industrializing Countries and the Decline of an Ideology.* New Amsterdam: New Amsterdam Books.

Hickey, Samuel/Mohan, Giles (eds.) 2004: *Participation: From Tyranny to Transformation? Exploring New Approaches to Participatory Development.* London: Zed.

Laclau, Ernesto/Mouffe, Chantal 1985: *Hegemony and Socialist Strategy: Towards a Radical Democratic Politics.* London: Verso.

Leal, Pablo Alejandro 2010: Participation: The Ascendancy of a Buzzword in the Neo-liberal Era. In: Cornwall, Andrea/Eade, Deborah (eds.) 2010: *Deconstructing Development Discourse: Buzzwords and Fuzzwords.* Bourton: Practical Action, 89–100.

Li, Tania Murray 2007: *The Will to Improve: Governmentality, Development, and the Practice of Politics.* Durham, NC: Duke University Press.

Macdonald, Laura 1995: NGOs and the Problematic Discourse of Participation: Cases from Costa Rica. In: Moore, David/Schmitz, Gerald J. (eds.) *Debating Development Discourse: Institutional and Popular Perspectives.* Basingstoke, Macmillan, 201–229.

Menzel, Ulrich 1992: *Das Ende der Dritten Welt und das Scheitern der großen Theorie*. Frankfurt: Suhrkamp.

Mohan, Giles/Stokke, Kristian 2000: Participatory Development and Empowerment: The Dangers of Localism. *Third World Quarterly* 21(2), 247–268.

Moore, David/Schmitz, Gerald J. (eds.) 1995: *Debating Development Discourse: Institutional and Popular Perspectives*. Basingstoke: Macmillan.

Mosse, David/Lewis, David (eds.) 2005: *The Aid Effect: Giving and Governing in International Development*. London: Pluto.

Myrdal, Gunnar 1981: Relief Instead of Development Aid. *Intereconomics* 16(2), 86–89.

Rahnema, Majid 1990: Participatory Action Research: The 'Last Temptation of Saint' Development. *Alternatives* 15(2), 199–226.

Rahnema, Majid 1992: Participation. In: Sachs, Wolfgang (ed.) *The Development Dictionary: A Guide to Knowledge as Power*. London: Zed Books, 116–131.

Rahnema, Majid (ed.) 1997: *The Post-development Reader*. London: Zed.

Rossi, Benedetta 2004: Revisiting Foucauldian Approaches: Power Dynamics in Development Projects. *Journal of Development Studies* 40(6), 1–29.

Sachs, Wolfgang (ed.) 1992a: *The Development Dictionary: A Guide to Knowledge as Power*. London: Zed Books.

Sachs, Wolfgang 1992b: Environment. In: Sachs, Wolfgang (ed.) *The Development Dictionary: A Guide to Knowledge as Power*. London: Zed Books, 26–37.

Sachs, Wolfgang (ed.) 1995: *Global Ecology: A New Arena of Political Conflict*. London: Zed Books.

Sachs, Wolfgang 1999: *Planet Dialectics: Explorations in Environment and Development*. London: Zed Books.

Scoones, Ian 2010: Sustainability. In: Cornwall, Andrea/Eade, Deborah (eds.) *Deconstructing Development Discourse: Buzzwords and Fuzzwords*. Bourton: Practical Action, 153–162.

Storey, Andy 2000: Post-Development Theory: Romanticism and Pontius Pilate Politics. *Development (SID)* 43(4), 40–46.

Toye, John 1987: *Dilemmas of Development: Reflections on the Counter-revolution in Development Theory and Policy*. Oxford: Blackwell.

White, Sarah 1996: Depoliticising Development: The Uses and Abuses of Participation. *Development in Practice* 6(1), 6–15.

Williams, Glyn 2004: Evaluating Participatory Development: Tyranny, Power and (Re)Politicisation. *Third World Quarterly* 25(3), 557–578.

World Bank 1989: *Sub-Saharan Africa: From Crisis to Sustainable Growth*. Washington, DC: Author.

World Bank 1992: *Governance and Development*. Washington, DC: Author.

World Bank 1993: *The East Asian Miracle: Economic Growth and Policy*. Washington, DC: Author.

World Bank 2002: A Sourcebook on Poverty Reduction Strategies: Overview. Online http://povlibrary.worldbank.org/files/5301_overview.pdf (October 17, 2006).

World Commission on Environment and Development 1987: *Our Common Future*. Oxford: Oxford University Press.

World Development Movement 2001: Policies to Roll-back the State and Privatize? Poverty Reduction Strategy Papers Investigated. UNU, WIDER discussion paper No. 2001/120.

Ziai, Aram 2013: The Discourse of 'Development' and Why the Concept Should be 'Abandoned'. *Development in Practice* 23(1), 123–136.

8 From 'development' to 'globalisation'

This chapter[1] is concerned with the academic and political fields of North-South relations, often circumscribed as 'development theory' and 'development policy' respectively. I argue that a shift from a discourse of development to a discourse of globalisation has occurred in recent years and that this shift is central to the changing ways in which knowledge about global relations of power and exchange has been conceptualised in the past two decades or so. A concise analysis of both discourses is relevant and insightful because notions of *development* and of globalisation are conceptualising social change in strikingly different ways and with different attitudes towards social engineering. A comparison of these latter qualities enables us to better decipher the social production of knowledge about changes in the global system.

Discourse analysis is particularly fruitful if discourses are understood as powerful and meaningful systems of representation that interlink the production of knowledge with material practices that are in turn justified and thus substantiated. As we have seen in earlier chapters, the discourse of development has already been dissected by scholars like Ferguson (1994) and Escobar (1995). These scholars focused on the historical constellation that facilitated its rise, its underlying assumptions and its effects. A similar dissection, however, remains to be done for the discourse of globalisation. Some scholars have identified shifts in development theory and policy during the past two decades (see especially Moore/Schmitz 1995 and Mosse/Lewis 2005). McMichael (2000) claims that the development project has been replaced by a globalization project. Gibson-Graham (1996) and Ho (2005) offer immensely interesting critiques of this latter project, which provide valuable points of reference for future analysis. However, little systematic discourse analysis has been carried out on the shift identified above. This article will attempt to engage these gaps – although it will certainly be impossible to close all of them, given how vast the field of analysis is.

One of the field's main challenges is reflected in the fact that the article deals primarily with the discourses of Western Europe and North America.[2] This focus is particularly relevant in the field of development aid, where in recent years – following the rise of China and others to the status of influential donor-countries – there has been some debate about a new plurality of actors. However, this supposedly new donor rivalry is something quite familiar from the Cold War period.

Only after 1989 the West had the monopoly on development aid, allowing it to pursue good governance policies and the like.

In order to establish my argument, the general hypothesis of the shift from a discourse of development to one of globalisation shall be elaborated and specified in the course of the following sections. First, it is necessary to outline more precisely what is to be understood by the term discourse. Then, the discourse of development and the reasons for its putative demise coinciding with the rise of the discourse of globalisation are sketched. The ensuing main section will highlight the differences between the discourses of development and globalisation with particular reference to the practices rendered possible or impossible by each of them respectively. Throughout these sections, I will indicate how both notions and knowledge about change have been altered in the course of the historical shift from development to globalisation as the driving force of global interaction.

Discourse, discourse analysis and the question of representing the world

Discourse will be understood here in a Foucauldian sense. What this means has been succinctly captured by Stuart Hall:

> By 'discourse' we mean a particular way of representing [. . .] A discourse is a group of statements which provide a language for talking about – i.e. a way of representing – a particular kind of knowledge about a topic. When statements about a topic are made within a particular discourse, the discourse makes it possible to construct the topic in a certain way. It also limits the other ways in which the topic can be constructed.
>
> (Hall 1992: 291, emphasis in the original)

This rather general definition stresses the constructivist point that 'to speak is to do something' (Foucault 1972: 209) (namely to construct social reality). This can be made more precise – as well as more complicated – by referring to Foucault himself. In the *Archaeology of Knowledge*, he identifies discourses as discursive formations and states that 'whenever, between objects, types of statement, concepts, or thematic choices, one can define a regularity (an order, correlations, positions and functionings, transformations), we will say [. . .] that we are dealing with a discursive formation' (ibid.: 39). Thus, discourses can be recognised due to the existence of these regularities – due to their rules of formation.

On the other hand, as poignantly expressed in the quote by Hall above, the existence of such regularities always implies exclusions. This nexus of regularity and exclusion is especially relevant for the link between discourse and power:

> Each society has its regime of truth, its 'general politics' of truth: that is, the types of discourse which it accepts and makes function as true; the mechanisms and instances which enable one to distinguish true and false statements, the means by which each is sanctioned; the techniques accorded

value in the acquisition of truth; the status of those who are charged with saying what counts as true.

(Foucault 1980: 131)

This perspective does not relate to truth as a question of the accurate representation of reality by language, but seeks to identify which discourses are accepted as true. Truth furthermore is always produced and embedded in relations of power.

If we agree with Foucault that the production of knowledge is a central task of discourses, and that this knowledge enables certain social and political practices while excluding others, we will see that the notions of and knowledge about change generated by the discourses of development and globalisation are highly significant for the material realities of the global system. As a standard criticism of Foucault's discourse analysis is that it fails to grasp the opposite influence of historical constellations in politics and the economy on discourses (which is justified only for the Archaeology of Knowledge, but less so for his later writings), we will also be dealing with the question which factors have made possible certain discourses.

The rise and decline of 'development' discourse

Development is a word that has been used to designate processes of change in numerous areas and disciplines. My discussion shall be confined to the *development* of societies, especially of non-Western societies. If we take a cursory glance at the history of this concept (among the vast literature see especially Nisbet 1969, Alcalde 1987, and Cowen/Shenton 1996 for thorough discussions), we can see how two discourses originating in the 19th century merged due to geopolitical constellations in the 20th century: social evolution and social technology.

The discourse of social evolution (which other than commonly assumed was not overly concerned with Darwin's theory) was influenced above all by the theories of Spencer, Marx and Comte. Its paradigmatic assumption is that there is a general evolution of human societies (a universal process realised along national paths, cf. Sidaway 2007: 350), which proceeds along a sequence of stages. This sequence was ultimately defined by the industrialised capitalist societies of the West that were positioned at the top of this evolutionary scale. In this perspective, the conditions in 'backward' areas corresponded with evolutionary stages through which Western European and North American capitalist societies had passed long before. One can thus say that Comte's 'comparative method' of looking at different societies in order to examine the process of evolution formed the backbone of a perspective, which translated 'geocultural differences into historical stages' (Nandy 1992: 146).

The second discourse of social technology was closely linked to the writings of Saint-Simon and his followers, who saw the task of a positive social science in devising social interventions that aimed at rationally reforming society and in the acceleration of its evolutionary transformation. These views sought to answer the problems created by capitalist development by reconciling order and progress.

A central role in these interventions was attributed to privileged actors: 'Only those who had the "capacity" to utilise land, labour and capital in the interests of society as a whole should be "entrusted" with them' (Cowen/Shenton 1996: 25). Thus, this discourse sanctioned state interventions based on the knowledge of expert groups as a means to positively stimulate social and economic change.

The merging of these two discourses is at the root of what Cooper and Packard call the 'ambivalence of development'. This ambivalence is grounded in *development* being a 'description of ongoing self-propelled processes of social change' on the one hand and a 'blueprint for action' on the other (Cooper/Packard 1997: 8). But the prominence that development discourse should gain in the second half of the twentieth century was built on preconditions structuring the global system. A number of historical events in the first half of the 20th century laid the foundations for its rise: The Russian revolution, the global economic crisis emerging in the 1920s, Roosevelt's New Deal policies of the 1930s, the World Wars, and the global upsurge of anti-colonial struggles, coupled with the idea that all human beings are equal, laid the foundations for Cold War policies of development aid. Despite its equality oriented dimension, such aid was foremost an instrument of enlarging the capitalist bloc's spheres of influence and securing access to raw materials (for a detailed account see Alcalde 1987). It was under these historical conditions that, in 1949, US President Harry Truman announced a 'bold new program for making the benefits of our scientific advances and industrial progress available for the improvement and growth of underdeveloped areas' (Truman 1949) and that new ministerial offices, departments, international organisations, and even academic disciplines were formed under the heading of *development*. Rahnema argues that the success of development discourse in the era of decolonisation was due to a convergence of aspirations between three quite different groups of actors:

> [T]he leaders of the independence movements were eager to transform their devastated countries into modern nation-states, while the 'masses' . . . were hoping to liberate themselves from both the old and the new forms of subjugation. As for the former colonial masters, they were seeking a new system of domination, in the hope that it would allow them to maintain their presence in the ex-colonies . . . The myth of development emerged as an ideal construct to meet the hopes of the three categories of actors.
>
> (Rahnema 1997: ix)

This myth of *development*, reflected in the early modernisation theories, proclaimed that the *underdeveloped* areas could become *developed* through the transfer of capital and knowledge within a few decades. Thereby global inequality was depoliticised as '[t]he effect of this powerful narrative was to transform a spatialised global hierarchy into a temporalised (putative) historical sequence' (Ferguson 2005a: 178). The Post-Development critics (see Esteva 1992 as the prime example) have highlighted not only the economic and political interests behind this construction, but especially its Eurocentrism: non-Western societies (in the terminology of postcolonial theory, the Other) were conceived as deficient versions of the ideal norm (the Self). Still, Cooper is right in pointing out a more positive aspect of this concept when he writes:

> Much as one can read the universalism of development discourse as a form of European particularism imposed abroad, it could also be read . . . as a rejection of the fundamental premises of colonial rule, a firm assertion of people of all races to participate in global politics and lay claim to a globally defined standard of living.
>
> (Cooper 1997: 84)

It is this point that helps to explain the popularity that the development discourse enjoys in the peripheries of the global system until today.[3]

And yet, this popularity seems to be on the decline since the 1980s at least. Leys (1996: 26) notes that the history of development theory and policy shows how its core ideals have progressively been altered and abandoned, from the ideal of catching up in the 1960s to redistribution with growth and basic needs in the 1970s and on to structural adjustment in the 1980s. The promise of improvement for the *underdeveloped* regions became more and more modest in the course of time. This has led the Post-Development school as far as to proclaim the end of the age of development: 'The idea of development stands like a ruin in the intellectual landscape' (Sachs 1992: 1). Its proponents give four reasons for this claim. First, once the ecological consequences of industrialisation had become obvious, it had become impossible to portray the *developed* societies as a model for the rest of the world. Second, with the end of the Cold War a central precondition of the discourse of development was lost and the benevolent dimension of the relationship between North and South came to be increasingly conceptualised in different frameworks (e.g., crisis prevention). Third, the project of transforming the *underdeveloped* areas into *developed* ones was proven unsuccessful in light of the growing gap between rich and poor countries – especially after development's 'lost decade', the 1980s. Fourth, the cultural homogenisation linked to the universalisation of the Western way of life came to be increasingly rejected (Sachs 1992).

Obviously, nondiscursive factors are seen as influencing discourses here in the first three points. It has to be noted that these four points refer to different dimensions or aspects of *development* and these dimensions need further evaluation. The first point highlights the ecological impossibility of universalising the Western way of life. But despite its validity, its recognition has hardly led to an abandonment of attempts to industrialise countries of the South. On the other hand, the ecological restructuring of the highly industrialised countries has so far produced only modest results. On a conceptual level nevertheless, the term *development* has since the Brundtland Report (1987) and the UN Conference on Environment and Development (1992) usually been coupled with the qualifier sustainable.[4] Concerning the second point referring to the impact of End of the Cold War, one must consider that the official development assistance (ODA) rate (measured as a percentage of the OECD countries' GNI) continuously declined throughout the 1990s (from 0.33 per cent to 0.22 per cent) and has only slightly risen since the turn of the century (to 0.28 per cent) (DAC 2008: 15). According to these statistics, *development* in terms of financial transfers from North to South has clearly lost in significance after the end of the Cold War and although the proclamation of the Millennium Development Goals in 2000 has had some effects, it has not offset the earlier loss.[5] Support from the Soviet Block (which was markedly less than the Western ODA) was also lost. Beyond these financial aspects, the peripheral countries lost in geopolitical significance due to the end of the Cold War and could not credibly threaten to join the rival camp any longer. As regards the third point, the growing gap between rich and poor countries can hardly be denied – although most countries in the South actually experienced improvements in social indicators such as life expectancy until the 1970s. A widespread disillusionment with *development* as a means to overcome global social inequality is certainly manifest at least since the 1980s. Concerning the fourth point, which refers to the putative effects of successful processes *of development* (and therefore seems somewhat contradictory to the preceding point), countless anthropologists have shown that not cultural homogenisation, but rather processes of hybridisation have taken place in the periphery – although this does not mean that the perception of cultural homogenisation as threatening was no important factor in the rise of some anti-Western social movements.

Still, other factors also contributed to the decline of the development discourse. Apart from the failure of development policy, manifest in the growing gap between rich and poor countries and the increase in absolute poverty in Sub-Saharan Africa and some other regions, another kind of failure or impasse of development theory, in particular of Marxist development theory, has been identified by Booth (1985). This impasse was the result of theoretical problems (Booth accuses Marxist development theory of economism and determinism) exemplified in the inability to explain the successful *development* of the East Asian Tiger states from a perspective, which had regarded the inclusion into the capitalist world system as the least promising way to achieve industrialisation and material improvements.[6] Another factor was the ongoing critique of development projects as top-down interventions caring little about the people who were supposed to benefit. That some projects instead supported corrupt dictatorships was part of the criticism voiced by Third World solidarity groups and nongovernmental organisations as well as by some individuals in the development institutions themselves.[7]

Another effort to explain the decline of development discourse adopts a more global approach and focuses on the predominance of the Fordist system (Arrighi 1999). Arrighi argues that as early as the late 1960s the Fordist capitalist world system evidently failed to deliver on its promise to increase the material well-being of the inhabitants of poor countries while at the same time failing its promise of increasing the prosperity of the people in the rich countries. He attributes this to the exhaustion of the system's capacities expressed in declining rates of profit and culminating in the crisis of capitalism in the 1970s. At the same time, a strategy for solving this crisis became prominent that would later be called neoliberalism. This included trade liberalisation, privatisation of state enterprises, the deregulation of markets and the increasing commodification of social relationships and nature (see Gledhill 2004). As we shall see in the next section, the rise of neoliberalism and the discourse of globalisation are intertwined with the decline of development discourse.

At the end of this section, it is important to note that *all* the factors mentioned above contributed to the decline of the development discourse. This means that the orthodox way of speaking and writing about *development* and the practices that were enabled thereby became increasingly rare and the ones that persisted became increasingly questioned during the 1990s. This is not to say that the development industry set up in the preceding decades ceased to exist, but that this industry had to react to a crisis that arose because of deficits in internal logics and changes in the wider global system, by integrating new discourses into its portfolio. As some of these discourses were not quite compatible with the rules of the traditional formation, we can identify a transformation of development discourse sui generis (see chapter 7).

These new discourses are too numerous to be dealt with in detail here.[8] But probably the most important factor in this transformation was the rise of neoliberal and globalisation discourse, which will be dealt with in the next section.

Thus, at the end of this section we can note that due to a number of factors – in particular the end of the Cold War, the disillusionment with the promise of transforming the *underdeveloped* into *developed* countries, the crisis of Fordism, the awareness of the ecological predicament and last but not least the rise of neoliberalism – the discourse of development was on the decline since the 1980s.

The structure and rise of globalisation discourse

In this section, the discourse of globalisation will be sketched out in light of its variations, related standardised phrases and the criticisms that have been voiced. In particular, we will be dealing with the historical rise of this discourse to its present prominent position. Special reference will be given to the phenomenon of so-called Newly Industrializing Countries (NICs) in East Asia and its heterogeneous interpretations. The next section will then discuss in how far the notion of change in the globalisation discourse differs from that within the above discussed development discourse and whether such a difference has enabled new political-economic practices and power structures.

Since the mid-1990s, globalisation has become the new buzzword in the social sciences. Although probably not (yet) comparable to the postwar omnipresence of *development*, a host of academic volumes, courses, conferences and new professorships bear witness to the catch-all qualities of globalisation. As a signifier, globalisation is linked to a variety of signifieds across different contexts. In order to provide some orientation in this confusing array, we can at least distinguish two usages: a general one, highlighting increasing global interconnectedness, and an economic one, highlighting increasing liberalisation of the world economy. The standard formula of the first variant is that since several years and as a result of flows of information, capital and people, the world has become more and more interconnected. In the spheres of media, economy, culture and ecology, actions and events in any part of the world are said to have consequences elsewhere and therefore no place or nation-state on the globe can regard itself or be regarded as isolated. This discourse is exemplified in the writings of Castells, for example:

> [T]his is indeed a time of change [. . .] In the last quarter of the twentieth century, a technological revolution, centered around information, transformed the way we think, we produce, we consume, we trade, we manage, we communicate, we live, we die, we make war, we make love. A dynamic, global economy has been constituted around the planet, linking valuable people and activities from all over the world.
>
> (Castells 2000: 1)

The other, more specific and probably more important variant employs a different standard formula, namely: As a result of advances in information technology and of the liberalisation of world trade, national economic policy became subject to (increasing) global competition compelling states to compete with one another for capital investment. Thus, states have to align their economic and fiscal policy according to the preferences of global financial markets and enterprises, which basically means that thereby a new structure of dependency is created. In turn, workers have to accept the necessities of global competition and adapt to harsher production regimes and reduced remuneration for reproduction. Key terms in this discourse, which has exerted considerable discursive and also conditioning power since the 1980s, are: liberalisation, deregulation, privatisation, welfare cuts and tax breaks for investors on the state level as well as global sourcing, just-in-time production, lean management and competitiveness on the enterprise level, and increased flexibility and reduced social security on the workers' level. Michel Camdessus, former Managing Director of the IMF, gave a paradigmatic statement illustrating this discourse:

> [I]t is now nearly universally accepted that the most effective economic strategies are private sector-led and outward-oriented. The strategies that have been systematically adopted in the OECD countries, with various shadings, have been the secret of success in East Asia, and they are in turn generating fresh opportunities in Latin America and other regions of the world. Conversely, there is ample evidence that when the state dominates the economy, resources are often misallocated, and private investment and growth suffer. [...] [C]ountries that hope to attract private capital inflows must pursue policies that the market believes will result in economic stability and growth.
>
> (Camdessus 1996)

Although some critics of globalisation like former Chief Economist of the World Bank Joseph Stiglitz and others (who will be referred to below) have painted a far gloomier picture of today's global environment, they mostly agree to the analysis. While Stiglitz fundamentally disagrees with Camdessus' positive judgement, he also sees globalisation characterised by the transnational flows of goods and capital and the inability of states to regulate these flows:

> Today, with the continuing decline in transportation and communication costs, and the reduction of man-made barriers to the flow of goods, services and capital [. . .] we have a process of 'globalization' analogous to the earlier processes in which national economies were formed. Unfortunately, we have no world government, accountable to the people of every country, to oversee the globalization process in a fashion comparable to the way national governments guided the nationalization process. Instead, we have a system [. . .] in which a few institutions [. . .] and a few players [. . .] dominate the scene, but in which many of those affected by their decisions are left almost voiceless.
> (Stiglitz 2003: 22)

It could be said that Stiglitz and others employ a critical economic variant in opposition to the affirmative economic variant of globalisation discourse presented in the Camdessus quote. Still, a discourse can be stabilised by those forms of critique which unquestioningly accept its foundations, and this applies for the critical economic variant as well. First of all, it is easy to realise that the flows of capital, information and people are still by no means evenly distributed around the globe, and that investment and internet-access are heavily concentrated in some areas. In this vein, Ferguson (2005b) has argued that many accounts of the process – Giddens (2002) or Held et al. (1999), but also supposedly critical ones by Stiglitz (2003), Sassen (1999) and Hardt and Negri (2001) – are largely ignoring the experiences of certain regions, notably Africa, which do not fit into the perception of a globalised world. Thus, such accounts are reproducing the questionable assumptions of the discourse they seek to criticise fundamentally. The general variant of globalisation discourse has also been subject to a trenchant critique by Anna Tsing (2000) who maintains that the discourse's assumptions of newness and globality obstruct a more accurate vision of historical continuities and local practices, for example by erecting unhelpful and all-too-simple dichotomies.

Concerning the economic variant, it has been argued that the increasing economic interdependence is vastly exaggerated, especially compared with the situation at the beginning of the 20th century, and the possibilities of political regulation are vastly underestimated (Hirst/Thompson 1996). Gibson-Graham (1996) observes that the standard script of this variant overstates corporate power and downplays the potential for negotiation and resistance other actors, particularly unions, still have. Another critique is voiced regarding the dismantling of the welfare state and the increasingly precarious and flexible character of wage labour as a result of globalisation. This perception has been called a 'legend of Fordism' by George Baca because it ignores that in the peripheral areas of the world economy, and even in some regions and sectors in the centre, the welfare state and social security have never been realised. This legend would thus conflate and idealise the post–World War II experience of the industrialised capitalist countries as a global experience (Baca 2004; see also Neveling 2006).

However, the questions to be answered here are: What happened to North-South relations as the globalisation discourse became the master narrative of global economic integration? And what effects can be identified in comparison to the earlier conception of social change under the heading *development*? The first question shall be dealt with in the following, while the next section is devoted to the second.

If we are talking about the rise of globalisation discourse we have to be aware that it is a popular, watered-down version of neoliberal discourse linked to the idea of globality and One World which became prominent after the end of the bipolar world order. Yet, the rise of neoliberal discourse in institutions of development policy was long underway at that time. In his study of this rise John Toye, at that time Director of the Institute of Development Studies (IDS) at Sussex University, called it 'the counter-revolution in development theory and policy' (1987), because it started as a countermovement against the Keynesian doctrine of state intervention in economic policy. In the neoliberal perspective, whose theoretical basis was to be found in neoclassical and monetarist economics, the perceived failures of development policy were attributed to flawed Keynesian strategies: the idea of the necessity and beneficial effects of state intervention was blamed for over-inflated public sectors, inefficient state enterprises, an overemphasis on the means of production, neglect of human capital development and price-distorting interventions in the market mechanism benefiting urban sectors over rural producers.[9]

When neoliberal discourse entered development theory and policy, it not only pointed out these problems but promoted its own formulae as solutions: the efficiency of the allocation of resources through market mechanisms and the welfare-increasing effects of competition, liberalisation, privatisation and deregulation in terms of lower prices and higher productivity, innovation and progress were stressed. These market-oriented strategies were vehemently promoted by the World Bank and the International Monetary Fund (IMF) as universally applicable in (and for) Third World countries.

The Asian tiger states as best-practice examples of neoliberalism?

In this respect, the appropriation of the unique success story of the Southeast Asian Tiger states by neoliberal discourse played an important role. The rapid processes of economic growth, industrialisation and technological progress in South Korea, Taiwan, Hong Kong and Singapore were interpreted as proof for the benefits of a neoliberal and world-market oriented development strategy.[10] These success stories already featured prominently in the quote by Camdessus above, whose author identified the private-sector led and outward-oriented strategies as the secret of success. While it is correct to point out that these states did at one point in time adapt an export-oriented economic strategy in contrast to a

concept of import-substituting industrialisation, which was only partly successful in Latin America, this emphasis omits several crucial points. Among these
points are the positive geographical (two of the Tigers are city states), historical
(Japanese colonisation did have some positive effects in terms of infrastructure),
geopolitical (they were massively supported by the USA during the Cold War)
and economic (relatively egalitarian distribution after land reforms) conditions
prevalent in some or all of these countries (Castells 2000: 256–306). Yet the most
important omission concerns the role of the state in the processes of economic
growth and industrialisation which can hardly be underestimated and is in direct
opposition to the neoliberal credo of rolling back the state and letting the market
rule. As Castells puts it in his section on the Tiger states:

> [A]ny serious, unbiased observer of the Asian Pacific scene knows that sys-
> tematic state intervention in the economy, as well as the state's strategic
> guidance of national firms and multinational corporations located in the
> country's territory, were fundamental factors in ensuring the transition of
> industrializing economies to each of the stages they were reaching in their
> developmental process . . . the 'developmental state' lies at the core of the
> experience of newly industrializing economies.
>
> (Castells 2000: 258)

Although Castells is a proponent of what I have labelled the general globalisation
discourse above, this quote shows the proximity of his work to the critical variant.
Adams (1993: 224–228) arrives at similar conclusions: the examples of the Asian
Tiger states 'suggest very strongly that at critical stages in the *development* process,
the free market solution may be incompatible with the desired objectives' (227).

The World Bank, however, did not see the experience of the Tiger states as the
definitive refutation of neoliberal strategies. In its 400-page study on the 'East
Asian Miracle', the World Bank argues that the states basically adopted the strategies of the Washington Consensus (Williamson 1990): 'The authors conclude
that rapid growth in each economy was primarily due to the application of a set
of common, market-friendly economic policies, leading to both higher accumulation and better allocation of resources' (World Bank 1993: vi). This conclusion can only be explained by the World Bank's remarkable skills in the 'art of
paradigm maintenance' (Broad 2006). Regardless of how justified this appropriation was, the example of the (South-)East Asian Tiger states as successful glo-
balisers played an important role in the rise of neoliberal globalisation discourse
in the field of development theory and policy and legitimised the promotion of
market-oriented strategies in poor countries all over the world.

The significance of economic factors in the rise of globalisation discourse has
already been referred to above. According to Arrighi, neoliberalism can be seen as
a strategy to overcome the crisis of Fordist capitalism. The importance of political
factors in this rise, notably of the coming to power of conservative governments
in the USA, Great Britain and Germany between 1979 and 1982, deserves to
be mentioned as well. Especially the Thatcher and Reagan administrations have

done their best to promote the assumptions of neoliberal globalisation discourse and discredit its rivals (Thatcher's slogan 'There is no alternative' became the rallying cry of this faction). Some scholars even go so far as to argue that the implementation of neoliberal policies in the South through the Structural Adjustment Programs (SAP) of the World Bank and the IMF were not primarily designed to reorient their economies to the maximisation of interest payments (as many critics claim), but to prevent the very policies that had allowed the newly industrialising economies to emerge as rivals to the industrialised states of the North:

> That the Reagan/Thatcher Neoliberal revolution has reversed the policies proved successful by the Asian NICs and has insisted that the rest of the Third World then implement them reveals something of the revolution's actual intentions. Their setting these new rules into place during the 1980s was a rational reaction to the quick rise of the Asian NICs by the world's traditionally wealthy countries in the 1970s. The real policy has been, and continues to be: 'No more NICs!'
>
> (Rowden 1998: 156)

This explanation builds on the historical fact that all the industrialised countries (with the partial exception of England as being the first-comer) have employed those protectionist strategies, which they later tried to prevent others from employing. Chang (2003) has described this method as 'kicking away the ladder'. Adams (1993: 223) outlined the strategies which were a standard feature of development policy before the rise of neoliberalism: government intervention to promote key industries and sectors, protectionist measures, special allocations, foreign exchange policies, etc. Most of them were outlawed by international agreements by 2000.

It cannot finally be clarified here to what extent the rise of the neoliberal discourse of globalisation in the realm of development theory and policy was a rational reaction to the shortcomings of Keynesian development economics and the convincing arguments of the neoliberal critics, or to what extent it was an economic process triggered by the economic crisis of Fordism, or to what extent it was a political means to maintain global inequality. Certainly all three elements played an important role.

In the previous section, we have discussed the characteristics of development discourse and the reasons for its decline. In this section, we have been dealing with the assumptions of globalisation discourse in its different variants and the factors contributing to its rise. Our main question now is: In what ways did this new perspective on processes of change differ from the old conception of *development*? This will be discussed in the next section.

From 'development' to 'globalisation' – different assumptions, different policies

While in the last section the characteristics and assumptions of globalisation discourse have already been mentioned, they will be more thoroughly and systematically discussed in the following. In order to examine how globalisation offers a different conception of social change than *development*, we will compare the two discourses in terms of their general principles, their assumptions regarding material improvements, the consequences of these assumptions for North-South relations and the policies and practices rendered necessary, possible or impossible by these consequences. This section thus constitutes the a first step towards a systematic comparison of *development* and globalisation as two concepts of change from the perspective of discourse analysis which up to now is still missing in the literature. The material used in my analysis represents central, programmatic and/or typical texts of both discourses.

Beginning with the general analytical principles, it is easy to see that the discourse of development is based on a fundamental dualism between *developed* and *underdeveloped* or *less developed* or *developing* countries, areas, states or nations. Thus Truman's inaugural address, which is often cited as the beginning of development discourse, envisioned a 'program of development' for 'making the benefits of our scientific advances and industrial progress available for the improvement and growth of underdeveloped areas' (Truman 1949). In the discourse of globalisation, this dualism is gone. Although differences in material wealth between countries are by no means denied, the world is not split up into two different kinds of international political entities that have to be treated differently: all states are equal before the market. There is only one world (not three), and, one might add, only one way to survive in this world. Thus when IMF Managing Director Camdessus[11] talks about the process of globalisation, he claims 'this sea change in policies and performance is associated with two phenomena of profound and universal significance; first, the changing role of the state, and second, the globalization of the international capital markets' (Camdessus 1996). As these phenomena constitute the global environment of all states alike, the developmental dualism is replaced by a universalism.[12]

Beyond the dimension of general world-view and the conception of one or two types of actors in the international arena, fundamental differences can also be traced in the construction of these subjects or actors' relation to historical processes. In development discourse, the ultimate goal was quite ambitious, the *development* of the *underdeveloped* areas, and therefore the socioeconomic transformation of the greater part of the world according to the model of the industrialised capitalist countries. Such enthusiasm did not survive the second half of the twentieth century but it is worthwhile to remember that in 1970 the UN resolution for the second development decade[13] announced what follows:

> In the conviction that development is the essential path to peace and justice, Governments reaffirm their common and unswerving resolve to seek a better and more effective system of international co-operation whereby the prevailing disparities in the world may be banished and prosperity secured for all.
>
> (UN 1970, par. 6)

This amounts to no less than a plan of action for eliminating global inequalities, with the international community as an acting subject shaping the global environment accordingly. Paragraphs 13ff go one step further, as they outline the exact rates of economic and population growth to be achieved for the different categories of countries (*developing/developed*). Thus, global social change can and must be planned in development discourse, and its second underlying principle can be identified as social technology, bearing witness to its theoretical roots discussed earlier.[14]

Neither this nor a resembling principle forms part of the discourse of globalisation. Here it is stated that global economic forces have changed and can no longer be objects of planned action. On the contrary, globalisation is constructed as an active force that leaves no society untouched. In many political speeches and texts of the mid and late 1990s and early 2000s, globalisation is portrayed as a natural phenomenon. Then-Director General of the World Trade Organization Renato Ruggiero (1998) told the European Commission at a conference on trade in services that 'globalization is an inescapable process' and repeated this claim many times. Bill Clinton claimed in 2000 that '[g]lobalization is not something we can hold off or turn off . . . it is the economic equivalent of a force of nature – like wind or water.'[15] So the only course of action available was to adjust to the new realities of the global economy on the levels of the state, the enterprise, and the worker as pointed out above. The authors of the highly influential 2002 World Bank publication 'Globalization, Growth, and Poverty' (which until today is the prime reference cited on globalisation on the World Bank's homepage)[16] state that: 'A century ago globalization seemed as inevitable as it does today' (World Bank 2002a: 4). The inevitability of the prescribed policies is underlined by the slogan referred to above: 'There is no alternative'. The structural adjustment programs (SAP), which delineate World Bank and IMF conditionalities concerning the economic and fiscal policy of Third World countries in exchange for loans, were based on the principle that national policies have to adjust to the inevitable realities of the global economy. Therefore, the second principle of the discourse of globalisation can be identified as adjustment. This principle is also rooted in the theoretical foundations of the discourse, as, according to neoclassical economics, the economic sphere is best left to work on its own (without state interventions apart from securing property rights).

Although both discourses deal with the possibility of material improvements for the poorer part of the world's population, their assumptions of how to achieve these improvements again differ significantly. While it is usually not mentioned explicitly, development discourse assumes that interventions in the market mechanism in favour of *less developed* countries are absolutely indispensable for achieving material improvements. A hotly debated question amongst development economists therefore was what kinds of interventions in the market mechanism were the most promising, but not whether this was a good idea in principle (see Martinussen 1997: 56–72). Globalisation discourse, on the other hand, argues in line with neoclassical economic theory and regards interventions in the market mechanism as the source of inefficient resource allocation resulting in higher prices and lower quality in goods and services. The principle paradigm of comparative advantage proves that free trade and specialising in those goods a country can produce best will be economically beneficial for all countries (ibid.: 20f). The 'invisible hand' of the market invoked by Adam Smith will thus help the poor far more than state interventions in the market. David Ricardo applied this idea to the international level with his concept of 'comparative advantage', arguing that international trade is beneficial for all countries under any circumstances as long as they specialise in exporting those goods (his classic example was wine for Portugal and cloth for England) they can produce most efficiently (i.e. in whose production they have a comparative advantage over other goods they can produce – not necessarily an absolute advantage over the production of other countries). Thus free trade is, according to Ricardo, the best option even for less competitive economies.

The application of such different principles in North-South relations raises awareness of the general structures of the global political economy once the link between development economics, development aid and the developmental state on the one hand and the alteration of the related principles under globalisation are considered. It is evident that as long as there is a notion of two groups of international actors, one of which is disadvantaged and lagging behind the other, special rules for these *less developed* countries (LDC) may very well be considered appropriate and necessary. In this case scientific practice, development economics, devoted to elaborating these rules and the conditions for material improvements in these handicapped countries, does make sense. If, on the other hand, one rejects the premise of different kinds of international actors, then the same rules can and should apply for all. Assuming that material improvements will be achieved only through market mechanisms, the main characteristic of these rules needs to be the liberalisation of these mechanisms from earlier constraints. In this line of thinking, the existence of development economics does not make sense, as there is only one economic theory that applies to all countries alike – be they in the North or in the South. Therefore Deepak Lal (1983) proclaimed the 'poverty of development economics'.

This leads us to the next point: In this view, state intervention in the working of a market economy (deriving from what Lal calls the 'dirigiste dogma') is ineffective and damaging, because it results in a situation where resources are allocated and prices are not set according to the laws of supply and demand but according to political preferences. Ultimately this means that producers will either make undeserved profits or will not get a fair price, while consumers will either pay too little or too much for the goods and services purchased. Opposed to this is the understanding of a developmental state as an indispensable tool to steer the economy, to interfere in market prices and to channel investment of state and private capital into priority sectors highlighting the (at least potentially) positive effects of capital and technology transfer into *less developed* countries. These are clearly interventions in the market mechanism, which is why the more consistent proponents of neoliberalism demand their abolition (the latest one being Dambisa Moyo [2009]).

Looking back at the historical record of development policy, it can be observed that the two discourses were not only theoretically rendering possible different sets of practices and policies, but that these policies were in fact implemented according to the discursive principles and assumptions. Of course, there is no clear-cut line separating an era of development from an era of globalisation (see McMichael 2000), but it is possible to argue that the different forms of knowledge about social change identified above were of varying influence during certain decades. Practices based on the discourse of development were dominant from the 1950s to the 1970s, while during the 1980s and 1990s, practices based on the discourse of globalisation became more and more influential – i.e. exerted discursive and then even conditioning power.

One arena that provides an obvious illustration of these changes is the global trading system and its institutional structure. The General Agreement on Tariffs and Trade (GATT) (which was ratified in 1948 as a framework for multilateral trade in the post–World War II era) includes clauses on Special and Differential Treatment (SDT) for *less developed* countries, reflecting the assumption of two different kinds of international actors with different capacities and needs and granting the LDCs exceptions and waivers. In 1964, a new clause, Part IV, was added to the GATT, which was designed to reconcile the right to *development* with international economic integration and firmly established the principle of nonreciprocity for LDCs – meaning that these countries would benefit from preferential market access to *developed* countries following the above outlined principle of market intervention. In 1979 (during the Tokyo Round of negotiations), the enabling clause legalised preferential (i.e. nonreciprocal) treatment for LDCs within the GATT (Rocher 1996: 45f).

The 1980s, the decade of the rise of neoliberal discourse in the field of North-South relations, saw 'a movement towards reappraisal and roll-back of the various privileges and special advantages that developing countries had enjoyed in the trading system' (Adams 1993: 191). For example individual countries were pressured to unilaterally renounce the right to import restrictions according to the balance-of-payments provision of GATT article 18-B, and a number of them, including Korea and Brazil, have in fact done so (ibid.: 192). Also, the entry conditions for *developing* countries in the GATT became much stricter in terms of tariff bindings and restrictions during the 1980s, and the required free trade commitments of new member states such as Mexico, Tunisia, Venezuela, El Salvador, Guatemala, Costa Rica and Bolivia, far exceeded those of older members, notably India (ibid.). The General System of Preferences (GSP) was often used to further this roll-back: threatening to withdraw its benefits was a practice regularly used above all by the US to extract concessions in relation to issues like intellectual property, services and investment which were not covered by the GATT (ibid.: 193). These issues were, however, on the agenda of the World Trade Organization.

In 1995 (in line with the 1986 commenced Uruguay Round of negotiations), the GATT was superseded by the World Trade Organization (WTO) as the new framework for multilateral trade – meaning that the GATT was now one in a bundle of agreements. Also the WTO regulations include special treatment for

LDCs,[17] but many critics maintain that it 'has suffered a massive dilution' (Lal Das 1998a: 4) and was 'drastically eroded' (Cuttaree 2002) in comparison to the era of the GATT.

The WTO is devoted not only to establishing a transparent, rule-based system of international trade, but also to the basic principles of free trade and nondiscrimination. In its own words:

> The trading system should be without discrimination – a country should not discriminate between its trading partners (they are all, equally, granted 'most-favoured-nation' or MFN status); and it should not discriminate between its own and foreign products, services or nationals (they are given 'national treatment').
>
> (WTO 1998: 5)

That is the WTO is designed to outlaw discrimination between foreign multinational companies and small local enterprises – the same rules have to apply for all. Therefore the special treatment still granted within the WTO is mostly confined to longer transition periods for LDCs before the nondiscriminatory WTO rules have to be implemented (see Lal Das 1998a, 1998b).

Another example is provided by the relationship between the EU/EC and the ACP-countries (the former colonies of Africa, the Caribbean and the Pacific). The treaties of Yaoundé (1963, 1969), Lomé (1975, 1979, 1984, 1990) and Cotonou (2000) between these two groups of states illustrate a major shift in their strategic cooperation (on the following see Raffer 2002). The first of these treaties established a nonreciprocal system of preferences for the ACP countries and included a contractual right to aid. Lomè I (which was ratified in 1975 as a concession of the European countries after the blockade of the New International Economic Order resolution ratified by the UN in 1974) introduced STABEX (System for the Stabilization of Export Earnings), a mechanism to stabilise the revenues of countries exporting raw materials and suffering from the high fluctuations in world market prices and supply. Lomé II added SYSMIN (System of Stabilization of Export Earnings from Mining Products), which provided similar assistance to the mining industries of countries strongly dependent on it. In Lomé IV (1990), the transformation of development discourse can already be observed: less aid is provided and Good Governance criteria are introduced. The Cotonou agreement (2000) is explicitly designed to be compatible with WTO rules ('Economic and trade cooperation shall be implemented in full conformity with the provisions of the WTO', EC and ACP 2000, Art. 34.4) and aims at establishing free trade agreements with parts of the ACP-countries (the Economic Partnership Agreements or EPAs) instead of the former system of preferences (ibid., Art. 36ff). STABEX and SYSMIN were abolished with the Cotonou agreement. Raffer concludes: 'The history of Lomé after 1975 has been characterised by a continuous and tenacious roll-back of the concessions once granted' (Raffer 2002: 172). The interventions of the 1970s into the market mechanisms have been abolished, and the rules of free trade are now applied to all contracting parties.

For the field of development aid we have already discussed the decline of financial transfers during the 1990s above. Of course one could correctly argue that the development institutions established in the era after World War II are still existent and active, which highlights the persistence of development discourse and the corresponding policies and practices. The prime examples would be the International Bank for Reconstruction and Development (IBRD) and its subsidiary, the International Development Association (IDA) – the two are better known as the World Bank. Especially the activities of the IDA – providing almost interest-free loans to low-income countries – clearly correspond to development discourse (market distortions, special rules for poorer countries). Still, the rise of neoliberal discourse has markedly changed policies and priorities in the World Bank. During the 1980s and 1990s, an increasing part of its lending was based on programme lending, not project lending. While development projects include planned socioeconomic interventions and the transfer of finance, knowledge and technology, programme or policy-based lending (the Structural and Sectoral Adjustment Loans of the SAPs) is more concerned with implementing sound economic policies in the receiving countries through lending conditions and to initiate policies to abolish interventions in the market mechanism and to roll back the developmental state (George/Sabelli 1994, Mohan et al. 2000).

One might object however, that such SAPs did not apply to all the countries, but merely to the poorer ones. And if the discourse of globalisation was so influential during the 1980s and 1990s, should we not expect to find similar conditionalities being applied to the industrialised countries? Indeed, we should. Apart from the WTO rules referred to above, the most striking example is probably the European Monetary Union (EMU). The Maastricht criteria, the provisions on the basis of which countries were eligible for the EMU, bear a striking similarity to the conditions of the SAP, especially in terms of fiscal austerity – and have had similar effects on the member-states' social policies. This can be observed in the experience of poorer EU countries, in particular Greece, in the financial crisis of recent years. The EMU criteria can thus be seen as a comparable form of disciplinary application of neoliberal policies in the North, as has been argued by Gill (2001, 2003).[18]

The differences between the discourses can thus be (incompletely) sketched in Table 8.1.

Social reality does not neatly fit into boxes, but the table tries to illustrate the differences in the two discourses on social change regarding the two basic principles (concerning the actors and the actions), specific principles and policy recommendations derived from these, and the corresponding status of the developmental state, development aid and development economics. Thus, the regularities of the discursive formations and the practices they render possible or impossible are highlighted.

Table 8.1 Characteristics of the discourses of 'development' and 'globalisation'

Discourse of:	'Development'	'Globalisation'
Basic principle (actors), patterns of change:	Dualism (developed vs. underdeveloped)	Universalism (One World)
Basic principle (actions), how to achieve change:	Social technology (transforming the LDC)	Adjustment (globalisation inevitable, TINA)
Derived principle (actors), policy recommendations:	Special rules for LDC (SDT, NIEO)	Same rules for all (SAP/ Maastricht, WTO)
Derived principle (actions), policy recommendations:	Interventions in market mechanism (Lomé)	No interventions, free trade (Cotonou)
Derived status of and recommendations towards developmental state:	Developmental state necessary or even crucial, to be strengthened	Developmental state ineffective or even damaging, to be pushed back or abolished
Derived status of and recommendations towards development aid:	Development aid necessary or even crucial, to be increased	Development aid ineffective or even damaging, to be decreased or abolished
Derived status of and recommendations towards development economics:	Development economics necessary or even crucial, to be supported	'Poverty of development economics', general economics is sufficient, dev. ec. is superfluous

Conclusion

In this chapter I have argued that two different discourses, *development* and globalisation, can be identified as successively dominating global North-South relations in the past decades. These discourses are based on different forms of knowledge about social change, work according to different rules and assumptions and correspond to different, even opposed, practices and policies. While development discourse was dominant from the 1950s to the 1970s, it lost importance with the rise of globalisation discourse in the 1980s. I have illustrated this shift with examples from international political economy ranging from the GATT and the EU-ACP-treaties to Structural Adjustment Programs of the IMF and the World Bank. One crucial conclusion that can be drawn from my observations is that the knowledge about historical change is itself subject to historical change – the changing conceptions of social change are part of social change itself.

Despite the important differences between the two forms of knowledge discussed in this chapter, my analysis of the respective discourses indicates that the institutional places where claims to knowledge are formed and substantiated mostly remain the same: international organisations concerned with North-South relations (above all the World Bank as the leading player) and a limited number of university departments. In this respect, continuities are dominant. Nevertheless, there are of course differences in the way globalisation discourse is formulated in different institutions – in the IMF and in the United Nations Conference on Trade and Development (UNCTAD) for example (and even within these institutions).

However, a few more recent developments have to be noted briefly. First, since the Report of the Commission on Global Governance ('Our Global Neighbourhood') appeared in 1995, the concept of Global Governance has become quite prominent at least in the political and academic arenas. Although it is in important aspects a new version of the neoliberal discourse on globalisation, it explicitly acknowledges the need to steer, shape or regulate the global economy in the light of the consequences of unmitigated neoliberalism (Brand 2005). Second, another reorientation took place in 1999, when the SAPs were renamed Poverty Reduction Strategy Papers (PRSPs) and restructured according to the principles of ownership and poverty reduction (World Bank 2002b).[19] Critics argue that despite the new rhetoric, the insistence of World Bank and IMF on sound economic policies has basically remained the same (World Development Movement 2001, Craig/ Porter 2003). (Chapter 9 will deal with the discourse of the World Bank.) Third, in the field of development policy, the rise of the Millennium Development Goals (MDGs) in recent years cannot be overlooked. While the relevant documents testify to a significant reverse regarding the declining importance of development discourse during the 1990s and heavily emphasise the need for development aid, they nevertheless accept neoliberal globalisation as a process to which individuals and states have to adjust to (UN Millennium Project 2005: 13; see also UN 2000, 2005). Chapter 11 will take a closer look on the MDG discourse.

The analysis presented above allows us to see that no new discourse is being formulated here. These recent developments can rather be seen as attempts to reconcile the two discourses by integrating aspects of one into the other and producing hybrid forms. It can be assumed that this merging of discourses presents a reaction to the massive antiglobalisation protests prevalent since the second half of the 1990s – but this remains to be examined in another article.

This chapter has tried to address the challenge formulated by Tsing (2000) of mapping the discourse of globalisation in a similar way as the discourse of development has been analysed. I have done so through a systematic comparison of these discourses in the field of North-South relations and highlighted their different regularities, principles and policy implications. However, regarding recent processes in this field, a merging of these discourses can be observed that deserves further research: Which elements of the two discourses are adopted by whom? Which institutional contexts seem more prone to one discourse than to the other and why? What is the relation between geopolitical and economic transitions and forms of knowledge about change? Questions like these can be addressed more specifically on the groundwork of the analysis presented here.

Notes

1 Many thanks to Patrick Neveling and also to the anonymous reviewers for a host of comments which have greatly improved the text.
2 This article relies mainly on sources and scholars from these regions. However, this should not be perceived as Eurocentrism. Just as people from the South (especially if educated in the North) are by no means immune to Eurocentric ideas, people from

the North are not necessarily prisoners to their cultural upbringings. Gayatri Spivak (1994) has convincingly warned against a cultural essentialism that emphatically jux-taposes First and Third World as it embraces and romanticises supposedly authentic Third World voices.

3   Failure to acknowledge this point often leads scholars to resort to theories of ideology and false consciousness as explananda, which means to regard large percentages of the Third World population as passive objects of manipulation (as is illustrated in the work of Rahnema and Esteva referred to earlier).

4   Both established the concept of sustainable development as a new kind of *development* that meets the needs of the present without compromising the ability of future genera-tions to meet their own needs.

5   The Millennium Development Goals (MDGs) have been proclaimed by the UN Gen-eral Assembly in 2000 and include (among others) the aim of halving the number of people living in extreme poverty until 2015. Other goals are concerned with universal education, gender equality, child health, maternal health, HIV/AIDS, environmental sustainability and a global partnership (see chapter 11).

6   This critique does not do justice to the more sophisticated accounts of Marxist and/or dependency theory like Cardoso and Faletto (1979), which left room for (world market-) dependent development. Second, this position may reflect the majority posi-tion but is still not shared by every scholar. Leys claims for example that the decline of dependency theory and the rise of neoliberalism were the results of transformations in the world economy instead of problems inherent to the theoretical position itself (1996: 19; see also my later reference to Arrighi's position). The example of the East Asian Tiger states will also be relevant in the third section of this chapter.

7   One faction of this civil society critique of *development* became what is now known as the Post-Development school around Esteva, Escobar and Rahnema (see earlier).

8   To name but a few: good governance and democratization emerged after the end of the Cold War and as a reaction to the critique by civil society; an emphasis on relief, crisis prevention, failed states, humanitarian interventions and even liberal imperialism as a reaction to the disillusionment with the promise of *development* (the Post-Development discourse can be seen as a rather different reaction to this factor); sustainable develop-ment and one world discourses as a reaction to the ecological predicament; participa-tion, civil society, ownership and empowerment as reactions to the critique of top-down approaches; and gender mainstreaming, human development, sociocultural issues and middle-range theories came up to deal with other critiques of development theory and policy – or, if you will, as the result of processes of institutional learning. Although these discourses here are presented as reactions to certain historical factors, their emergence is of course a multicausal and somewhat more complicated issue. For example the one world discourse owes its existence not only to the realization of the reach of ecological problems, but also to the end of the bipolar world order – and even the photographs of the earth taken from space. For a more thorough examination, see Ziai (2007: 66–94).

9   The latter point had been described by Michael Lipton (1977) as 'urban bias'. Lipton at that time also worked at the IDS and later contributed to World Bank and UNDP (United Nations Development Programme) reports.

10 Sometimes other countries are also subsumed under the heading Asian Tigers, such as Indonesia, Malaysia and Thailand, but most scholars refer primarily to the four coun-tries mentioned here.

11 As has already been mentioned, the IMF was at the forefront of the neoliberal coun-terrevolution during the 1980s and '90s.

12 By this I mean that the assumptions of the discourse claim to be universally valid as its subjects or actors are not divided by the dualism of its predecessor in two different kinds of countries/states/regions/economies (*developed/underdeveloped*). In another dimension, globalisation discourse does of course employ dualisms, above all, the dichotomy between the global and the local (see Tsing 2000). Although this is a spatial distinction with connotations similar to *development* (e.g. modernity/tradition), the discourse of globalisation claims to be universally applicable, in contrast to the discourse of development, which was targeting the *less developed* parts of the world. Therefore it seems justified to attribute a universalism to globalisation discourse.

13 This declaration can be seen as a landmark in development policy because it introduced the commitment by the industrialised countries to devote at least 0.7% of their GDP to development assistance – a promise never kept except for the Netherlands and the Scandinavian countries.

14 In the second section of this chapter, we have identified the concept of social engineering as one of the two sources of development discourse.

15 http://thinkexist.com/quotes/top/last-name/clinton/ (December 27, 2008)

16 http://www1.worldbank.org/economicpolicy/globalization/ (December 27, 2008)

17 To be precise, the WTO rules mention two groups: *developing* countries and *least developed* countries (WTO 1998). Here, both are referred to as LDCs.

18 Although one might be tempted to point out that the Maastricht criteria have not been implemented too rigorously in comparison to the SAP, the study by Mosley et al. (1991) reveals that at least the World Bank has surprisingly often been not very strict in enforcing its conditionalities either.

19 World Bank and IMF demand PRSPs from the receiving countries, in which the government with the participation of civil society should outline its economic policies and poverty reduction strategies. The World Bank now gives out Poverty Reduction Strategy Credits (instead of Structural and Sectoral Adjustment Loans), and the IMF's Enhanced Structural Adjustment Facility is now called Poverty Reduction and Growth Facility.

Bibliography

Adams, Nassau A. 1993: *Worlds Apart: The North-South Divide and the International System*. London: Zed Books.

Alcalde, Javier Gonzalo 1987: *The Idea of Third World Development: Emerging Perspectives in the United States and Britain, 1900–1950*. Lanham, MD: University Press of America.

Arrighi, Giovanni 1999: The Global Market. *Journal of World-Systems Research* 5(2), 217–251.

Baca, George 2004: Legends of Fordism: Between Myth, History, and Foregone Conclusions. *Social Analysis* 48(3), 169–178.

Booth, David 1985: Marxism and Development Sociology: Interpreting the Impasse. *World Development* 13(7), 761–787.

Brand, Ulrich 2005: Order and Regulation: Global Governance as a Hegemonic Discourse of International Politics? *Review of International Political Economy* 12(1), 155–176.

Broad, Robin 2006: Research, Knowledge, and the Art of 'Paradigm Maintenance': The World Bank's Development Economics Vice-Presidency (DEC). *Review of International Political Economy* 13(3), 387–419.

Camdessus, Michel 1996: Argentina and the Challenge of Globalization. Online http://www.imf.org/external/np/sec/mds/1996/mds9611.htm (November 28, 2008).

Cardoso, Enrique/Faletto, Enzo 1979: *Dependency and Development in Latin America*. Berkeley: University of California Press.

Castells, Manuel 2000: *End of Millennium. The Information Age: Economy, Society and Culture*, Vol. 3. 2nd ed. Oxford: Blackwell.

Chang, Ha-Joon 2003: *Kicking Away the Ladder: Development Strategy in Historical Perspective*. London: Anthem.

Cooper, Frederick 1997: Modernizing Bureaucrats, Backward Africans, and the Development Concept. In: Cooper, Frederick/Packard, Randall (eds.) 1997: *International Development and the Social Sciences: Essays on the History and Politics of Knowledge*. Berkeley: University of California Press, 64–92.

Cooper, Frederick/Packard, Randall 1997: Introduction, In: Cooper, Frederick/Packard, Randall (eds.) 1997: *International Development and the Social Sciences: Essays on the History and Politics of Knowledge*. Berkeley: University of California Press, 1–41.

Cowen, Michael P./Shenton, Robert W. 1996: *Doctrines of Development*. London: Routledge.

Craig, David/Porter, Doug 2003: Poverty Reduction Strategy Papers: A New Convergence. *World Development* 31(1), 53–69.

Cuttaree, Jayen Krishna 2002: Rules Issues and Special and Differential Treatment. Online http://www.inwent.org/ef-texte/wto02/cuttaree.htm (November 30, 2008).

DAC (Development Aid Committee of the OECD) 2008: Are Targets Slipping Out of Reach? Online http://www.oecd.org/dataoecd/47/25/41724314.pdf (November 27, 2008).

EC/ACP 2000: Partnership Agreement Between the Members of the African, Caribbean and Pacific Group of States and the European Community and Its Member States (Cotonou Agreement). Online http://ec.europa.eu/development/icenter/repository/agr01_en.pdf (November 30, 2008).

Escobar, Arturo 1995: *Encountering Development: The Making and Unmaking of the Third World*. Princeton, NJ: Princeton University Press.

Esteva, Gustavo 1992: Development. In: Sachs, Wolfgang (ed.) 1992: *The Development Dictionary: A Guide to Knowledge as Power*. London: Zed Books, 6–25.

Ferguson, James 1994: *The Anti-politics Machine: 'Development', Depoliticization and Bureaucratic Power in Lesotho*. Minneapolis: University of Minnesota Press.

Ferguson, James 2005a: Decomposing Modernity: History and Hierarchy After Development. In: Ferguson, James 2006: *Global Shadows: Africa in the Neoliberal World Order*. Durham, NC: Duke University Press, 176–193.

Ferguson, James 2005b: Globalizing Africa? Observations From an Inconvenient Continent. In: Ferguson, James 2006: *Global Shadows: Africa in the Neoliberal World Order*. Durham, NC: Duke University Press, 25–49.

Foucault, Michel 1972: *The Archaeology of Knowledge & The Discourse on Language*. New York: Pantheon Books.

Foucault, Michel 1980: *Power/Knowledge: Selected Interviews & Other Writings 1972–1980*. New York: Pantheon Books.

George, Susan/Sabelli, Fabrizio 1994: *Faith and Credit: The World Bank's Secular Empire*. Harmondsworth: Penguin.

Gibson-Graham, J. K. 1996: Querying Globalization. In: *The End of Capitalism (As We Knew It). A Feminist Critique of Political Economy*. Minneapolis: University of Minnesota Press, 120–147.

Giddens, Anthony 2002: *Runaway World: How Globalization Is Reshaping Our Lives*. London: Routledge.

Gill, Stephen 2001: Consitutionalising Capital: EMU and Disciplinary Neo-liberalism. In: Bieler, Andreas/Morton, Adam David (eds.) 2001: *Social Forces in the Making of the New Europe: The Restructuring of European Social Relations in the Global Political Economy*. Houndmills: Palgrave, 47–69.

Gill, Stephen 2003: Globalization, Market Civilization and Disciplinary Neo-liberalism. In Gill, Stephen 2003: *Power and Resistance in the New World Order*. Houndmills: Palgrave Macmillan, 116–142.

Gledhill, John 2004: Neoliberalism. In: Nugent, David/Vincent, Joan (eds.) *A Companion to the Anthropology of Politics*. Oxford: Blackwell, 332–348.

Hall, Stuart 1992: The West and the Rest. In: Gieben, Bram/Hall, Stuart (eds.) *Formations of Modernity*. London: Polity Press, 276–320.

Hardt, Michael/Negri, Antonio 2001: *Empire*. Cambridge, MA: Harvard University Press.

Held, David/McGrew, Anthony/Goldblatt, David/Perraton, Jonathan 1999: *Global Transformations: Politics, Economics, Culture*. Stanford, CA: Stanford University Press.

Hirst, Paul/Thompson, Grahame 1996: *Globalization in Question: The International Economy and the Possibilities of Governance*. Cambridge: Polity Press.

Ho, Karen 2005: Situating Global Capitalisms: A View from Wall Street Investment Banks. *Cultural Anthropology* 20(1), 68–96.

Lal, Deepak 1983: *The Poverty of 'Development Economics'*. London: Institute of Economic Affairs.

Lal Das, Bhagirath 1998a: *An Introduction to the WTO Agreements*. Penang, Malaysia: Third World Network.

Lal Das, Bhagirath 1998b: *The WTO Agreements: Deficiencies, Imbalances and Required Changes*. Penang, Malaysia: Third World Network.

Leys, Colin 1996: *The Rise and Fall of Development Theory*. London: James Currey.

Lipton, Michael 1977: *Why Poor People Stay Poor: Urban Bias in World Development*. London: Temple Smith.

Martinussen, John 1997: *Society, State and Market: A Guide to Competing Theories of Development*. London: Zed Books.

McMichael, Philip 2000: *Development and Social Change: A Global Perspective*. 2nd ed. Thousand Oaks, CA: Pine Forge Press.

Mohan, Giles/Brown, Ed/Milward, Bob/Zack-Williams, Alfred B. 2000: *Structural Adjustment: Theory, Practice and Impacts*. London: Routledge.

Moore, David/Schmitz, Gerald J. (eds.) 1995: *Debating Development Discourse: Institutional and Popular Perspectives*. Basingstoke: Macmillan.

Mosley, Paul/Harrigan, Jane/Toye, John 1991: *Aid and Power: The World Bank and Policy-based Lending*. Vol. 1. London: Routledge.

Mosse, David/Lewis, David (eds.) 2005: *The Aid Effect. Giving and Governing in International Development*. London: Pluto Press.

Moyo, Dambisa 2009: *Dead Aid: Why Aid Is Not Working and How There Is Another Way for Africa*. London: Penguin.

Nandy, Ashis. 1992: *Traditions, Tyranny, and Utopias: Essays in the Politics of Awareness*. Delhi: Oxford University Press.

Neveling, Patrick 2006: Spirits of Capitalism and the De-alienation of Workers: A Historical Perspective on the Mauritian Garment Industry. SCM Online Paper Series, No.2, MLU Halle-Wittenberg. Online http://www.scm.uni-halle.de/gsscm/die_graduiertenschule/online_papers/2006/mauritian_garment_industry/.

Nisbet, Robert 1969: *Social Change and History: Aspects of the Western Theory of Development*. Oxford: Oxford University Press.

Raffer, Kunibert 2002: Cotonou: Slowly Undoing Lomé's Concept of Partnership. *Journal für Entwicklungspolitik* 18(2), 171–184.

Rocher, Joseph 1996: *The GATT in Practice: Understanding the World Trade Organisation.* Paris: RONGEAD/La librairie FPH.

Rowden, Rick 1998: Developing Savages, Spreading Democracy: Popular Conceptions of North-South Relations. *Berkeley Journal of Sociology* 43, 149–187.

Ruggiero, Renato 1998: Towards GATS 2000 – A European Strategy, Address to the Conference on Trade in Services, organized by the European Commission in Brussels, 2 June 1998. Online http://www.wto.org/english/news_e/sprr_e/bruss1_e.htm (December 27, 2008).

Sachs, Wolfgang 1992: Introduction. In: Sachs, Wolfgang (ed.) *The Development Dictionary: A Guide to Knowledge as Power.* London: Zed Books, 1–5.

Sassen, Saskia 1999: *Globalization and its Discontents: Essays on the New Mobility of People and Money.* New York: New Press.

Sidaway, James D. 2007: Spaces of Postdevelopment. In: *Progress in Human Geography* 31(3), 346–361.

Spivak, Gayatri 1994: Can the Subaltern Speak? In: Williams, Patrick/Chrisman, Laura (eds.) *Colonial Discourse and Post-Colonial Theory: A Reader.* New York: Columbia University Press, 66–111.

Stiglitz, Joseph 2003: *Globalization and its Discontents.* 2nd ed. New York: W.W. Norton.

Toye, John 1987: *Dilemmas of Development: Reflections on the Counter-revolution in Development Theory and Policy.* Oxford: Blackwell.

Truman, Harry 1949: Inaugural address, Thursday, January 20, 1949. Online http://www.let.rug.nl/usa/P/ht33/speeches/truman.htm (October 1, 2008).

Tsing, Anna 2000: The Global Situation. *Cultural Anthropology* 15 (3), 327–360.

UN 1970: *International Development Strategy for the Second United Nations Development Decade,* Resolution 2626.

UN 1974: *Declaration on the Establishment of a New International Economic Order,* Resolution 3201.

UN 2000: *United Nations Millennium Declaration,* Document A/RES/55/2.

UN 2005: *In Larger Freedom: Towards Development, Security and Human Rights for All.* Report of the Secretary-General, Document A/59/2005.

UN Millennium Project 2005: *Investing in Development: A Practical Plan to Achieve the Millennium Development Goals.* Overview. New York: UNDP.

Williamson, John 1990: What Washington Means by Policy Reform. Online http://www.iie.com/publications/papers/print.cfm?doc=pub&ResearchID=486 (December 27, 2008).

World Bank 1993: *The East Asian Miracle: Economic Growth and Policy.* Washington, DC: World Bank/Oxford University Press.

World Bank 2002a: *Globalization, Growth, and Poverty: Building an Inclusive World Economy.* Washington, DC: World Bank/Oxford University Press.

World Bank 2002b: A Sourcebook on Poverty Reduction Strategies. Overview, Online http://povlibrary.worldbank.org/files/5301_overview.pdf (October 17, 2006).

World Development Movement 2001: *Policies to Roll-back the State and Privatize? Poverty Reduction Strategy Papers Investigated.* UNU: WIDER discussion paper No. 2001/120.

WTO 1998: Trading Into the Future. Introduction to the World Trade Organisation. Geneva: Author.

Ziai, Aram 2007: *Globale Strukturpolitik? Die Nord-Süd Politik der BRD und das Dispositiv der Entwicklung im Zeitalter von neoliberaler Globalisierung und neuer Weltordnung.* Münster: Westälisches Dampfboot.

9   World Bank discourse and poverty reduction

The critical literature on Neoliberalism, or the neoliberal discourse of globalisation, as we have termed it in the last chapter, usually sees the World Bank as a stronghold of this discourse (e.g. Peet 2003: 23). A closer look at the World Bank and its discourse on development and poverty reduction reveals that this view sometimes tends to overlook both the historical changes in this discourse and competing variants of this discourse in the World Bank. So, after some introductory remarks about neoliberalism and the World Bank, this chapter will engage with the shifts and variants that can be discerned within this institution's discourse. The next section will compare WB discourse in three important publications in its history (the 1973 study *Redistribution with Growth*, the 1981 report *Accelerated Development in Sub-Saharan Africa: An Agenda for Action* and the 1989 *From Crisis to Sustainable Growth: Sub-Saharan Africa – A Long-Term Perspective*), before examining more in detail the ambivalent *World Development Report 2000/2001: Attacking Poverty* and briefly contrasting it with the 2002 study *Globalization, Growth and Poverty*.

Neoliberalism and the World Bank

As we have seen in the last chapter, a coherent neoliberal discourse of globalisation opposes interventions in the market mechanism, special rules in world trade for poorer countries a developmental state, development aid and even a separate discipline of development economics. The neoliberal case against all this aid has been presented already in the 1960s and 1970s by Peter Bauer (Bauer 1974, 1981), restated by Deepak Lal and others like Ian Little, Bela Balassa and Harry Johnson in the 1980s (Lal 1983a, 1983b, 1985, Toye 1987) and somewhat unoriginally repeated by Dambisa Moyo in the 2000s (Moyo 2009). Apart from the reproach that development aid has the 'disastrous tendency to politicise life in poor countries', that is to 'increase the power, resources and patronage of governments compared to the rest of society' (Bauer 1974: 268) and subsidises rent-seeking elites as well as 'classes of beneficiaries of official aid in the donor countries (exporters, consultants, civil servants, and academics)' (ibid.: 271), the economic core of the criticisms is that development interventions distort market prices (leading to an ineffective allocation of resources) and create wrong incentives. In the words of

Lal, instruments of government policy usually 'induce economic agents to behave less efficiently' (1983a: 285): if there are financial transfers for those below a certain threshold of income (or increased taxes for those above), this provides an incentive for individuals not to raise their income in order not to lose this transfer. The same holds true for those transfers to low-income countries called development aid. Thereby all of these 'bureaucratic failures' impair productive efficiency and lead to 'welfare losses' (ibid.: 284).

Institutions of development aid which are engaged with financial transfers to poorer countries are therefore, from a neoliberal perspective, at best ineffective in relation to the goal of poverty reduction, at worst damaging, because they maintain structures in the global economy (and polity) which prevent self-sustaining growth processes. Dambisa Moyo charges these institutions with upholding a 'vicious cycle of aid' which 'chokes off desperately needed investment, instils a culture of dependency, and facilitates rampant and systematic corruption, all with deleterious consequences for growth' (Moyo 2009: 49). So now the question appears: if the World Bank is (as the left critics say) a stronghold of neoliberalism, but as it is also an institution delivering development aid, which makes it (as the neoliberal critics say) opposed to neoliberalism: how does all of this fit together?

Let us start by briefly taking a look at the World Bank's characteristics (for the following see George/Sabelli 1994, Rich 1994, Kapur et al. 1997, Goldman 2005, Marshall 2008, Toussaint 2008). The International Bank for Reconstruction and Development (IBRD), which later became known as the World Bank, was devised in 1944 at the conference on the postwar economic order in Bretton Woods, New Hampshire, in the US. Its initial role was to finance the reconstruction of war-torn Europe through long-term loans, but soon (after the introduction of the Marshall Plan) its focus turned to the global South. Here, it functioned as a manifestation of Truman's promise to support the efforts of *less developed* countries to become *developed* by financing projects, primarily in the field of infrastructure. As already mentioned in chapter 6, since 1960 it has been supported by the International Development Association (IDA), which gave out loans not on market conditions, but with extremely low interest rates to the poorest countries. IBRD and IDA are usually seen as the World Bank, while the World Bank group also comprises the International Finance Corporation (IFC), focusing on private investment, the Multilateral Investment Guarantee Agency (MIGA) and the International Centre for the Settlement of Investment Disputes (ICSID). The President of the World Bank is traditionally a US citizen (while the Managing Director of the IMF is European). The World Bank is governed by the Board of Directors, in which 24 representatives of the 185 member states are taking decisions, their voting power is calculated according to the capital shares of their countries (in contrast to the 'one country, one vote' system of the UN). In 2014, it had more than 10,000 employees in more than 120 offices worldwide,[1] and its lending commitments amounted to US$40.84 billion.[2] Given that and the widely recognised intellectual leadership, the World Bank is certainly 'the most important development institution in the world' (Peet 2003: 111).

Turning to the question of neoliberalism, it can be observed that the IBRD does not provide grants, but primarily loans at market interest rates to middle-income countries, so in this respect is actually not guilty as charged by its neoliberal critics. The IDA, however, does provide almost interest-free loans, i.e. financial transfers on concessional, not market terms (Marshall 2008: 36f), which are not compatible with the discourse of neoliberalism. Further, the debt relief for the Highly Indebted Poor Countries (HIPC), which was funded also by IDA and IBRD (Marshall 2008: 156f), cannot be reconciled with a rigid neoliberal position either (Bauer 1974: 272f). On the other hand, the World Bank has used its position as the largest and most influential donor to achieve changes in the economic policy of recipient countries in the course of the structural adjustment loans, changes guided by the discourse of neoliberalism and the 'Washington Consensus':[3] liberalisation of trade and capital markets, deregulation of the economy, privatisation of public institutions, etc. (Hayter/Watson 1985, Cornia et al. 1987, George 1988, Sparr 1994, World Bank 1996, Mohan et al. 2000, SAPRIN 2004). Thus our first look at the Bank leaves us with an ambivalent picture. A strictly neoliberal position would demand the abolishment of development institution, but this might be too strict a demand for a development institution incompatible with the institutional interest in survival. Rather, the World Bank opted for the middle path of trying to implement market reforms while not abiding by market principles itself and using financial transfers to further these reforms.[4] In the next section, we will examine the discourse of the World Bank and its relation to neoliberalism more in detail.

World Bank discourse: from redistribution to adjustment

The number of World Bank publications far exceeds the capacity of a single researcher in a single chapter. Therefore I will concentrate in this and the following section on some of them which have been widely read and cited. I will start with the study *Redistribution with Growth. Policies to improve income distribution in developing countries in the context of economic growth*, which was a joint study by the World Bank's research centre and the Institute of Development Studies in Sussex (Chenery et al. 1973). It starts with the statement: 'It is now clear that a decade of rapid growth in underdeveloped countries has been of little or no benefit to perhaps a third of their population' (Chenery et al. 1973: xiii), delivered by the World Bank's vice-president for development policy. There was 'evidence of growing inequality in the Third World' because this growth was 'very unequally distributed among countries, regions within countries, and socio-economic groups' (ibid.) – an unambiguous indictment of trickle-down assumptions. Yet the study also warns of policies which would prioritise redistribution and neglect the significance of growth altogether: this 'new conventional wisdom seems to be almost as misleading as the old' (ibid.).[5]

On the other hand, the study recommends the policies of countries 'in which the poor have shared equitably in income growth', such as Israel, Yugoslavia, Taiwan, Korea, Sri Lanka, Costa Rica and Tanzania (ibid.: xv). These consist of improving access to modern-sector employment through education, redistribution of land and public investment targeted at the poor (ibid.). At least the latter point does not seem quite consistent with a neoliberal discourse relying strictly on market forces and decrying the welfare losses produced through government policy providing what is seen as false incentives. The inconsistence becomes a clear contradiction when the study claims that elements of public and private ownership are needed: 'laissez faire instruments of taxation and price policy as well as the socialist instruments of state ownership and direct intervention' (ibid.: xvii). Far from being opposed to markets, the study claims: 'While we advocate maximum use of instruments that operate through factor and product markets, often they will not be sufficient for this purpose [poverty reduction]' (ibid.). Policy measures suggested include controversial ones such as land reform (59f), consumption transfers (64f) and nationalisation (61f). It is even mentioned that there are 'market mechanisms that discriminate against low-income groups' (17). The message could hardly be clearer: reliance on market mechanisms alone will not reduce poverty, redistribution in favour of the poor is indispensable.

As it is deemed 'necessary to evaluate the results of any development policy in terms of the benefits it produces for different socio-economic groups' (ibid.: 39), an index of economic performance is developed which measures the growth rate of each income quintile and thus potentially poverty weighted welfare increases (note that welfare is identified with economic growth). The study explicitly mentions the possibility of giving weight to economic growth in inverse proportion to income levels (ibid.: xvi), i.e. focusing on the progress of the poor. Yet even the equally weighted measurement would imply that an income increase of $1 in a household with an income of $100 were seen as significant as an increase of $10 in a $1,000 household – something which is not the case in unspecific statistics taking the state as a unit of analysis.

As regards the role of international aid agencies, the study proposes their firm endorsement of redistributive policies and corresponding support for such policies on the national level (175), a diversification of funds to mitigate large donor influence (ibid.), achievement and increase of the 0.7 per cent target (ODA in relation to GNP) (177), untying of aid (178) and giving 'much greater priority . . . to countries whose development policies showed an open and effective commitment to poverty-focused strategies' (ibid.). It even stresses 'the need to alter the framework of international economic relationships' (175) to achieve the objective of redistribution. In other words, the policy recommendations are clearly rooted in the discourse of development, emphasising the necessity to achieve or at least approach global equality through financial transfers and interventions in market mechanisms.

A mere eight years later, the tide had turned, and the World Bank increasingly saw its role as a promoter of market-oriented policies in the structural adjustment programmes. One of the first hallmarks of this turn was the report *Accelerated Development in Sub-Saharan Africa* (World Bank 1981), nicknamed Berg report after its coordinator Eliot Berg.[6] Already the foreword by World Bank President Clausen emphasised 'more efficient use of scarce resources' and suggested that 'governments can more effectively achieve their social and development goals by reducing the widespread administrative overcommitment of the public sector and

by developing and relying more on the managerial capacities of private individuals and firms' (World Bank 1981: v). This echoes Lal's (and others') opposition to
the developmental state's government intervention which was based on neoclassical economic theory.

The report sees weak growth in Africa as the problem and 'domestic policy
inadequacies' (4) as 'sources of lagging growth', next to other factors (among
them the 'economic disruption that accompanied decolonization and postcolonial consolidation', but not the economic disruption that accompanied colonialism), and here in particular protectionism, overextended public sectors and a bias
against agriculture (ibid.). The central policy actions advocated to cure these ills
are market oriented: devaluation in exchange rates, deregulation, privatisation
and liberalisation in the public sector and in agricultural policies (5). While all
this is in line with neoliberal discourse, the report also demands 'a commitment
to larger aid flows in the 1980s', more specifically 'a doubling of aid in real terms'
by the end of the decade (7) – which is clearly contrary to it. The aid should,
however, be 'targeted to improve efficiency of resource use', (ibid.) which in the
historical context of structural adjustment can easily be read as 'used as leverage
for neoliberal reforms'.

Inequality, however, does not feature prominently in the Berg report. In fact,
it is mentioned *not once* in the 217 pages. The market, in contrast, is mentioned
around 230 times. (To compare: in the 1973 study, which was also concerned
with growth and poverty reduction, the market was mentioned 137 times and
inequality 117 times.) Market-oriented reforms are seen as the crucial instrument
for attaining the goal of economic growth. In line with the classical theory of
comparative advantage, the report argues:

> Economic growth implies using a country's scarce resources – labor, capital,
> natural resources, administrative and managerial capacity – more efficiently.
> Improving efficiency requires, first, that a country produces those things
> which it can best produce as compared with other countries and, second,
> producing them with the least use of limited resources.
>
> (24)

Therefore great emphasis is given to calculating the domestic resource costs
(DRC) per unit of foreign exchange in export crops for African countries (65)
in order to identify the goods in which the specific countries have a comparative
advantage and in whose exports they should specialise. This World Bank advice
reflects the following assumptions:

Local production should be geared to earn foreign exchange. This constitutes
the rationale of the structural adjustment programmes which were, after all,
designed to solve the debt crisis by enabling the debtor countries in the South
to pay their debts to the Banks in the North – the purpose of local production
should not be to address the basic needs of the population.

Countries should produce whatever they are able to efficiently produce in the
present. This does not take into account how their production structure has been

shaped in the past by the needs of European colonialism. Neither does it take into account the problematic aspects of being locked into a colonial division of labour as an exporter of primary goods (see Singer 1950), nor that all industrialised countries have at one point in their history decided to focus on industrial production – against their comparative advantage in agricultural production (see Chang 2003). So the World Bank recommendations end up in 'freezing countries in existing patterns of production which are, on the whole, the ones left over from colonialism' (George/Sabelli 1994: 65f).

The present world market prices will remain more or less stable. This assumption neglects not only the usual volatility, but in particular the consequences of the Bank's own actions. If it pushes all the recipients of structural adjustment loans in the Third World towards exporting more primary goods, oversupply will reduce the prices. And this is just what happened during the 1980s. Unsurprisingly, the Bank's projections of world market prices turned out to be too optimistic on a regular basis (George/Sabelli 1994: 79–95). This can be seen as a consequence of methodological nationalism which sees single countries as the units of analysis.[7]

Another eight years later, another influential report on Sub-Saharan Africa was published by the World Bank, entitled *Sub-Saharan Africa: From Crisis to Sustainable Growth* (World Bank 1989). It is noteworthy that only two years after the Brundtland report introduced the new catchphrase 'sustainable development', the World Bank adopted it, but transformed it to 'sustainable growth'. It continued the argument on adjustment and neoliberal reforms, stressing from the outset a new buzzword from the discourse of globalisation, competition:[8] 'We have come to appreciate that fundamental structural change is needed to transform African economies and make them competitive in an increasingly competitive world. The adjustment efforts must be continued and the reforms broadened and deepened' (World Bank 1989: xi). This was necessary to achieve economic growth of 'at least 4 or 5 percent annually' which was a requirement for 'a modest improvement in living standards', jobs and food security (ibid.). However, 'although sound economic policies and an efficient infrastructure are essential', they are not sufficient:

> A root cause of weak economic performance in the past has been the failure of public institutions. Private sector initiative and market mechanisms are important, but they must go hand-in-hand with good governance – a public service that is efficient, a judicial system that is reliable, and an administration that is accountable to its public.
>
> (xii)

Thus even three years before the influential *Governance and Development*, the World Bank introduced the concept which was to become a central concept in development policy during the 1990s.

It has been noted that the new emphasis on good governance can be seen as a convenient explanation of the failures of structural adjustment (Abrahamsen

2000). Whereas the neoliberal reforms were heralded as the way forward at the beginning of the decade, the report cannot but realise that 'Sub-Saharan Africa as a whole has now witnessed almost a decade of falling per capita incomes, increasing hunger and accelerating ecological degradation. The earlier progress made in social development is now being eroded' (World Bank 1989: 1). In a situation where the majority of African countries have been undergoing structural adjustment, the failure of these policies to improve lives or even spur economic growth can now be attributed to 'weak public sector management' leading to 'loss-making public enterprises, poor investment choices, costly and unreliable infrastructure, price distortions . . . and hence inefficient resource allocation' (3) – instead of blaming the economic reforms themselves. In this way, the argument for good governance actually affirms the legitimacy and necessity of neoliberal reforms and the concept becomes 'synonymous with sound development management' (World Bank 1992: 1). Other elements of good governance – rule of law, accountability, democracy, etc. – are thus merely seen as means to the end of market-oriented reforms and a stable and attractive environment for investors (World Bank 1989: 9, 11, 15, 126).

The measures proposed by this agenda of neoliberal reform and good governance – among them the introduction or raising of fees for health care (6, 64, 67f), water provision (7, 53, 55, 86, 165), schooling (7, 80–82) and even fuelwood (11), the freezing or lowering of wages (5, 12, 29, 42, 49, 75, 110, 167, 175, 186, 191) and the cutting of social services (and instead using women's unpaid work) (7, 46, 64, 86) – are purportedly

> aimed at empowering ordinary people, and especially women, to take greater responsibility for improving their lives – measures that foster grassroots organization, that nurture rather than obstruct informal sector enterprises, and that promote nongovernmental and intermediary organizations . . . development must be more bottom-up.
>
> (xii; see also 1, 4, 55, 187)

Thus empowerment was envisioned as a dismantling of supposedly corrupt and overregulating states to allow for entrepreneurial individuals who would take over the responsibility for improving their lives. Here, we have a clear rejection of the trusteeship of developmental states and the corresponding elements of the discourse of development. And although of course the existence of development aid and development institutions is again not called into question (and even more ODA and debt reductions are recommended, 13f), the report warns that in 'the long term, dependency on aid and technical assistance must be reduced' (xii). Inequality is again a nonissue: the term is not to be found on the 322 pages.[9]

We find that while the World Bank in the 1973 study was still firmly anchored in the discourse of development, in the 1981 and the 1989 report, it has adopted most elements of the discourse of neoliberal globalization – except for the demand to abolish development aid and development organisations, which would be against its own interests of institutional survival. Yet the principled rejection of the developmental state in general and interventions in the market mechanism in particular on the grounds that they distort prices and provide false incentives is as pervasive as the advocacy of liberalisation, privatisation and deregulation and the corresponding orientation to competition and the world market. These elements could not be found in the 1973 study. Another significant finding is that the World Bank's concern with the question of inequality visible here – a topic not entirely unexpected when dealing with questions of growth and poverty reduction – has disappeared entirely in the 1980s. That inequality is something negative and a concern for politics is a view which Friedrich August Hayek, the Austrian economist and mentor of neoliberalism, has fought vehemently again and again.[10] The increasing inequality as a result of neoliberal adjustment (Mohan et al. 2000, SAPRIN 2004) thus is not a coincidence and during the 1990s led to an increasing crisis of legitimacy of those global economic institutions promoting these policies, above all IMF, World Bank, and the World Trade Organization (WTO).

Contested neoliberalism: the World Bank report on poverty

When the World Bank celebrated its 50th anniversary in 1994, it was met by protesters from civil society proclaiming '50 years in enough!' and demanding the shutdown of the institution (Danaher 1994). When World Bank president James Wolfensohn took office in 1995, he seemed determined to take action regarding this crisis of legitimacy. He launched the headline 'Our dream is a world free of poverty' on the World Bank homepage, initiated internal reforms, engaged the critics of adjustment in dialogue and even joint research,[11] and made Joseph Stiglitz, who was more of a Keynesian than a neoliberal, Chief Economist of the Bank. The 1997 World Development Report *The State in a Changing World* (World Bank 1997) coordinated by Stiglitz already aroused some attention as it saw a more positive role of states in the process of economic growth and *development*, whereas a few years earlier, the World Bank had still maintained that the impressive successes of the East Asian Tiger states came about *despite* and not because of massive state intervention in the economy (World Bank 1993).

In this context, the World Development Report 2000/2001 *Attacking Poverty* deserves special attention. The World Development Reports are the World Bank's flagship publications, at least 50,000 copies are printed, it is translated into seven languages and it can be downloaded for free on its website. The 2000/2001 report was to be coordinated by Ravi Kanbur at the behest of Joseph Stiglitz. The report drew heavily on the 'Voices of the Poor', a combination of participatory studies by the Bank involving 60,000 people in 60 countries, and although it did not deny the significance on growth for poverty reduction, its draft from January 2000 stressed that liberalisation and deregulation had sometimes worsened the situation of the poor and proposed to focus on the three areas of empowerment, security and opportunity. It even advocated capital controls to avoid financial crises. The draft unsurprisingly provoked serious opposition from the hard-core neoliberal faction at the Bank as well as from some economists and the US treasury. Kanbur yielded to the critics to a certain extent but then decided that further amendments would go too far and resigned in the face of insistent demands. He then refused all press interviews, not dissociating himself from the Bank in order not to legitimise further revisions of the report. The final version of the report which was published in September 2000 differed in some respects from the January draft – the pro-market position was strengthened – but still had enough original elements to make it a strange mixture and probably the most progressive outline of World Bank policy to date (Wade 2001).

Already in the first sentence – 'Poor people live without fundamental freedoms of action and choice that the better-off take for granted' (World Bank 2000: 1) – the question of liberty is linked to that of material deprivation. This linkage (echoing the work of Amartya Sen, see chapter 12) is an important move in the context of the preeminence given to political rights in the West to the detriment of economic and social rights. It is also remarkable that according to the report we live in 'a world where political power is unequally distributed and often mimics the distribution of economic power' (1) – an argument which can be used by Marxists to question the democratic credentials of the existing political and economic system. The frequent quotes of poor people, although often not mentioned by name, also introduce a new, participatory element in the report. However, the selectivity of the quotes cannot be evaluated without a major study of the extensive data. Concerning the important question of state intervention for the sake of the weak, the report clearly demands 'effective national action to manage the risks of economic shocks and effective mechanisms to reduce the risks faced by poor people . . . It also requires . . . providing a range of insurance mechanisms . . . from public work to stay-in-school programs and health insurance' (7).

Probably the most obvious sign of the partial deviance from the neoliberal orthodoxy can be found in the surprisingly prominent role given to inequality. In stark contrast to its complete absence in the 1981 and 1989 reports, the term appears around 110 times and also figures in the heading of chapter 3. In this chapter, we learn that 'income inequality between countries has increased sharply over the past 40 years' and that inequality among individuals has also risen (51). Related to this, power and powerlessness are frequently invoked as explanations for poverty and inequality, and 'empowerment of poor people – by making state and social institutions more responsive to them' is described as 'key to reducing poverty' (3). 'Social barriers such as class stratification and gender division' have to be tackled according to the report (10), just as 'legal discrimination' against 'disadvantaged ethnic and social groups' has to be eliminated (7). It is even asserted that '[m]any development programs are inherently political and powerful vested interests can be expected to mobilise against reforms that seek to erode their position in the name of poor people' (131). These statements may seem to refute Ferguson's hypothesis of the development apparatus functioning as an 'anti-politics machine' which reduces poverty and inequality to technocratic problems to be solved by unpolitical interventions side-lining the question of power and the political dimension of the state (Ferguson 1994: 69, 256).

However, a closer look reveals that a depoliticising function can in fact be found in the discourse present in the WDR 2000/2001. First of all, because on a number of occasions the report claims that there is no conflict between the objectives of growth and poverty reduction but, on the contrary, there are 'reinforcing effects from economic development to human development and back' (World Bank 2000: 58). The report goes on to assert that the 'interests of the poor and the nonpoor are intertwined in many ways' because 'efforts to reduce poverty can promote social and economic development for the whole nation, thereby also raising the living standards of the nonpoor' (108). Not only are promoting market opportunities for the poor, facilitating their empowerment and reducing their vulnerability beneficial both to the poor and to the growth process (7), even environmental protection (52), participation (113) and gender equality (39, 49, 119) are conducive to growth – and thus to poverty reduction. Repeatedly, a link or even an equivalence between market-friendly reforms, economic growth and development or poverty reduction is discursively constructed: '[T]here is now substantial evidence that open trade regimes support growth and development . . . Trade reforms have delivered growth, and thus poverty reduction' (70). Sometimes this equation is also used to construct the identities of reformers as well-meaning and democratic, in implicit opposition to those opposed to these reforms: 'Well-functioning markets are important in generating growth and expanding opportunities for poor people. That is why market-friendly reforms have been promoted by international donors and by developing country governments, especially those democratically elected' (61). Or it is used to explicitly delimit the discourse of poverty reduction to the space of neoliberal reforms: 'The debate about reforms is therefore not over a choice between reforms or no reforms: the absence of reforms to develop vibrant, competitive markets and create strong institutions condemns countries to continued stagnation and decline' (62).[12]

Second, and in line with the quotes above, power is discussed only in relation to the state, not in relation to enterprises or market forces. The negative consequences of neoliberal reforms in different contexts which are mentioned on page 65 are e.g. attributed to flawed state institutions (corruption, inadequate public investment, excessive bureaucracy), but not once to the simple workings of market mechanisms (65) – as if the market itself cannot fail. Participation in markets is always constructed as beneficial, exclusion from markets as a barrier to improvement (39, 76, 115, 179). There is a deafening silence on transnational companies and no hint in the report that they might be involved in creating or worsening poverty. Merely some vague 'forces affecting poor people's lives . . . beyond their control' are mentioned (16). Even when negative consequences of neoliberal reforms are mentioned, it is (inconsistently) claimed that they are a) inevitable and b) their alternative had even worse consequences: In an economic crisis, 'restrictive fiscal and monetary policies are inevitable and less costly than the alternative of delaying such measures' (162). And even when parts of the population will suffer as a consequence of these reforms, this must not be used as an argument against these reforms: 'In view of the urgent need to get countries into dynamic, job-creating development paths, it is critical that the difficulty of reform and the impossibility of compensating every loser not lead to policy paralysis' (76). So the decision to undertake neoliberal reforms is presented as rational and inevitable, not as a contingent political decision. The market thus takes on the character of a force of nature – the anti-politics machine has been dismantled only in respect to the state. And all of this has to be seen in the context of a report which aroused serious unrest within the World Bank because of its deviation from the neoliberal orthodoxy.

However, the next important World Bank report on the topic released shortly afterwards – *Globalization, Growth and Poverty* by Collier and Dollar (World Bank 2002) – was painting a clearer, less ambivalent picture: 'Globalization generally reduces poverty because more integrated economies tend to grow faster and this growth is usually widely diffused' (World Bank 2002: 1). Given the crisis of legitimacy mentioned at the beginning of the section, it cannot avoid recognising that '[g]lobalization also produces winners and losers', but the responsibility for the latter lies with unfavourable geographies, weak policies, institutions and governance or civil war (2) – not with the market mechanism. Inequality is still an issue in the report (around 100 mentions), but increased inequality as a consequence of liberalisation is either denied (6) or attributed to inadequate participation in the world market (7). Power and empowerment are redefined in a similar manner as participation: 'The combination of strong education for poor people and a more positive investment climate is critical for empowering poor people to participate in the benefits of a more strongly expanding economy' (20). The meaning of empowerment is thus limited to participating in the growing market economy through wage labour – a rather reductionist version of empowerment. The message is clear: the problems of liberalisation and globalisation have to be addressed, but certainly not by questioning liberalisation and globalisation, but by integrating the poor into the world economy: 'Many poor people are benefiting from globalisation. The challenge is to bring more of them into this process' (22). That their inclusion in the world economy on asymmetrical terms may be a reason of their poverty is thus conveniently excluded. We thus find a clearer commitment to the principles of neoliberal discourse, with the usual exception of demanding more foreign aid (20) and even debt relief for poor countries – which would contribute to 'enabling them to participate more strongly in globalization' (21). This kind of participation seems to be the universal recipe for growth and poverty reduction.

Looking back at the two reports, it can be observed that the moderate neo-classical faction in the World Bank (the Post-Washington-consensus advocates around Stiglitz and Kanbur) did suffer a defeat, but managed to retain some of its views in the WDR 2000/2001. In particular the clear statements about the relation between power and poverty seem remarkable, as they highlight that poverty is also closely related to discrimination and denial of freedom. Yet the relations of power implicit in a capitalist economy and the market mechanism are usually ignored even where the World Bank is at its most progressive.

Conclusion

Even the relatively brief and cursory analysis in this chapter has shown the vast differences in the World Bank publications over time and hinted at the existence of different factions within the institution. Whereas the 1973 study was firmly rooted in the discourse of development and advocated a mixture of market-oriented instruments and state ownership to achieve the objective of growth and poverty reduction, the tide had clearly turned in the 1980s. The 1981 and 1989 reports were unambiguous and vehement in their promotion of market-oriented policies and their rejection of the developmental state and its interventions. Inequality was a nonissue in these reports and the policy recommendations of neoliberalism were put forward with unbroken confidence – with the exception of the question of development aid. Here, the World Bank deviated from rigid neoliberalism for obvious reasons. In the reports of the new century, the confidence has been substituted by an awareness of the discontents of globalisation, coupled with the conviction that the market still provides the best of solutions, but that the task of institutions is to create an environment where people will benefit from the market mechanism. This results in what can be called a neoliberal discourse of development: the task of poverty reduction is (contra Hayek) seen as the prime objective, but liberalisation and private initiative are seen as the most effective instruments to achieve it. Development aid and assistance to the poor are (contra Bauer) necessary, yet they should be as market-oriented as possible (as in the strategies of opportunity, empowerment and security). Yet the controversy around the WDR 2000/2001 has shown that this discourse is contested within the World Bank: next to the still dominant faction that continues to promote growth and liberalisation as still the best cure, there is a faction whose trust to the market is less than complete and whose awareness of relations of power and inequality is far more *developed* than that of the orthodox neoliberals.

Notes

1 http://www.worldbank.org/en/about/what-we-do (December 19, 2014)
2 http://www.worldbank.org/projects (December 19, 2014)
3 John Williamson, who coined the phrase Washington Consensus to describe the political reforms demanded both by the US government and the IMF and the World Bank, differentiates between this more general consensus and the more hard-line position he regards as neoliberalism (Williamson 1993).
4 That its efforts to achieve market reforms in recipient countries have sometimes been thwarted by the pressure to lend (giving out loans was more important to the institution than strict adherence of the recipients to the letter of intent), was a highly interesting result of the research by Mosley et al. (1991).
5 Actually, this new conventional wisdom is not spelled out precisely, but the context suggests the meaning assumed here.
6 Evidently, the report was an answer to the Lagos Plan of Action, a strategy for *development* adopted by the African heads of state at the meeting of the Organization of African Unity 1980 (World Bank 1981: 1).
7 Here, the theoretical contribution of dependency and world-system approaches becomes obvious.
8 Competition and competitiveness appear 147 times in the 1989 report. The terms appeared 13 times in the 1973 study and 31 times in the 1981 report.
9 However, there are a few instances where the report is concerned with unequal distribution of livestock, natural energy resources or regional integration benefits across the continent (97, 128, 161) – not of property, land or income though.

10 'Inequality is not regrettable, but highly enjoyable. It is simply necessary . . . Precisely
   the differences in remuneration bring the individuals to actions which give rise to the
   national product' (Hayek 1981: 36, translation AZ).
11 Together with a number of NGOs, Wolfensohn initiated the Structural Adjustment
   Participatory Review Initiative (SAPRI), where World Bank representatives together
   with their critics chose local experts to assess the results of structural adjustment programmes in selected countries. When it turned out that the results would confirm
   the views of the critics more than its own, the World Bank withdrew from and even
   obstructed the review (SAPRIN 2004).
12 Bachrach and Baratz (1962) have termed such attempts to prevent controversy and
   further a particular agenda in this way as nondecisions.

Bibliography

Abrahamsen, Rita 2000: *Disciplining Democracy. Development Discourse and Good Govern-
ance in Africa*. London: Zed Books.
Bachrach, Morton/Baratz, Peter 1962: Two Faces of Power. *American Political Science
Review* 56(4), 947–952.
Bauer, Peter T. 1974: Foreign Aid, Forever? In: Chari, Sharad/Corbridge, Stuart (eds.)
2008: *The Development Reader*. London: Routledge, 265–278.
Bauer, Peter T. 1981: *Equality, the Third World and Economic Delusion*. London: Weidenfeld
and Nicolson.
Chang, Ha-Joon 2003: *Kicking Away the Ladder: Development Strategy in Historical Perspec-
tive*. London: Anthem Press.
Chari, Sharad/Corbridge, Stuart (eds.) 2008: *The Development Reader*. London: Routledge.
Chenery, Hollis/Ahluwalia, Montek S./Bell, C.L.G./Duloy, John H./Jolly, Richard 1973:
*Redistribution With Growth: Policies to Improve Income Distribution in developing Countries
in the Context of Economic Growth*. Oxford: Oxford University Press.
Cornia, Andrea/Jolly, Richard/Stewart, Frances (eds.) 1987: *Adjustment With a Human
Face: Protecting the Vulnerable and Promoting Growth*. 2 Volumes. Oxford: Clarendon
Press.
George, Susan 1988: A Fate Worse than Debt: A Radical New Analysis of the Third
World Debt Crisis. Harmondsworth: Penguin.
George, Susan/Sabelli, Fabrizio 1994: *Faith and Credit: The World Bank's Secular Empire*.
Harmondsworth: Penguin.
Goldman, Michael 2005: *Imperial Nature: The World Bank and Struggles for Social Justice in
the Age of Globalization*. New Haven, CT: Yale University Press.
Hayek, Friedrich August 1981: Ungeichheit ist nötig. Interview with F.A. von Hayek.
Wirtschaftswoche, March 6, 1981, 36–40.
Hayter, Theresa/Watson, Catherine 1985: *Aid: Rhetoric and Reality*. London: Pluto.
Kapur, Devesh/Lewis, John P./Webb, Richard (eds.) 1997: *The World Bank: Its First Half
Century*. 2 Volumes. Washington, DC: Brookings Institution Press.
Lal, Deepak 1983a: The Dirigiste Dogma. In: Chari, Sharad/Corbridge, Stuart (eds.) 2008:
The Development Reader. London: Routledge, 279–287.
Lal, Deepak 1983b: *The Poverty of 'Development Economics'*. London: Institute of Eco-
nomic Affairs.
Lal, Deepak 1985: The Misconceptions of 'Development Economics'. In: Corbridge, Stu-
art (ed.) 1995: *Development Studies. A Reader*. London: Edward Arnold, 56–63.
Marshall, Katherine 2008: *The World Bank: From Reconstruction to Development to Equity*.
London: Routledge.

Mohan, Giles/Brown, Ed/Milward, Bob/Zack-Williams, Alfred B. 2000: *Structural Adjustment. Theory, Practice and Impacts*. London: Routledge.

Mosley, Paul/Harrigan, Jane/Toye, John 1991: *Aid and Power: The World Bank and Policy-Based Lending*. 2 Volumes. London: Routledge.

Moyo, Dambisa 2009: *Dead Aid: Why Aid Makes Things Worse and How There Is Another Way for Africa*. London: Penguin.

Peet, Richard 2003: *Unholy Trinity: The IMF, the World Bank and WTO*. London: Zed Books.

Rich, Bruce 1994: *Mortgaging the Earth: The World Bank, Environmental Impoverishment, and the Crisis of Development*. Boston, MA: Beacon Press.

SAPRIN (Structural Adjustment Participatory Review Network) 2004: *Structural Adjustment: The SAPRI Report. The Policy Roots of Economic Crisis, Poverty and Inequality*. London: Zed Books.

Singer, Hans 1950: The Distribution of Gains Between Investing and Borrowing Countries. In: Chari, Sharad/Corbridge, Stuart (eds.) 2008: *The Development Reader*. London: Routledge, 179–185.

Sparr, Pamela (ed.) 1994: *Mortgaging Women's Lives. Feminist Critiques of Structural Adjustment*. London: Zed Books.

Toussaint, Eric 2008: *The World Bank: A Critical Primer*. London: Pluto Press.

Toye, John 1987: *Dilemmas of Development: Reflections on the Counter-revolution in Development Theory and Policy*. Oxford: Basil Blackwell.

Wade, Robert H. 2001: Making the World Development Report 2000: Attacking Poverty. *World Development* 29(8), 1435–1441.

Williamson, John 1993: Democracy and the 'Washington Consensus'. In: Chari, Sharad/Corbridge, Stuart (eds.) 2008: *The Development Reader*. London: Routledge, 288–296.

World Bank 1981: *Accelerated Development in Sub-Saharan Africa: An Agenda for Action*. Washington, DC: Author.

World Bank 1989: *Sub-Saharan Africa: From Crisis to Sustainable Growth. A Long-Term Perspective Study*. Washington, DC: Author.

World Bank 1992: *Governance and Development*. Washington, DC: Author.

World Bank 1993: *The East Asian Miracle: Economic Growth and Policy*. Washington, DC: Author.

World Bank 1996: *Social Dimensions of Adjustment: World Bank Experience, 1980–93*. Washington, DC: Author.

World Bank 1997: *World Development Report 1997: The State in a Changing World*. Washington, DC: Author.

World Bank 2000: *World Development Report 2000/2001: Attacking Poverty*. Washington, DC: Author.

World Bank 2002: *Globalization, Growth and Poverty: Building an Inclusive World Economy*. Washington, DC: Author.

10 'Development'

Projects, power and a poststructuralist perspective

In the late 1980s and especially during the 1990s, the Post-Development school in development theory became widely known (see above all Esteva 1987, Sachs 1992, Ferguson 1994, Escobar 1995, Rahnema 1997). Its argument, in a nutshell, was that the concept of *development* is Eurocentric because it implicitly clings to colonial assumptions of the superiority of Western societies and that it reproduces power relations between *developed* and *less developed* regions or individuals – even in well-meaning development projects aiming at poverty reduction (DuBois 1991). Going beyond a neo-Marxist critique that development projects actually serve as means for exploiting the periphery, the Post-Development school fundamentally questioned the endeavour of industrialising, modernising and uplifting the Third World, emphasising cultural difference against Western universalism and exposing what Cowen and Shenton (1996) have described as trusteeship: the authoritarian exercise of power based on expert knowledge at the root of development policy with the aim of improving society on behalf of poor and ignorant people. It was time, the Post-Development authors argued, to look for alternatives to *development* which could be found in grassroots movements and in the informal sector of the periphery.

Many critics have criticised or even rejected the Post-Development stance (Corbridge 1998, Kiely 1999, Nanda 1999, Nederveen Pieterse 2000). Most of the criticisms can be argued to be only valid for what could be called the neopopulist variant of Post-Development (Ziai 2004). However, one important criticism concerns the historical place of the Post-Development criticism and thus turns one of its major arguments against it. While the Post-Development school has argued that *development* was a child of the Cold War era (the geopolitical interests of the US are seen as a midwife of the concept), one could return that its critique may be appropriate for the 1970s and 1980s, but overlooks the profound transformations which have taken place in development policy since then.

Undoubtedly there has been a transformation in development discourse which includes the rise of neoliberalism, good governance, sustainable development, global governance, civil society, participation and partnership (IDS 2001, Mosse 2005). The latter are especially relevant in this context, because these elements directly contradict the view that *development* was a top-down, authoritarian programme. The article therefore pursues the question whether this transformation can also be observed on the level of development projects and whether and how it affected the implicit power relations.

In the following section, the concepts and the method of the argument will be outlined. After that, I will discuss several development projects as empirical examples before proceeding to the analysis of power relations and drawing some preliminary conclusions.

Concepts and method

When examining the power relations inherent in development projects, the first step is evidently to define these concepts. Development projects shall be defined as spatiotemporally limited formal measures in *developing* or *less developed* or *underdeveloped* countries aiming officially at improving the standard of living of the resident population. This is a rather broad definition which does not confine development projects to the practice of international development or aid organisations but does include measures taken by national governments or even private initiatives should they be sufficiently formalised (although this will not be relevant in this article). It does not preclude the result of these measures (whether they have in fact improved the standard of living) but takes as a defining factor the formal intention to do so. However, it excludes measures in *developed* countries as well as continuous or geographically unlimited government policies designed to improve the standard of living.

Reflecting on power in the social sciences, one can hardly avoid the classic definition given by Max Weber: According to him, 'Power denotes any chance to implement one's will in a social relation also against resistance' (Weber 2006: 62, translation: AZ). This definition appears less than ideal for our purposes for the following reasons: It confines power to social relations between individuals, leaving aside less personalised workings of power. Furthermore, it takes the occurrence of resistance as a defining factor of a power relation, neglecting the fact that power can operate to prevent resistance – through fear, distorted information or ideologies, for example. A more encompassing definition is needed.

One more suitable definition is provided by the work of Michel Foucault. In his later work he differentiates between three types of power: sovereign, disciplinary and governmental power.[1] Whereas sovereign power operates through repression and laws, disciplinary power works through training, repeated practices and conditioning. Governmental power refers to the 'conduct of conduct', thus emphasises the free will of the individual as an object of power relations. According to Foucault, power is exercised in general through the production of knowledge and – this is particularly relevant for our topic – through the structuring of possible fields of action.[2] Power, in this view, does not necessarily mean to coerce someone,[3] but power is also present where individual decisions are taken voluntarily in a field of action which is structured in a specific way, or where a discourse provides only certain ways of constructing social reality. Power does not only preclude certain actions or information, it is also productive, creating certain ways of behaving or knowing. It has correctly been pointed out that according to this definition, power is ubiquitous. This does not free critical scholars from the obligation of analysing its operations.

So power shall be defined here as the structuring or restructuring of fields of action in political, economic, social or ecological spheres. It aims at changing the practices of individuals and can be exercised through sovereign, disciplinary or governmental mechanisms – or, if we use the more precise terms of chapter 2, through representing, conditioning or subjectivising mechanisms.

Returning to our research question, we have to ask how a possible transformation of development policy on the level of projects and on the level of power relations can be observed. Obviously only by examining empirical examples of development projects, but equally obviously it is beyond the scope of a single paper to provide a thorough overview over the myriads of projects. Some examples have to be selected. The criteria here have been the following: the cases have to fit into the definition, they have to cover the relevant time span from the 1980s to the present, should represent different continents and different types of countries (large/small, different levels of industrialisation) and be somewhat typical of the time and the region. Practically, the projects must be also have been documented by scholars and the results published (or otherwise accessible). In spite of these criteria, a certain element of arbitrariness in the selection of examples inevitably remains and has to be borne in mind when formulating the conclusions.

These projects shall be presented in the following way: their name, content and measures will be portrayed as well as the relevant political context, the donors financing them and the time span during which they took place. Then we will focus on their implementation and the attempted (re)structuring of fields of action in different spheres and on their success in changing the practices of the target group. In the ensuing section, the results will be analysed.

Development projects: examples

Lesotho: integrated rural development[4]

The Thaba-Tseka Integrated Rural Development Project was implemented in Lesotho during 1975 and 1984. It comprised measures in the areas of infrastructure, agriculture, administration and health and was financed by the World Bank and the Canadian Development Agency CIDA.

As the project took place in a mountain area, heavy emphasis was laid on livestock and range development: the increase of commercial livestock production was a (if not the) central goal. In order to facilitate the supply of inputs and the marketing of farm produce, two components were seen as crucial: the construction of an all-weather road linking Thaba-Tseka with the capital city of Maseru and the construction of a regional centre at Thaba-Tseka, comprising office buildings, staff housing, warehouse and workshop facilities as well as a Farmers' Training Centre. In the area of administration, a new district (Thaba-Tseka) was formed and Village Development Committees were entrusted with hiring local labourers for the project. On top of that, there were also attempts to introduce new crop farming techniques, health and educational training programmes, the establishment of a transport pool for vehicles and a number of other measures.

Due to the geopolitical and economic insignificance of Lesotho, it can safely be assumed that the project in question was not designed to serve the interests of donor countries in a strict sense.[5] There are no signs indicating this might be the case. The project measures did not result in an improvement of the standard of living of the population in the target area, nor did they manage to introduce new relations of production: The attempted commercialisation of livestock production was utterly unsuccessful because it did not take into account the economic and cultural context of the target population. It ignored 1) that most of the cattle farmers were not classical farmers, but predominantly migrant labourers who also owned cattle; 2) that cattle functioned as a form of old-age pension for this group; 3) that cattle was imbued with symbolic value and therefore not a commodity to be freely traded like all others but instead was a manifestation of prestige and also a place-holder for absent males which could be borrowed by fellow villagers in need, making it an unselfish – and gendered – form of wealth; 4) that the commercial practices (above all enclosure of range areas) amounted to an attack on the communal land and were perceived as anti-social.

Despite this failure, the project had far-reaching effects which were not intended by the donors. The ruling party BNP (Basotho National Party) was able to acquire and instrumentalise resources provided by the project on a broad scale. The Village Development Committees were in fact party organisations promoting its cause and privileging its supporters. The measures in the areas of infrastructure and administration did not lead to a change in agricultural production, but allowed for an intensified control by the government in an area that had been quite remote from the capital and known to be a stronghold of the oppositional BCP (Basotho Congress Party).

So we can observe a restructuring of the fields of action in the political and economic sphere (e.g. by offering economic incentives for commercial cattle farming or by providing resources for the ruling party) which however is not always identical with donor intentions. The attempts to change the behaviour of the target group related to this restructuring were largely unsuccessful.

Guatemala: security and development[6]

In 1982, the new military regime under Rios Montt presented the 'National Plan for Security and Development' (*Plan Nacional de Seguridad y Desarrollo*). In its name, numerous projects were implemented during the next years especially in the Ixcan and other highland regions where the guerrilla were active. It included above all the establishment of development poles, model villages, civic patrols and inter-institutional coordinations – mostly measures in the areas of infrastructure and administration, only a few in agriculture and the social sector. Many of these projects were supported by food aid from the World Food Program (WFP) and USAID, from 1987 onwards – after the military conceded formal political authority to a civilian government – also by financial and technical aid from the European Community (EC).

The measures have to be seen in the context of the revolutionary movement against the military regime and the ruling elites, the civil war and an estimated one million of refugees as a result of the army's scorched-earth policy in the years before. Since the democratic government of Arbenz (a social democrat who had expropriated unused land from United Fruit) had been removed by a military coup backed by the CIA, the USA had been an ally of the regimes in Guatemala and after 1979 was determined to prevent a second Nicaragua in Central America.[7]

The development poles are microregions (largely identical with areas of conflict) in which the government tried to foster infrastructure and export-oriented agriculture, although this transformation of agricultural production (a goal emphasised in US foreign policy documents concerning the region) was not the priority – all in all a rather vague concept. The model villages are far more concrete: through food-for-work programmes homeless and starving refugees are brought to build villages in strategic locations (usually in the vicinity of a military camp) and thus resettled. Resources for the model villages usually come from international development aid. Then the males between 18 and 60 are recruited in formally voluntary[8] civic patrols, paramilitary groups which aid the army by accompanying them on their missions, keeping villagers under surveillance or cutting wood and building roads for the next military camp. The civic patrols replace former administrative units on the local level, establishing a new, militarised and hierarchical political structure. A similar function can be attributed to the inter-institutional coordinations, new administrative units which constitute a parallel structure controlled by the military and are used to collect development aid funds and channel them into the strategically important areas.

It can easily be observed that the measures financed by development aid were an integral part of a counterinsurgency campaign designed to control the population and stabilise the regime. It can be assumed that the donors were well aware of this. A massive political and economic restructuring took place (e.g. through offering food-for-work programmes and pressuring people to participate in the civic patrols). The measures were successful in inducing a change in behaviour of the target population, mainly as a result of force or threat thereof.

India: Narmada Valley Development project[9]

The Narmada Valley Development project comprises the impressive number of 3,200 dam projects, of which the vast majority are small, 135 are medium and 30 are major dams. The biggest of these is the Sardar Sarovar in Gujarat with a proposed height of 136.5 m. According to the government of India, this multi-purpose dam (irrigation, power production, flood-control) would irrigate more than 1.8 million hectares and bring drinking water to drought prone areas. Opponents claim that these benefits are vastly exaggerated and that more than 300,000 people have to be displaced without adequate compensation. Between 1985 and 1993, the project was financed above all by the World Bank ($280 million), but Japanese development aid was also involved (27 billion Yen).

The Japanese loan consisted of tied aid, it was linked to the purchase of turbines from Sumitomo Corporation. The report of an independent review commission (the Morse Report), which was called into being by the World Bank as a consequence of massive protests against the dam, came to the conclusion that the criticisms raised by the opponents were justified. Environmental and social impacts had not been adequately considered let alone addressed, and it would be best to withdraw from the project – which the Bank management was not willing to do but its Executive Directors agreed to after several months of debate and bad publicity.[10]

The government of Gujarat decided to pursue the project on its own, used fraud and deception to implement its resettlement schemes, occasionally resorted to violent means to oppress the protests and was taken to the Supreme Court by the opponents (organised in the Narmada Bachao Andolan (Save the Narmada movement) which has so far allowed a raise of the dam to 121 m. Concerning the benefits of the dam, one has to note that the irrigation schemes will by all probability benefit primarily the sugar cane agriculture and industry close to the river, and not the drought prone areas further away. Concerning the displacements, it has to be remarked that almost 60 per cent of the estimated 300,000 persons losing their home are Adivasis, indigenous people, who constitute only 8 per cent of the population of India. Even more will be and are already negatively affected by the impact of the dam on the ecosphere on which they make their living. Many resettled people have left their new homes because they were unable to survive there and now live either in the slums of one of the big cities or in their old villages to be submerged soon.

What we find here is again a major restructuring of fields of action in the spheres of economy and ecology (through flooding the areas concerned and offering or implementing resettlement schemes). The change of behaviour was the result of force, which in contrast to Guatemala can at least claim to be democratically legitimated.

Peru: family planning and reproductive health[11]

Under President Fujimori the National Programme for Reproductive Health and Family Planning (*Program Nacional de salud reproductiva y planificación familiar*) was established in Peru between 1996 and 2000. Fujimori promoted it explicitly as a means of fighting poverty. It comprised projects and measures in the field of health and population policy and was financed by USAID, the World Bank, and the United Nations Fund for Population Activities (UNFPA). Some Peruvian women's NGOs cooperated with the government and were partly integrated in the implementation of the programme through a large reproductive health project of USAID.

The measures taken were not confined to the improvement of maternal health care (to which only a small part of the budget was devoted) and the provision of a broad range of contraceptive methods, but included 'sterilisation festivals' which took place especially in rural or poorer urban areas. Women were enticed to take part by offering them free dental treatment, free haircuts and music bands. In hospitals, women were exempted from the high costs of in-patient childbirth if they agreed to be sterilised. But also pressure and threats were used: they would be refused medical treatment in the health centre if they did not agree, and nurses and doctors had to fulfil quotas. Although at the International Conference on Population and Development in Cairo 1994 such measures had been banned, they were regularly applied in Peru, and not without success: between 200,000 and 300,000 persons have been sterilised in the course of the programme, 90 per cent of which were women.

The government thus managed to restructure the field of action predominantly of its female population in the area of reproduction in a way that led to the desired change in behaviour – not through the direct use of force, but through conditioning and disciplinary measures (incentives offered for compliance and sanctions used against dissident conduct).

Indonesia: sustainable development[12]

The Central Sulawesi Integrated Area Development and Conservation Project was started in 1998. It is financed mainly by the Asian Development Bank and is pursuing several objectives: the sustainable use of natural resources, an improvement in agricultural productivity, as well as the conservation of biodiversity in and around the Lore Lindu National Park.

In marked contrast to the project in Lesotho, the political, economic, ecological and cultural context was well researched by a design study and an environmental assessment, although some results were ignored in the actual project plan – results indicating that conservation and *development* are not at all easy to combine in the present situation. And in contrast to the all of the earlier projects, participation of the target group is seen as important, and local NGOs are integrated as organisations implementing the project. While improving protection of the biodiversity and natural resources of the park was a priority, the project sought to provide alternative sources of income for those dependent on the park's land and forest resources for economic sustenance.

However, achieving the project's goals proved extremely difficult, not only because police and army collaborated in the illegal extraction of timber from the park, but especially because the target group was very keen on improving their livelihoods but not in the sustainable manner envisioned by the experts. Instead of planting economically useful native tree species, they resorted to monocropping cacao and collecting rattan within the park and protested against the attempted enforcement of its boundaries. The NGOs hired to educate the farmers, introduce participatory monitoring and bring them to sign community conservation agreements, were not able to achieve these goals either, and even coercive exclusion from the park by arresting farmers and burning huts and crops could not stop these practices in the light of increasing landlessness. Following the example of indigenous communities successfully struggling against eviction, in 2001 about 1,000 families calling themselves the Free Farmers Forum went so far as to occupy land in the park.

The restructuring of economic and ecological fields of action visible here (enclosures, incentives, sanctions) failed to achieve the intended change in behaviour in the target group – conditioning power did not lead to subjectivising power. That the government did not resort to large-scale violence to implement the project has to be seen in the context of the recent democratic transition in Indonesia after the fall of the Suharto regime in 1998.

Nepal: microcredits for women[13]

In 1998, the Asian Development Bank (ADB) established the Rural Microfinance Development Centre (RMDC) to implement the Nepal Rural Microfinance Project. Its main objective is to reduce rural poverty and empower women, concretely: to channel international and national resources to rural poor households, especially to women by borrowing from the government and lending (at market interest rates) to smaller microfinance institutions (MFIs) who then lend to the target group. The RMDC has access to 12 million SDR (special drawing rights) of loan fund from the ADB and is active in 47 out of the 75 districts of Nepal. Between 2000 and 2006, it has disbursed loans of the amount of 982 million Nepalese rupees (NR) to about 370,000 clients (all of them women), with a loan recovery rate of 100 per cent. Apart from that, the RMDC holds workshops, trains MFI staff, supervises its partner organisations, and tries to promote a market-friendly environment and spread best practices between MFIs and develop the microfinance industry.

The standard model of lending is the so-called Grameen Bank model: the credit system is based on a survey of the social background and peer groups of five members which are then incorporated into centres of up to 10 groups. Weekly or fortnightly meetings are held to collect compulsory payments: savings as well as loans. Loans are initially made to two members, the others follow subsequently, and the group members guarantee each other for loan repayments – as a substitute for collateral which the rural poor do not possess. The loans are used for different purposes, but the most important and certainly the one advised by the RMDC is the setting up of small enterprises by the women.

Obviously, we are confronted with a market-oriented *development* scheme: the availability of capital and the access to financial markets are supposed to reduce rural poverty and empower the women. The sources indicate that to a certain limited extent this seems to have been the case. Apart from that, it can be observed that the specific lending model reduces the costs of the lending institution by outsourcing the activities of information gathering on the borrower and motivating timely payments to the peer groups (also called solidarity or borrower groups). What is also worth noting is that the members of the group develop an economic interest in surveilling the financial practices of the other members and their enterprises, the groups assume as their primary objective the financial health of the microcredit programme (instead of the welfare of their members), and their empowerment is seen as achieved through participation in the market. They learn to act as the rational economic agents envisioned by neoliberal theory.

The reports indicate that the restructuring of the economic field of action in rural Nepal by offering microcredits attached to certain conditions has been quite successful in inducing a change in behaviour. This has not been achieved through repressive or disciplinary measures, but through relying on the voluntary actions of individuals, the rational and responsible conduct of the target group responding to their needs and the incentives provided. Conditioning power led to subjectivising power.

Bolivia: political participation[14]

In 2002 the British and Swedish development agencies (DFID and SIDA) launched a project designed to improve political participation in the Bolivian elections ('Towards an Inclusive Election Process') which proved somewhat controversial because the Bolivian government disagreed with it. The Danish and Dutch agencies initially involved as well left the project after the Bolivian government had made its disapproval clear and referred to the project as donor-driven, which was clearly in contrast to the commitment of the donor community and the Comprehensive Development Framework spearheaded by the World Bank which aims at putting the recipient country in the driver's seat. The other two donors continued their engagement, pressed by the Bolivian civil society consortium that had planned the project (the Pro Citizens' Participation Consortium consisting of 15 local NGOs and three grassroots organisations).

While the problem that a large part of the indigenous population did not participate in the elections was undeniable, the government deemed it sufficient to tackle the problem through educational programmes in the mass media. When some donors announced that they were going to support grassroots organisations trying to mobilise people to use their rights as voters, the government saw this as an interference in internal political matters and denounced the project for lack of ownership. Despite some hindrances, the project went ahead and showed that over 90 per cent of the clients (around 26,000 inhabitants of rural and peri-urban communities) did not even possess adequate personal documentation as a precondition for the right to vote and pointed to the link between lack of voice and social exclusion. Consequently, the project explained their citizens' rights to them and supported their claims to an identity card, the right to vote and political participation in general vis-à-vis the state bureaucracy.

The project seems to have successfully restructured the political field of action for its target group and induced a change in behaviour. Again, this was accomplished through offering possibilities for action and appealing to self-interest (though this time rather collective than individual self-interest).

Analysis

In the following I am going to analyse the empirical examples first in relation to the hypothesis of a transformation of development policy and second from a specifically poststructuralist perspective. Right at the outset it has to be stated that the small amount of examples given here is by no means a sufficient basis for wholesale assertions concerning development policy in general. Yet they allow for some interesting observations which can serve as a groundwork for further research.

Concerning the question in how far the transformation of development discourse since the 1980s can be observed on the level of development projects, sweeping statements are misplaced. All aspects of the transformation cannot be discussed here, but the crucial rise of catchwords like participation, civil society and ownership can also be traced in the project examples. Participation of the people who were affected by the project was not an issue in the plans of the Narmada Valley project and their protests were deliberately overheard as long as possible. Guatemala demonstrates an extreme case of authoritarian measures in the field of development policy.[15] In Lesotho one could at best talk of a participatory role of the Village Development Committees, which were in fact front organisations of the ruling party, but not of participation by the persons affected. In Peru, NGOs were already seen as playing a role and attempts were made to coordinate governmental policy with them. In Indonesia, NGOs and participation by the target group constituted important elements of the project (although participation was of course limited to the implementation of the project). In Nepal, the borrower groups have been described by the donors as self-help civil society organisations and they were obviously crucial to the project. In Bolivia, the project was conceived of, pushed forward and implemented by local NGOs and the donors took their support serious enough to annoy the government. The examples indicate that the hypothesis that the transformation of development discourse concerning participation since the 1980s is matched by a parallel transformation on the level of development projects seems a reasonable basis for further research.[16]

If we address the question of power relations, it can be seen that all projects imply a restructuring of the field of action of affected persons in the economic, political, social, reproductive or ecological spheres. On top of the intentional restructuring planned by the donors we also remark the possibility of unintended but nevertheless far-reaching restructurings as in Lesotho. Here the widely differing effectiveness of the respective restructurings becomes obvious. Only some of them managed to achieve the intended change in behaviour in their target group, and the power relations employed to do so can be differentiated between the three types presented in the first section: sovereign, disciplinary and governmental mechanisms.

In Lesotho, we find that the restructuring intended by the donors did not manage to induce a lasting change in behaviour among many people. In Guatemala, there was a successful restructuring enforced by repression (sovereign mechanisms of power). In India, the restructuring also changed the behaviour of the target group in the last instance only through the force of law – and even then resistance took place (sovereign power). In Peru, the combination of incentives and threats in the restructuring of reproductive policy can be identified as quite successful and as based on disciplinary power. In Indonesia, the restructuring ended in a failure as the governmental and disciplinary mechanisms employed were not able to achieve a change in behaviour and the government shied away from decisively using repressive means. In Nepal, subtle mechanisms of power have been applied in the restructuring of the economic field of action for rural women and the 'conduct of conduct', the government through the voluntary actions of the responsible individual, has been successful. Likewise, the restructuring of the political field of action in Bolivia has also relied on governmental relations of power – although of a very different political quality: the subjectivities produced were not those of rational entrepreneurs, but of democratic citizens claiming their rights.

Summing up the results, it seems fairly safe to say that the increasing importance of participation and civil society in development projects (whether as part of a general transformation or not) seems to be accompanied by a shift in the mechanisms of power to be found in these projects from sovereign and disciplinary to governmental ones, from repressive to subjectivising power.

It can also be observed that the deployment of mechanisms of power – even of brutal force – was legitimated in a recurring pattern: the measures took place in the name of *development*, they were constructed as somehow leading to improvements in the standard of living. This brings us to our second point of analysis: I argue that a poststructuralist perspective on *development* can highlight aspects of this use of this concept which otherwise remain unnoticed.

Poststructuralism is discussed in chapter 2. How can it contribute to the analysis of *development*? If we take a look at the projects sketched above it becomes clear that the signifier *development* is taken to be synonymous with concepts like progress, improvement, positive social change, poverty reduction and better standard of living. This can be denoted as a chain of equivalences which exists between the signifiers. But what is also obvious is that the signifier *development* refers to completely different projects and thus signifieds: infrastructure projects, resettlement and counterinsurgency, dam building and irrigation, birth control, biodiversity protection and promotion of sustainable agriculture, microcredit provision and small enterprise promotion, improvements in electoral participation – all these heterogeneous signifieds have been linked with the signifier *development* in the examples mentioned above – and further examples with again different signifieds could be found easily. *Development* can thus be termed an empty signifier which can be filled with almost any content.

In the terminology of Laclau's poststructuralist theory of discourse, we could say that *development* is not a floating signifier incapable of being wholly articulated to a discursive chain (Laclau/Mouffe 2001: 113) because the term is at the centre of the discourse of development theory linking *developed*, modern, industrialised, affluent and a number of other concepts. Neither is the term privileged signifier wholly adequate: although *development* is at the centre of the discourse, it does not 'fix the meaning of a signifying chain' (Laclau/Mouffe 2001: 112), but rather allows for a plurality of meanings to be linked with it. Therefore, the term 'empty signifier' (Laclau 1996) seems more appropriate, with its connotation of a component of a hegemonic struggle in which a particular content comes to

signify universal interests – in this case on a global scale. Moreover, an empty signifier, according to Laclau, 'has no content, because it only exists in the various
forms in which it is actually realised . . . [it] is present as that which is absent; it
becomes an empty signifier, as the signifier of that absence. In this sense, various
political forces can compete in their efforts to present their particular objectives
as those which carry out the filling of that lack' (Laclau 1996: 44).

From a poststructuralist perspective, it therefore seems futile to engage in discussions over the true meaning of *development*. As the relation between signifier and signified is arbitrary, the term has no real or essential meaning – the
controversies whether *development* is a 'mission to achieve global equality' or 'a
project of cultural imperialism' make sense only in their political, not their epistemological dimension. In this perspective, it becomes also clear that the discourse of development – just like that of civilisation in the preceding era – was
an important element in constituting the identity of the West as progressive,
industrialised, democratic, wealthy etc. The idealised picture of the Self constituted the universal norm according to which the deficiencies of the Other (the
under- or *less developed* societies) could be proven.

However, the empty signifier *development* does not, as indicated by Laclau,
constitute an antagonism between and in-group and excluded others. Rather, it
serves to link the concrete practices with the signifiers mentioned in a chain of
equivalences (progress, improvement, etc.) and legitimates hierarchies between
experts and beneficiaries. Returning to our examples, not only the heterogeneity of the measures but also the similarity of their legitimation is remarkable.
All the restructuring and all the demands to change one's behaviour were made
in the name of *development* in the sense of a process towards a universally desirable state of society which would result in the improvement of the lives of all its
members – and thus the 'filling of the lack of development'. The representation of
the measures to attain this state also had another quality in common: they were
based on supposedly technical expert knowledge, i.e. nonpartisan, nonpolitical
knowledge.

These similarities in the techniques of legitimising the use of power in the
field of *development* suggest that despite the arbitrary content with which the
concept can be filled, this content has to assume a certain form: the form of a
technical intervention leading to an improvement in the standard of living of all
members of society, as *development* denotes a process which usually takes place in
units like society-state complexes. Although its content is vague and arbitrary,
the function of the signifier *development* is clear: it is to legitimise certain interventions as beneficial. Metaphorically speaking, *development* works as an 'empty
plus'.[17]

That the discourse of development constructs the otherwise arbitrary content
in a certain way can be explained with institutional constraints. As Ferguson has
argued, a development agency tends to ignore analyses that locate the problem of
poverty in the spheres of political and economic structures, because this sphere
is outside its mandate. Its job is to improve agricultural productivity, not tackle
the unequal distribution of land, to improve school enrolment of girls, not to

take on government elites. The latter activities would be perceived as politics, as affairs which are not the business of development organisations. This is why they are prone to construct the problem of poverty in such a way that their nonpolitical development projects seem promising (Ferguson 1994: 68f). The discourse of development thus allows, as we have seen, for the depoliticisation of measures implying far-reaching restructurings in political, economic and other spheres. Similarly, it depoliticises the phenomenon of social inequality, because it frames it as a result of a historical stage and a fundamentally technical problem (lack of knowledge, education, infrastructure or technology) to be solved by nonpolitical interventions – not as a political problem requiring a change in asymmetrical power relations.

The example of Bolivia demonstrates the vivacity of these constraints: as the government of Bolivia learned of the donor plans to support grassroots organisations in investigating and mitigating political exclusion of certain segments of society, it denounced the project as political interference from the outside, in other words as a measure which was not technical, apolitical and for the benefit of all but partisan and for the benefit of the opposition. That the government's intervention was only halfway successful (only two of the four donors abandoned the project), indicates three things: that the discourses of participation and civil society are indeed changing the rules of the development game, that these same discourses can be turned against progressive changes (the government invoked the idea of ownership to fend off the project plans) – and that personal engagement by grassroots organisations and DFID staff is also a relevant factor. According to the poststructuralist perspective, the rules of the discourse are not set in stone, but have to be reproduced continuously. Nevertheless, the institutional constraints are still very much alive and kicking.

Conclusion

The chapter has argued that the transformation of development discourse since the 1980s leading to the rise in significance of concepts like participation and civil society is also visible in the examples of development projects that have been examined. The measures taken in these projects have been analysed as restructurings of fields of action of the people affected by them, thus as implying relations of power in the Foucauldian sense. It could be shown that the increasing emphasis laid on participation went hand in hand with a tendency to abandon sovereign, repressive mechanisms of power in favour of governmental, subjectivising techniques. Lastly, from a poststructuralist perspective the concept of *development* was analysed as an empty signifier which can be filled with almost any content. However, the institutional constraints of development discourse prescribe the form that this content must take: that of a technical, apolitical intervention based on expert knowledge which will benefit all members of society, that is bring about *development*. Thus, the signifier *development* can be described as an empty plus, a discursive shell capable of modifying and legitimising its largely arbitrary content in a certain manner.

Notes

1 See Foucault 1991, 1980 and 1983. On the theoretical problems of Foucault's interpretive analytics see Dreyfus/Rabinow 1983.
2 Although Foucault mainly identifies the structuring of possible fields of action of others with a relation of government (Foucault 1983: 221), his description of disciplinary measures reveals that their operation of power relies on sanctions and incentives and does leave room for individual decisions not to comply, and this even holds true for laws (the archetypical sovereign mode of a relation of power) which can always be broken.
3 In this view power is only present where physical force is absent and choice is possible: 'Power is exercised only over free subjects, and only insofar as they are free. . . . slavery is not a power relationship when [a] man is in chains' (Foucault 1983: 221).
4 For the following see Ferguson 1994.
5 One might argue that the project was intended to stabilise the capitalist world system by reducing global inequalities, or to promote commercialisation and the substitution of subsistence activities through market-oriented activities, and that the donor countries governments had an interest in these effects. This, however, is applicable to most development projects and shall not be termed interests in the strict sense. This category shall be reserved for interests in stabilising regimes allied to the donor government (especially but not only during the Cold War) and for interests in improving the economic opportunities of Transnational Companies of the donor country.
6 For the following see Barry/Preusch 1988, Sacher 1991, Schultz 1992 and Wilson 1993.
7 Although it has to be noted that the government of Carter was markedly more reluctant to support the military dictatorship than that of Reagan.
8 Many witnesses tell of threats, punishments and torture as elements of recruitment procedures.
9 For the following see Mehta 1994, Rich 1994, Caufield 1996 and Roy 1999.
10 Officially, it was the Indian government that withdrew after the Bank had given it another deadline to meet the conditions based on the report.
11 For the following see Schultz 2000 and Coe 2001.
12 For the following see Li 2007.
13 For the following see Rankin 2001 and Majorano 2007.
14 For the following see Leon et al. 2003, Eyben/Ferguson 2004, and Eyben/Leon 2005.
15 The example of Guatemala reminds us of the fact that not all measures implemented in the name of *development* do automatically benefit their target group, although of course it cannot at all be seen as representative for the whole of development aid.
16 That the transformation also includes a rise in the significance of gender, sustainability and market relations can be assumed, but in the light of the few examples must remain hypothetical.
17 Sachs 1995: 30. The phrase has been translated as 'curious plus' (Sachs 1990: 6) in the one and simply skipped in the other English translation (Sachs 1999: 7).

Bibliography

Barry, Tom/Preusch, Deb 1988: *The Soft War. The Uses and Abuses of US Economic Aid in Central America*. New York: Grove Press.
Caufield, Catherine 1996: *Masters of Illusion. The World Bank and the Poverty of Nations*. New York: Henry Holt.

Coe, Anna-Brit 2001: CHANGE: Promoting Women's Sexual and Reproductive Health in Peru. *Women's Health Journal* 4/2001, 61–66. Online http://www.genderhealth.org/pubs/RevistaEng.pdf (September 28, 2008).

Corbridge, Stuart 1998: Beneath the Pavement Only Soil: The Poverty of Post-Development. *Journal of Development Studies* 34(6), 138–148.

Cowen, Michael P./Shenton, Robert W. 1996: *Doctrines of Development*. London: Routledge.

Dreyfus, Hubert L./Rabinow, Paul 1983: *Michel Foucault. Beyond Structuralism and Hermeneutics*. Chicago: University of Chicago Press.

DuBois, Marc 1991: The Governance of the Third World: A Foucauldian Perspective on Power Relations in Development. *Alternatives* 16(1), 1–30.

Escobar, Arturo 1995: *Encountering Development. The Making and Unmaking of the Third World*. Princeton, NJ: Princeton University Press.

Esteva, Gustavo 1987: Regenerating People's Space. *Alternatives* 12, 125–152.

Eyben, Rosalind/Ferguson, Clare 2004: How Can Donors Become More Accountable to Poor People. In: Groves, Leslie/Hinton, Rachel (eds.) *Inclusive Aid: Changing Power and Relationships in International Development*. London: Earthscan, 163–180.

Eyben, Rosalind/Leon, Rosario 2005: Whose Aid? The Case of the Bolivian Elections Project. In: Mosse, David/Lewis, David (eds.) *The Aid Effect. Giving and Governing in International Development*. London: Pluto Press, 106–125.

Ferguson, James 1994: *The Anti-Politics Machine: 'Development', Depoliticisation and Bureaucratic Power in Lesotho*. Minneapolis: University of Minnesota Press.

Foucault, Michel 1980: *Power/Knowledge: Selected Interviews and Other Writings 1972–1977*. New York: Pantheon.

Foucault, Michel 1983: The Subject and Power. In: Dreyfus, Hubert L./Rabinow, Paul (eds.) *Michel Foucault. Beyond Structuralism and Hermeneutics*. Chicago: University of Chicago Press, 208–226.

Foucault, Michel 1991: Governmentality. In: Graham Burchell/Colin Gordon/Peter Miller (eds.) *The Foucault Effect: Studies in Governmentality*. Chicago: University of Chicago Press, 87–104.

IDS 2001: *The New Dynamics of Aid: Power, Procedures and Relationships*, IDS Policy Briefing 15. Sussex: Institute of Development.

Kiely, Ray 1999: The Last Refuge of the Noble Savage? A Critical Assessment of Post-Development Theory. *European Journal of Development Research* 11(1), 30–55.

Laclau, Ernesto 1996: Why Do Empty Signifiers Matter to Politics? In: Ernesto Laclau (ed.) *Emancipation(s)*. London: Verso, 34–46.

Laclau, Ernesto/Mouffe, Chantal 2001 (1985): *Hegemony and Socialist Strategy: Towards a Radical Democratic Politics*. London: Verso.

Leon, Rosario/Goulden, Jay/Rea, Carmen/Salinas, Humberto/Medrano, Luis/Schollaert, Jan 2003: *Social Exclusion, Rights and Chronic Poverty in Bolivia*. Paper presented at the Chronic Poverty and Development Conference in Manchester (2003), online version: http://www.chronicpoverty.org/pubfiles/LeonGoulden.pdf (September 28, 2008).

Li, Tania Murray 2007: *The Will to Improve. Governmentality, Development, and the Practice of Politics*. Durham, NC: Duke University Press.

Majorano, Francesca 2007: *An Evaluation of the Rural Microfinance Development Centre as a Wholesale Lending Institution in Nepal*. Asian Development Bank Working Paper Series No. 8 (2007). Online http://www.adb.org/Documents/Papers/NRM/wp8.pdf (September 28, 2008).

Mehta, Pradeep S. 1994: Fury Over a River. In: Danaher, Kevin (ed.) *50 Years is Enough. The Case Against the World Bank and the International Monetary Fund.* Boston, MA: South End Press, 117–120.

Mosse, David 2005: Global Governance and the Ethnography of International Aid. In: Mosse, David/Lewis, David (eds.) *The Aid Effect. Giving and Governing in International Development.* London: Pluto Press, 1–36.

Mosse, David/Lewis, David (eds.) 2005: *The Aid Effect. Giving and Governing in International Development.* London: Pluto Press.

Nanda, Meera 1999: Who Needs Post-development? Discourses of Difference, Green Revolution and Agrarian Populism in India. *Journal of Developing Societies* 15(1), 5–31.

Nederveen Pieterse, Jan 2000: After Post-development. *Third World Quarterly* 20(1), 175–191.

Rahnema, Majid (ed.) 1997: *The Post-development Reader.* London: Zed Books.

Rankin, Katharine N. 2001: Governing Development: Neoliberalism, Microcredit, and Rational Economic Woman. *Economy and Society* 30(1), 18–37.

Rich, Bruce 1994: *Mortgaging the Earth: The World Bank, Environmental Impoverishment and the Crisis of Development.* London: Earthscan.

Roy, Arundhati 1999: The Greater Common Good. *Frontline* 16(11). Online http://www.hinduonnet.com/fline/fl1611/16110040.htm (September 27, 2008) or www.narmada.org.

Sacher, Danuta 1991: EG-Entwicklungspolitik im Dienst der Aufstandsbekämpfung in Guatemala. In Wilhelm Kempf (ed.) *Verdeckte Gewalt. Psychosoziale Folgen der Kriegsführung niedriger Intensität in Zentralamerika.* Hamburg: Argument, 84–91.

Sachs, Wolfgang 1990: The Archaeology of the Development Idea. *Interculture* 23(4), Nr. 109, 1–37.

Sachs, Wolfgang (ed.) 1992: *The Development Dictionary: A Guide to Knowledge as Power.* London: Zed Books.

Sachs, Wolfgang 1995: *Zur Archäologie der Entwicklungsidee.* 2nd ed. Frankfurt: IKO – Verlag für Interkulturelle Kommunikation.

Sachs, Wolfgang 1999: *Planet Dialectics. Explorations in Environment and Development.* London: Zed Books.

Schultz, Susanne 1992: *Guatemala: Entwicklungspolitik im Counterinsurgency-Staat. Das Fallbeispiel Food-For-Work-Projekte.* Diploma thesis, Free University of Berlin.

Schultz, Susanne 2000: Leise Diplomatie. Die Politik feministischer Nicht-Regierungs-Organisationen zur Sterilisationskampagne in Peru. In Gabbert, Karin et al. (eds.) *Jahrbuch Lateinamerika. Analysen und Berichte 24. Geschlecht und Macht.* Münster: Westfälisches Dampfboot, 55–65.

Wilson, Richard 1993: Continued Counterinsurgency: Civilian Rule in Guatemala. In: Gills, Barry/Rocamora, Joel/Wilson, Richard (eds.) *Low Intensity Democracy. Political Power in the New World Order.* London: Pluto Press, 127–160.

Weber, Max 2006 (1922): *Wirtschaft und Gesellschaft.* Paderborn, Germany: Voltmedia.

Ziai, Aram 2004: The Ambivalence of Post-development: Between Reactionary Populism and Radical Democracy. *Third World Quarterly,* 25(6), 1045–1061.

11 Millennium Development Goals
Back to the future?

The Millennium Development Goals (MDGs) constitute more or less a normative consensus in the development community of the beginning of the 21st century. Apart from some scattered critics, the overwhelming majority seems to agree that to attain these eight goals and 18 targets are a worthwhile cause or even the most urgent challenge humanity faces today. Who would disagree? Who would be against reducing the proportion of people suffering from hunger or the under-five mortality rates? Hardly anyone of sound mind. Still, it must be permitted to scrutinise and critically analyse the MDGs without being reproached of promoting world hunger. The chapter attempts to examine the MDGs from the perspective of poststructuralist discourse analysis and to situate them in their specific historical context. A historical comparison between the key documents reveals how development discourse has shifted between 1970 and the beginning of the 21st century in terms of topics and priorities, objectives and lines of causation, responsible actors and proposed measures.

The article proceeds as follows: in the first part the exact object of analysis, the analytical background, the research question and the method will be clarified. The second section will analyse the texts in relation to the question, while the third introduces the historic dimension by comparing the MDG documents to the UN declaration 2626 which spearheaded the Second Development Decade in 1970 and introduced the 0.7 per cent goal, which is still referred to today.

As objects of analysis, the following texts can be identified as the most important documents concerning the MDGs: the UN Millennium Declaration (UN 2000), the report of the then Secretary-General for the 2005 World Summit entitled 'In Larger Freedom' (Annan 2005), and the report by the UN Millennium Project headed by Jeffrey Sachs (UN Millennium Project 2005). They are the points of reference cited most often in political as well as academic texts concerned with the MDGs and figure prominently on the website www.un.org/millenniumgoals.

Concerning the analytical background (research does not start from nowhere but takes place in a specific context), it seems promising to relate an examination of the MDGs to the hypothesis asserting a transformation in development discourse since the 1980s. The most radical of its proponents were arguably the Post-Development authors (above all Sachs 1992, Escobar 1995, Rahnema 1997) who claimed that with the end of the Cold War and with the realisation of the ecological predicament, the ever-rising global inequalities between countries and the cultural homogenisation accompanying the post–World War II development enterprise, no one believed or was interested in *development* anymore – the era of development was over, or at least about to end. Superpower rivalry would no longer bribe peripheral countries with aid to join their side, the model of the industrial nations could obviously not be universalised, the gap between rich and poor had been growing instead of shrinking, and cultural diversity was seen as valuable and threatened by the homogenisation brought by the development project. Other works would not go that far, but still acknowledge the productivity of a discourse analysis of *development* and subscribe to the thesis that after the crisis in development theory and policy and the lost decade of the 1980s, a profound transformation was taking place in development discourse, introducing new (or sometimes not-so-new) buzzwords like sustainability, participation, good governance, poverty reduction, gender, globalisation, market-orientation, ownership and the like (Crush 1995, Moore/Schmitz 1995, Cooper/Packard 1997, IDS 2001, Mosse/Lewis 2005). At the end of the 1990s, it seemed reasonably plausible to assert that these new issues were becoming more and more important in North-South relations, and that not only the Official Development Assistance, but also the concept of *development* itself was on the decline.

With the advent of the MDGs this seems to have changed, although rather gradually than with a big bang. Already in 1996, the Development Aid Committee (DAC) of the OECD presented a paper called 'Shaping the 21st Century', in which several measures and a timetable were proposed to halve the number of the absolute poor until 2015 (Development Assistance Committee 1996). The Millennium Declaration in 2000, the Monterrey Conference on Finance for Development in 2002, and the MDG world summit in 2005 were the landmarks of the goals' rise to prominence.

Thus, from a point of view which asserts the decline of the *development* concept because of structural factors, the MDGs must appear anachronistic, remnants of a bygone era which are now heralded as the way into the future. From the perspective of poststructuralist discourse analysis, the article examines whether this is really the case. This perspective (see Belsey 2002 for a good introduction) investigates the relation between signifier and signified and identifies signifying systems which construct reality as discourses. Poststructuralist discourse analysis thus sets out to examine these discourses, their rules of formation, their continuous transformations, their story lines and the subjectivities they produce. Of special interest in this context is the relationship between discourse and power: how do power relations in the field of the economy, politics, gender and culture in general influence the production of discourses? Which discourses are recognised as scientific and true, and which remain marginal? What are the effects of certain discourses in terms of reproducing or transforming relations of power and structuring what can be said and done and what is excluded? (see Foucault 1972, 1980, 1983).[1]

Analysis of the documents

This section will analyse how the problem of human suffering (e.g. poverty) and the corresponding solutions (e.g. poverty reduction, *development*) are constructed in the MDG documents. While the analysis will start with the titles of the documents and the MDGs themselves, the next subsections will deal with the central themes and story lines of the three publications, that is with the way certain signifiers are related to each other and to certain signifieds and the way these relations are justified.

The titles of the documents are not uniform: The United Nations Millennium Declaration (MD) does not hint at a specification of its topic and its sections cover a wide range of issues ('Peace, security and disarmament', 'Development and poverty eradication', 'Protecting our common environment', 'Human rights, democracy and good governance', 'Protecting the vulnerable', 'Meeting the special needs of Africa', 'Strengthening the United Nations'). Although it introduces what later became the MDGs, it is not called Millennium Development Declaration. The Report of the Secretary-General (as a follow-up to the outcome of the Millennium Summit) bears the title 'In larger freedom: towards development, security and human rights for all' (ILF). Here, the three latter issues are united under the umbrella of larger freedom, which already indicates a liberal commitment in contrast to other conceivable headings for a report on the MDGs like 'Towards development for all' or 'Implementing the right to development'. The Report to the Secretary-General by the Millennium Project (headed by Jeffrey Sachs) is entitled 'Investing in Development. A Practical Plan to Achieve the Millennium Development Goals' (IID), framing the task in economic terms of investment and planning.

The perspective of planning, of deliberate interventions in economy and society with the aim of achieving improvements, is also at the basis of the MDGs themselves. The eight goals ('Eradicate extreme poverty and hunger', 'Achieve universal primary education', 'Promote gender equality and empower women', 'Reduce child mortality', 'Improve maternal health', 'Combat HIV/AIDS, malaria and other diseases', 'Ensure environmental stability', 'Develop a global partnership for development') are operationalised in 18 targets, 10 of which contain quantitative targets to be achieved at a certain point in time (usually 2015). The last goal, which deals with actions to be taken not on the national, but on the international level, is operationalised in seven targets alone, all of which are nonquantitative. Obviously the emphasis on concrete, measurable progress is abandoned when it comes to the necessary reform of global trade and debt issues. This becomes even clearer when the Millennium Project lists the uneven and insufficient progress towards the MDGs in a table of 20 measurable targets, only one of which refers to goal eight ('A global partnership for development'), and this target is the improvement of youth unemployment (IID, 3) – not the cancellation of debt or another of the original MDG eight targets concerned with reforms of the global economy.

Story line 1: poverty reduction, development and growth

In the MDG documents we find numerous occasions where the signifiers *develop-ment* and poverty reduction are closely linked or even used synonymously, such as the following:

> We will spare no effort to free our fellow men, women and children from the abject and dehumanising conditions of extreme poverty . . . We are commit-ted to making the right to development a reality for everyone and to freeing the entire human race from want.
>
> (MD par. 11)

Often, however, a chain of equivalences is established between these two signi-fiers and another, economic growth: 'Our goal is to eradicate poverty, achieve sustained economic growth and promote sustainable development' (IID, 5). Sometimes this growth is specified as being private-sector growth dependent on foreign direct investment and on policies of good governance:

> In order to reduce poverty and promote global prosperity for all . . . (i) Devel-oping countries should recommit themselves to taking primary responsibility for their own development by strengthening governance, combating corrup-tion and putting in place the policies and investments to drive private-sector led growth and maximise domestic resources to fund national development strategies.
>
> (ILF Annex, par. 5)

This line of argument – in order to reduce poverty, *development* has to be achieved and the way to do so is through economic growth – has a very familiar ring within development theory and is reminiscent of 1950s and 60s trickle-down-assumptions (Martinussen 1997, ch. 5). However, a new element can be found in quotes like 'meeting the Goals for hunger, education, gender equality, environment, and health is vital for overall economic growth and development' (IID, 4f): Here, the causality is reversed. Not only growth is necessary for poverty reduction, but poverty reduction or the provision of basic needs is a contribution to economic growth. This argument (which is repeated on p. 13 of IID) is familiar from the World Bank's WDR 2000/2001 on poverty (World Bank 2000) and constructs a harmonious, mutually reinforcing relationship between poverty reduction and economic growth and thus the proponents of either goal as allies. The relationship between the different signifiers becomes especially clear in the following quote:

> Achieving the [Millennium Development] Goals is largely about making core investments in infrastructure and human capital that enable poor peo-ple to join the global economy, while empowering the poor with economic, political and social rights that will enable them to make full use of infra-structure and human capital, wherever they choose to live. . . . Both villages

and cities can become part of global economic growth if they are empowered with the infrastructure and human capital to do so. If every village has a road, access to transport, a clinic, electricity, safe drinking water, education, and other essential inputs, the villagers in very poor countries will show the same determination and entrepreneurial zeal of people all over the world.

(IID, 15)

Development and poverty reduction are thus understood as joining the global economy and becoming part of global economic growth, and the necessary means are investments in infrastructure and human capital which empower the poor. In contrast to a meaning of empowerment as a change in power structures initiated by the disempowered (e.g. Friedmann 1992), empowerment is reduced to public investments which will allow the poor to escape poverty by unleashing their entrepreneurial zeal and joining the global economy. Power structures do not seem to be present, reducing poverty is merely a matter of mobilising resources for the right investments, afterwards market forces and entrepreneurship will do the job – structures present in the market economy leading to unequal distribution of profits are completely neglected. This fits to the specifications about how to achieve growth in the previous quote: through investments, the private-sector, good governance and the maximisation of resources for *development*. This leads to the next element of the MDG discourse.

Story line 2: development as a technical problem

Achieving *development*, meeting the MDG targets and reducing global poverty are presented not as political, but as technical problems: 'The unprecedented combination of resources and technology at our disposal today means that we are truly the first generation with the tools, the knowledge and the resources to meet the commitment, given by all States in the Millennium Declaration, "to making the right to development a reality for everyone and to freeing the entire human race from want"' (ILF par. 27). The main problem seems to arise from a lack of resources: 'We are concerned about the obstacles developing countries face in mobilising the resources needed to finance their sustained development' (MD par.14). But how are these resources to be used? The answer given here is:

The key to escaping the poverty trap is to raise the economy's capital stock to the point where the downward spiral ends and self-sustaining economic growth takes over. This requires a big push of basic investments between now and 2015 in public administration, human capital (nutrition, health, education), and key infrastructure (roads, electricity, ports, water and sanitation, accessible land for affordable housing, environmental management).

(IID, 19)

A big push in investments should raise the capital stock to the (potentially calculable) point where self-sustaining growth sets in.[2] Again we are reminded of the

1950s-era theories of unbalanced growth and necessary savings rates, although it has to be noted that investments in basic needs and education are given a more significant role here. Apart from mentioning the issues of governance and corruption, the documents contain no hints concerning political obstacles, social conflicts or parties whose interests would be harmed by a shift in policy on a national and international level prioritising the achievement of the MDGs. *Development* seems as a consensual, nonconflictive goal to be achieved by technical processes to which no one can object.[3] In the light of the link between poverty reduction and growth, one could even argue that the achievement of the MDGs is presented as being in everyone's interest. This point is stressed by Kofi Annan in the conclusion to his report as well: 'We are united both by moral imperatives and by objective interests' (ILF, par. 220). Achieving the MDGs is prescribed not only from the ethical point of view, but also from that of economic interest. The reason for this is not only the harmonious relationship between poverty reduction and growth, but also that between security and *development*, or in a more general formulation: the interconnectedness of all peoples in the age of globalisation.

Story line 3: globalisation, security and development

The term globalisation is linked with two slightly different signifieds in the documents: in a more general meaning with something like global interconnectedness, in a more specific one with global economic liberalisation. Although global economic liberalisation is by no means rejected, a significant departure from the neoliberal discourse prevalent in the 1990s in many official texts on *development* and poverty reduction can be observed in the following quotes:

> We believe that the central challenge we face today is to ensure that globalisation becomes a positive force for all the world's people. For while globalisation offers great opportunities, at present its benefits are very unevenly shared, while its costs are unevenly distributed.
>
> (MD, par. 5)

> But when individuals and whole economies lack even the most basic infrastructure, health services, and education, market forces alone can accomplish little. Households and whole economies remain trapped in poverty, and fail to reap the benefits of globalisation. Without basic infrastructure and human capital, countries are condemned to export a narrow range of low-margin primary commodities based on natural (physical) endowments, rather than a diversified set of exports based on technology, skills, and capital investments. In such circumstances, globalisation can have significant adverse effects . . . rather than bring benefits through increased foreign direct investment inflows and technological advances.
>
> (IID, 13)

While in neoliberal discourse the standard formulae had been 'globalisation is inevitable and we have to adjust' and 'globalisation brings huge opportunities and benefits', both documents now also mention the costs and the uneven distribution of the benefits. Nevertheless, the process of global economic liberalisation is still seen as a potentially beneficial force, and the Millennium Project sees its task less in reforming (or even stopping) it, but in adapting the actors to the process, in building people's and economies' capacities so that they can reap the benefits. These benefits are thereby assumed to be naturally existent and the failure to attain them lies within the responsibility of the actors and is not the fault of the process of liberalisation.

The basic attitude towards free markets is also visible in Target 12 of the MDGs which explicitly demands an 'open, rule-based, predictable, nondiscriminatory trading and financial system' (IID, xv). Nondiscriminatory – in the context of WTO trading rules – means that it is not allowed to discriminate against certain (usually foreign) economic actors in favour of other actors. Thus supporting less competitive, local enterprises and protecting them from the often overwhelmingly superior competition of transnational corporations (a practice that can be observed in nearly every successful process of industrialisation in history, see Chang 2003) is constructed as an activity usually associated with racism or patriarchy (discrimination).

The other sense of globalisation conveys increasing global interconnectedness, as in the following quote:

> As the world's only universal body with a mandate to address security, development and human rights issues, the United Nations bears a special burden. As globalisation shrinks distances around the globe and these issues become increasingly interconnected, the comparative advantages of the United Nations become ever more evident.
>
> (ILF, par. 21)

So according to the report, the shrinking distances cause a mutually reinforcing relationship between *development*, security, and human rights:

> This relationship has only been strengthened in our era of rapid technological advances, increasing economic interdependence, globalisation and dramatic geopolitical change. While poverty and denial of human rights may not be said to 'cause' civil war, terrorism or organised crime, they all greatly increase the risk of instability and violence. Similarly, war and atrocities are far from the only reasons that countries are trapped in poverty, but they undoubtedly set back development. Again, catastrophic terrorism on one side of the globe, for example an attack against a major financial centre in a rich country, could affect the development prospects of millions on the other by causing a major economic downturn and plunging millions into poverty.
>
> (ILF, par. 16)

This construction of linkages aims at a reconceptualisation of interests and identities, which can, in a slightly simplified manner, be sketched as follows: if poverty increases the risk of violence and terror which can affect the centre, it is in
the interests of the rich countries to assist the poor. And if attacks like in September 2001 bring about a recession which also affects the periphery, it is in the
interests of the poor countries to help preventing them. Thus the convergence of
interests compels another construction of identity than the one based on nations:
an identity based on perceiving oneself as first and foremost part of humanity,
part of 'one world':

> If we act boldly – and if we act together – we can make people everywhere
> more secure, more prosperous and better able to enjoy their fundamental
> human rights. . . . All the conditions are in place for us to do so. In an era of
> global interdependence, the glue of common interest, if properly perceived,
> should bind all States together in this cause, as should the impulses of our
> common humanity.
>
> (ILF, pars. 1–2)

Thus we can observe the construction of a Self (we) which comprises the entire
human race as an actor driven to reforms for the improvement of *development*
and security and human rights not only by ethical motives but at least equally by
self-interest: 'In a world of interconnected threats and challenges, it is in each
country's self-interest that all of them are addressed effectively' (ILF, par. 18).

This construction is problematic in several respects: if the link between problems in the South and well-being in the North turns out to be less strong in
concrete examples as is suggested here, e.g. because the UN manages to contain
conflicts and refugee flows on a regional scale, the argument loses its force. From
the point of view of enlightened self-interest, wars and misery in the periphery
do not pose a threat if they have no detrimental effects for those in the centre. Further, the construction assumes an objective interest without taking into
account the diverse subjective conceptions of interest and well-being and, what's
more, the different positions occupied by individuals in the global society. Probably global warming is a less pressing problem for people dying from malaria or
AIDS in Africa or for those who can still afford to go skiing at a higher place,
just as the financial markets crash is maybe less significant for those searching the
waste dumps of Sao Paulo for something to eat.[4] The political consequence of the
assumption of an actor called humanity united by common interest is that one
loses sight of the numerous conflicts of interests within this humanity, of the vast
differences in resources, power and influence, and of their deadly effects.

The only precondition for humanity to solve the problems of *development* and
poverty, security and human rights, seems to be that the leaders 'make the right
choice' and Annan encourages them 'to transcend their differences' and calls
for 'wisdom' and 'firm, clear-sighted leadership' in order to achieve 'a visionary
change of direction in our world' (ILF, par. 222). So the problem boils down
to leaders finding the courage to act in favour of the MDGs – no structural

constraints, no conflicts, no power, merely a potential lack of courage and wisdom which can hopefully be defeated by the urgent appeal of the Secretary-General of the United Nations. If the political is defined as an area of contestation where conflicting interests engage in order to arrive at binding rules, we are clearly confronted with a depoliticisation of poverty in the central MDG documents. This, however, has already been identified as a central feature of traditional development discourse (Ferguson 1994). Returning to our question, we can observe that the theoretical concepts underlying the MDG documents are reminiscent of old-fashioned growth theory coupled with basic needs strategies and economic liberalisation. A historical comparison will provide a more precise picture of the continuities and discontinuities in development discourse that can be observed in the MDG.

Historical comparison

It could be argued that the depoliticising quality of the MDG documents is not untypical of UN documents and reports in general, especially if we deal with declarations requiring the consensus of all represented governments, and of development policy programmes in particular. This would be a rather broad criticism, but in order to further specify the analysis, it seems useful to compare the Millennium Declaration of 2000 to the International Development Strategy for the Second Development Decade of 1970 (UN 1970, hereafter IDS). This can illuminate elements of the transformation of development discourse which took place during these 30 years. Both documents are UN declarations adopted by the General Assembly and both are programmatic texts dealing with problems of global inequality interpreted under the heading of *development*. These two texts shall be compared regarding their topics and priorities, objectives and lines of causation, responsible actors and proposed measures.

Topics and priorities

Comparing the two documents in terms of their topics, it is conspicuous that the IDS is far more focused on *development*, and mostly in a narrow sense of economic development and growth. International trade is given a priority role in this respect and is dealt with specifically in paragraphs 21–40 and 53–55, that is in more than a quarter of the whole document. Another prominent topic is (unsurprisingly) development aid respectively 'financial resources for development' (par. 41–52). The document also deals with the specific problems of the 'least developed' and 'land-locked developing' countries (par. 56–59), with science and technology (par. 60–64) and with various topics subsumed under the heading human development: population growth (65), employment (66), education (67), health (68), nutrition (69), youth and children (70), housing (71), and the environment (72). In a section on 'expansion and diversification of production' it also covers agricultural strategies (among others land reform and rural credit provision) (75), industry (76) and infrastructure (77). The declaration also calls for an end to apartheid and colonialism, for general and complete disarmament, and equal political, economic, social and cultural rights for all (5) and somewhere even mentions that 'The full integration of women in the total development effort should be encouraged' (par. 18 h).

Although it introduces what became the MDGs, the term *development* is significantly less in the centre of the MD. It has sections on 'Peace, security and disarmament' (par. 8–10), 'Development and poverty eradication' (11–20), 'Protecting our common environment' (21–23), 'Human rights, democracy and good governance' (24–25), 'Protecting the vulnerable' (26), 'Meeting the special needs of Africa' (27–28) and 'Strengthening the United Nations' (29–32). Notwithstanding the fact that the section on *development* is (in terms of paragraphs) by far the largest, it is merely one among several in the MD. Although many (not all) of the topics addressed in the other sections have already been present in the IDS, it seems that they are no longer seen as aspects of *development*, but as issues in their own right and are thus attributed more space in document, independent of the section on *development*. The significance of *development* as a universal signifier for global improvements has obviously declined.

Some of the topics of the MD are in fact new, while others are not new but are taken more seriously. Other topics have disappeared or severely lost in significance. Three topics that are new are 'international terrorism', 'the world drug problem' and 'trafficking as well as smuggling in human beings' (MD par. 9). These three in particular (others include HIV/AIDS, migration, human rights, good governance and small arms trade) are significant insofar as they are all referring to problems usually constructed in terms of the South being the origin of threats against which the North has to protect itself, through a 'war on terror' in Afghanistan and Iraq and the London underground,[5] through a 'war on drugs' in Colombia and elsewhere, and through stricter controls at the borders of the EU and the US. This hints at a change in the perception of North-South relations already evident after the end of the Cold War, but certainly intensified after September 11, which has been described in the following way: 'Third World countries are now risk zones. All kinds of dangers are to be found there, as the newspapers and television keep telling us . . . even the stronghold of the North is not immune from the threat of immigration, . . . drug traffic, terrorism and war . . . In these circumstances, the "development" concept . . . slowly . . . is being substituted by the concept of "security"[6] – from the North's viewpoint' (Sachs 1999: 21f). Even if the concept of *development* is not entirely substituted, it is increasingly linked to the concept of security (see section 1). Good governance and human rights, it should be added, also became important issues only after the end of the Cold War, during which both superpowers generously overlooked the despotic and nondemocratic nature of some of their allies.

One topic which was mentioned only marginally in the IDS is the issue of gender. It appears three times in the MD: In par. 25 it is resolved to 'combat all forms of violence against women and to implement the Convention on the Elimination of All Forms of Discrimination against Women'; in par. 19 the goal of reducing maternal mortality is formulated; and in par. 20 it is resolved to 'promote gender equality and the empowerment of women as effective ways to combat poverty, hunger and disease and to stimulate development that is truly sustainable'. This illustrates at first glance the shift from a Women-in-Development approach which aimed at integrating women in an otherwise unchanged *development* process ('The full integration of women in the total development effort should be encouraged') (IDS, par. 18 h, see Boserup 1970) to a Gender-and-Development approach (see Kabeer 1994). On a second glance, the concept of gender is limited to achieve women's equality, and, on top of that, women's empowerment (see the above discussion of the content of the term) is merely seen in an instrumental perspective as a means to combat poverty, not as a goal on its own.

Topics which have disappeared in 2000 include the strategy of land reform (IDS par. 75) and a more equitable distribution of income (18). What is more remarkable is that the issue of international trade has severely lost its significance. From being the clearly dominant topic in the IDS to one not even addressed in an own section, but merely mentioned in passing in a few paragraphs (14, 15, 28). Here, a significant shift in development discourse can be observed on the level of topics: international trade and the distribution of assets do no longer appear as issues which deserve political debate and regulation. Other important differences between the documents can be found in the different position of the concept of development and the new prominence of security issues in North-South relations.

Objectives and lines of causation

Despite the different significance attributed to the term, one could argue that both documents adopt development as their main objective. However, scope and content of this objective are not quite identical and neither are the causal mechanisms with which it is assumed to be achieved. The perception of the problem is still relatively similar in both texts:

> [T]he level of living of countless millions of people is still pitifully low. These people are often still undernourished, uneducated, unemployed and wanting in many other basic amenities of life. While a part of the world lives in great comfort and even affluence, much of the larger part suffers from abject poverty, and in fact the disparity is continuing to widen. This lamentable situation has contributed to the aggravation of world tension.
>
> (IDS, par. 3)

In the last sentence, the alleged relationship between security and *development* discussed in the previous section is hinted at. In the MD, the corresponding passage reads:

> We will spare no effort to free our fellow men, women and children from the abject and dehumanising conditions of extreme poverty, to which more than a billion of them are currently subjected. We are committed to making the

right to development a reality for everyone and to freeing the entire human race from want.

(par. 11)

It is conspicuous that the view on the poor in the first document puts them in the context of comfort and affluence and sees inequality as the problem, whereas the picture drawn in the second document does not – poverty is seen as an absolute, not a relative condition, independent of wealth in other places. The first view is reinforced in other paragraphs, notably in the following passage:

> In the conviction that development is the essential path to peace and justice,[7] Governments reaffirm their common and unswerving resolve to seek a better and more effective system of international co-operation whereby the prevailing disparities in the world may be banished and prosperity secured for all.

(IDS, par. 6)

Here, the ambitious objective of eliminating global inequalities is articulated. The MD adopts far more modest objectives, above all to halve 'the proportion of the world's people whose income is less than one dollar a day and the proportion of people who suffer from hunger and . . . the proportion of people who are unable to reach or to afford safe drinking water' (par. 19). However, for these as well as the other goals (ensure primary schooling, drastically reduce maternal and child mortality, halt and reverse the spread of HIV/AIDS and Malaria, and others) a concrete time frame ('by the year 2015') is mentioned. For the elimination of global disparities in the IDS, it was not. Still, the document did mention a time frame ('not later than 1975') for the obligation of the *developed* countries to provide financial transfers of 1 per cent or at least 0.7 per cent of its GNP (par. 43).

Concerning the contents of the signifier *development*, the goals mentioned above sum up the MD position quite well. Equality is mentioned as an objective in the MD as well, as an equality 'at the global level' (par. 2) and as the 'equality of all states' (4). However, in the enumeration of fundamental values in par. 5 ('Equality. No individual and no nation must be denied the opportunity to benefit from development. The equal rights and opportunities of women and men must be assured.') it is specified primarily as an equality of opportunity. Affluence existing next to poverty or inequality in the distribution of wealth are nowhere seen as problems in the MD. In contrast, to this, in the IDS *development* is also linked again to the question of inequality: 'If undue privileges, extremes of wealth and social injustices persist, then development fails in its essential purpose' (IDS, par. 7). In the view prevalent in the IDS, a change in the international situation or even the world order is required to achieve this objective: 'The success of international development activities will depend in large measure on improvement in the general international situation' (IDS, par. 5) 'Governments designate the 1970s as the Second United Nations Development Decade and pledge themselves, individually and collectively, to pursue policies designed to create a more just and rational world economic and social order' (par. 12). References to a more just world order cannot be found in the MD, and the closest phrase is: 'We resolve therefore to create an environment – at the national and global levels alike – which is conducive to development and to the elimination of poverty' (MD, par. 12).

What is worth mentioning is that in the IDS, the overcoming of inequality and the achievement of *development* is closely linked to improvements in economic growth. In the section on Goals and Objectives, in the paragraphs 13–17, it lists the detailed numbers which rates of growth are required:

> The average annual rate of growth in the gross product of the developing countries as a whole during the Second United Nations Development Dec-ade should be at least 6 per cent . . . The average annual rate of growth of gross product per head in developing countries should be about 3.5 per cent . . . The target for growth in average income per head is calculated on the basis of an average annual increase of 2.5 per cent in the population of developing countries . . . An average annual rate of growth of at least 6 per cent in the gross product of developing countries during the Decade will imply an aver-age annual expansion of a) 4 per cent in agricultural output. . . . there should be an average annual expansion of: a) 0.5 per cent in the ration of gross domestic saving to the gross product so that this ration rises to around 20 per cent by 1980; b) Somewhat less than 7 per cent in imports and somewhat higher than 7 per cent in exports.

We are thus confronted with a detailed concept of socioeconomic planning dis-playing an impressive amount of confidence regarding the possibility to politi-cally control the economy which under the present circumstances and Zeitgeist appears almost anachronistic.

However, the most important shift in terms of objectives and lines of causa-tion is to be found in a new modesty concerning the goals and the disarticulation between *development* and equality. Whereas in the IDS, *development* was conceiv-able only in a context of a movement towards global equality and poverty was perceived in relation to affluence, this view is no longer present in the MD.

Responsible actors

Who are the actors supposed to achieve these objectives? Again, we find marked differences between the two documents. In the MD, the dominant subject is 'We', specified in paragraph 1 as 'heads of State and Government'. (The implications of this conception have been discussed in the previous section.) In every single of the 32 paragraphs this unified collective actor appears (altogether 49 instances), usually in formulations like 'we resolve', 'we are determined' or 'we will spare no effort'. In contrast to this, in the IDS the actors are often specified as *developed* or *developing* countries, although there are also many passive constructions avoid-ing an explicit subject (e.g. 'The well-being of children should be fostered', IDS, par. 18 f) and occasionally the international community is invoked (8), as it is in the MD. While in the MD only in rare instances the *developing* and industrialised countries are addressed separately (par. 5, 15), in the IDS we find different positions and obligations of *developed* and *developing* countries in 64 out of the 84 paragraphs. Thus in the MD, the common convictions and interests are emphasised, while in the IDS the different needs and interests of rich and poor countries were stressed. Although paragraph 11 announces 'The primary responsibility for the development of developing countries rest upon themselves', the IDS is very explicit about the obligations of the OECD world – in stark contrast to the MD.

Another point worth mentioning is that in both documents states are the dominant types of actors and multilateral organisations also appear occasionally (MD par. 29–32, IDS 21, 24, 32, 51). In the MD, two new groups of actors turn up: the private sector and civil society organisations as potential partners 'in pursuit of development and poverty eradication' (par. 20). That capitalist enterprises can be partners in eradicating poverty is a view certainly not shared by all, but this point (indicating a shift in development discourse) cannot be pursued here.

Concerning the responsible actors mentioned in the document, it is clear that between 1970 and 2000 a shift has taken place in the direction of a more harmonious, nonantagonistic relation between rich and poor countries. Whereas the IDS continuously emphasises different needs and obligations of these actors, the MD merges them into a benevolent international 'we'.

Proposed measures

A detailed comparison of all the proposed measures cannot be provided, but the main principles and announcements of the two declarations should be addressed here. In the MD, the proposed measures for reducing poverty and achieving development are above all: 'good governance within each country', 'good governance at the international level' (whatever that might mean – fighting corruption at the UN?), 'transparency in the financial, monetary and trading systems', 'an open, equitable, rule-based, predictable and non-discriminatory multilateral trading and financial system' (par.14), mobilise sufficient resources the *developing* countries need 'to finance their sustained development', 'a policy of duty- and quota-free access for essentially all[8] exports from the least developed countries' in the industrialised countries, to grant more development assistance especially to countries 'that are genuinely making an effort to apply their resources for poverty reduction' and to deal with the debt problems of 'low and middle-income developing countries' (15, 16).

The policy measures proposed in the IDS are more numerous and more detailed. They include commodity agreements between producer nations to regulate outputs and prices (par. 21, 22), buffer stock mechanisms to stabilise prices through regulation of supply (23), pricing policies aimed at 'securing stable, remunerative and equitable prices with a view to increasing the foreign exchange earnings from exports of primary products from the developing countries' (24) and the use of bilateral and multilateral development assistance to support the attempts of *developing* countries to 'accelerate the diversification of their economies with a view to the expansion of the production and exports of semi-manufactures and manufactures, as well as semi-processed and processed commodities' (28). Strong emphasis is given to the preclusion and reduction of protectionist measures of the *developed* countries ('No new tariff and non-tariff barriers will be raised nor will the existing ones be increased by developed countries against imports of primary products of particular interest to developing countries') (25). 'Developed countries will accord priority to reducing or eliminating duties and other barriers to imports of primary products, including those in processed or semi-processed form' (26),[9] 'Developed countries will not, ordinarily, raise existing tariff or non-tariff barriers to exports from developing countries, not establish new tariff or non-tariff barriers or any discriminatory measures, where such action has the effect of rendering less favourable the conditions of access to the markets of manufactured and semi-manufactured products of export interest to developing countries.' (33) and correspondingly to the promotion of nonreciprocal preferential treatments for exports from the South to the North (32). Other measures are the general prevention of tied aid (45),[10] the establishment of a World Bank scheme providing financial assistance 'for dealing with the problem of disruption of development arising from adverse moments in the export proceeds of developing countries' (51).

Already these brief quotes allow for the recognition of the following points concerning the proposed measures of the documents: Many measures proposed in the IDS aim at regulating global trade in a manner beneficial for exporters of primary products while others aim at supporting the diversification and industrialisation of their economies, having recognised the structural problems they are confronted with under the present structures of the international economy. The measures were also concerned with abolishing protectionist measures, but first and foremost those in the North harming the export revenues of the South. These measures have almost completely disappeared in the MD. What remains is the call for tariff-free access of essentially all exports of the *least developed* countries and apart from that for a nondiscriminatory trading system. This can be interpreted as testifying the influence of neoliberal thinking which sees the political regulation of trade (especially the control of prices) as economically harmful and is committed to a level playing field and getting the prices right. Another point worth mentioning is that in the MD, the industrialised countries appear less as dominant actors in the global economy which are politically and morally obliged to change their behaviour and the structures of the global economy (as they did in the IDS), but as benign actors giving out aid to those poor countries that have deserved it by proving their intents to govern responsibly and reduce poverty. Although the MD mentions the right to *development* twice (par. 11, 24), development aid is not seen as an unconditional right of a peripheral country, no matter how its government acts, but as a favour given in response to good conduct. This has the positive aspect of preventing the financing of corrupt dictators and at the same time the negative ring of continued dominance by ex-colonial powers assuming the pedagogical role of parent subjects. So it can be stated that in comparison to the IDS, the discourse present in the MD is characterised by a rejection of market interventions and a basic commitment to neoliberal economic thinking and by a markedly more benign portrayal of the industrialised countries and their relationship to the periphery. These results indicate significant shifts in power relations that took place between the writing of these two documents.

Conclusion

The analysis of the key documents relating to the MDGs yields the following results (which can only be summarised in a slightly simplified form): on various occasions, a chain of equivalences is established between the signifiers *development*, poverty reduction and economic growth which is reminiscent of early modernisation theories, although as new elements noneconomic factors are mentioned as well and poverty reduction is also seen as a contribution to economic growth (not only vice versa). Meeting the MDGs is primarily constructed as a technical problem, as a challenge in terms of mobilising sufficient resources. Conflicts of interests are hardly mentioned, resulting in a depoliticised view of the problem of global inequality. The global harmony of interests is seen as a consequence of increasing global interconnectedness and the ensuing mutually reinforcing relationship between *development*, security and human rights leading to a reconceptualisation of interests and identities – a rather fragile construction downplaying the vast differences in resources and power within the collective actor assumed here (humanity).

The comparison of the Millennium Declaration with the International Development Strategy of 1970 places these results in a historical perspective and indicates that the features identified here are not specific to UN documents on the topic in general. It illustrates that the term *development* is less relevant in today's debates, linked to more modest objectives and portrays the problem of poverty in absolute instead of relative terms, thus disarticulating *development* and inequality. The most conspicuous element identified in the comparison is the predominance of efforts to regulate global trade as a strategy to promote *development* in the IDS which has almost disappeared in the MD. The numerous differentiations between *developing* and *developed* states as actors and their corresponding needs and obligations have also disappeared. The proposed measures today are far more concerned with free trade than with intervening in the market mechanisms of the global economy in favour of peripheral countries or reforming world order.

It can be stated that in the documents we are confronted with manifestations of a significant shift in discourse that has taken place between 1970 and 2000, a shift in favour of neoliberal, market-oriented measures to counter global poverty and in favour of a nonantagonistic conception of the global community of states which precludes demands for global regulation of trade or redistribution. This must not only be seen as a shift in power relations between North and South after the end of the Cold War reflected in discourse, but the prevalent discourse reproduces and constitutes these power relations, providing depoliticised conceptions of poverty and confining poverty reduction measures to those compatible with market-oriented solutions. To return to our initial question: in some respects the current discourse does indeed seem anachronistic, especially in focusing on mobilising large resources (big push) and in the close relation implied between poverty reduction and economic growth, neglecting a wide range of scholarship since the 1970s. In other respects, there are marked differences to old-school concepts: MDG discourse tries to incorporate significant neoliberal elements into development discourse and has abandoned attempts of what could be called global Keynesianism to regulate the global economy for the benefit of poorer countries.

Notes

1 Of course there are significant differences between the different concepts of discourse used by Foucault, but the view put forward here is that an archaeological examination of the rules of formation is compatible with an analysis of the link between power and knowledge.
2 A more thorough critique of the 'legend of the Big Push' is provided by Easterly 2006, ch. 2.
3 Thus we are faced with a strategy of depoliticisation, which has been analysed by Ferguson 1994 and Murray Li 2007 as a structural feature of development discourse.
4 The words probably and maybe are crucially important here unless one wants to imply a theory of objective interest.
5 On July 22, 2005, a Brazilian man was shot dead (in the head at close range) in a London tube station by the Metropolitan Police who misidentified him as a terrorist (see http://en.wikipedia.org/wiki/Jean_Charles_de_Menezes, January 11, 2009).
6 Cynthia Enloe (1989) has clearly demonstrated that these interpretations of security are patriarchal, neglecting threats to security, e.g. from marital violence.
7 Again, a link between security and *development* is postulated.
8 Which of course means: not quite all – significant ones have been excepted.
9 This phrase refers to the tariff escalation practiced by industrialised countries which charges higher tariffs for processed primary products – a measure directed against building up processing industries in the South.
10 Aid which is given under the condition of using it to purchase certain goods or services from enterprises of the donor country is referred to as tied aid.

Bibliography

Annan, Kofi 2005: *In Larger Freedom: Towards Development, Security and Human Rights for All.* Report of the Secretary-General. UN document A/59/2005.
Belsey, Catherine 2002: *Poststructuralism: A Very Short Introduction.* Oxford: Oxford University Press.
Boserup, Ester 1970: *Women's Role in Economic Development.* London: Allen & Unwin.
Chang, Ha Joon 2003: *Kicking Away the Ladder: Development Strategy in Historical Perspective.* London: Anthem Press.
Cooper, Frederick and Packard, Randall (eds.) 1997: *International Development and the Social Sciences: Essays on the History and Politics of Knowledge.* Berkeley: University of California Press.
Crush, Jonathan (ed.) 1995: *Power of Development.* London: Routledge.
Development Assistance Committee 1996: *Shaping the 21st Century: The Contribution of Development Co-operation.* Paris: OECD.

Easterly, William 2006: *The White Man's Burden: Why the West's Efforts to Aid the Rest Have Done So Much Ill and So Little Good.* London: Penguin.

Enloe, Cynthia 1989: *Bananas, Beaches and Bases: Making Feminist Sense of International Relations.* Berkeley: University of California Press.

Escobar, Arturo 1995: *Encountering Development: The Making and Unmaking of the Third World.* Princeton, NJ: Princeton University Press.

Ferguson, James 1994: *The Anti-politics Machine: Development, Depoliticisation and Bureaucratic Power in Lesotho.* Minneapolis: University of Minnesota Press.

Foucault, Michel 1972: *The Archaeology of Knowledge and the Discourse on Language.* New York: Pantheon.

Foucault, Michel 1980: *Power/Knowledge: Selected Interviews and Other Writings 1972–1977.* New York: Pantheon.

Foucault, Michel 1983: The Subject and Power. In Dreyfus, Hubert L./Rabinow, P. (eds.) *Michel Foucault Beyond Structuralism and Hermeneutics.* Chicago: University of Chicago Press, 208–226.

Friedmann, John 1992: *Empowerment: The Politics of Alternative Development.* Cambridge: Blackwell.

IDS 2001: *The New Dynamics of Aid: Power, Procedures and Relationships.* IDS Policy Briefing 15. Sussex: Institute of Development.

Kabeer, Naila 1994: *Reversed Realities: Gender Hierarchies in Development Thought.* London: Verso.

Martinussen, John 1997: *Society, State and Market: A Guide to Competing Theories of Development.* London: Zed Books.

Mosse, David/Lewis, David (eds.) 2005: *The Aid Effect. Giving and Governing in International Development.* London: Pluto Press.

Moore, David/Schmitz, Gerald J. (eds.) 1995: *Debating Development Discourse. Institutional and Popular Perspectives.* Basingstoke: Macmillan.

Murray Li, Tania 2007: *The Will to Improve: Governmentality, Development and the Practice of Politics.* Durham, NC: Duke University Press.

Rahnema, Majid (ed.) 1997: *The Post-development Reader.* London: Zed Books.

Sachs, Wolfgang (ed.) 1992: *The Development Dictionary: A Guide to Knowledge as Power.* London: Zed Books.

Sachs, Wolfgang 1999: *Planet Dialectics: Exploration in Environment and Development.* London: Zed Books.

UN General Assembly 1970: *International Development Strategy for the Second United Nations Development Decade.* UN Resolution no. 2626.

UN General Assembly 2000: *United Nations Millennium Declaration.* UN document A/RES/55/2.

UN Millennium Project 2005: *Investing in Development. A Practical Plan to Achieve the Millennium Development Goals. Overview.* New York: United Nations Development Programme.

World Bank 2000: *World Development Report 2000/2001: Attacking Poverty.* Oxford: Oxford University Press.

12 Justice, not development

Sen and the hegemonic framework for
ameliorating global inequality

Amartya Sen's work *Development as Freedom* can be regarded as development
theory's best-seller of the last decade, and the 'capability approach' put forward
in it (as in some other books by him and Martha Nussbaum) is certainly a contender for the most influential approach within the discipline at the moment. It
appears to be equally influential within institutions of development policy like
the United Nations Development Program (UNDP) or indeed the World Bank
where Sen worked as an advisor and research fellow. This article points out some
merits, but also some problems of Sen's version of this approach and argues that
the problems are related to Sen's uncritical adoption of the discourse of development. This discourse is the hegemonic framework for ameliorating global inequality today but limits our thinking and action on the question of global justice
and therefore should be abandoned.

In the first part of the chapter, I will be discussing the merits and flaws of
Sen's *Development as Freedom*, highlighting positive as well as negative aspects.
In the second part, I will link the problems identified in the approach to the discourse of development which constitutes the hegemonic framework for discussing questions of global inequality since the mid-20th century. Finally, I will point
out which questions of global justice are neglected by adopting this hegemonic
framework.

Sen's approach and its problems

Sen's *Development and Freedom* has earned much praise since its publication in
1999, and certainly a great deal of it is justified. Before starting to criticise it,
some of its merits have to be remembered. By seeing *development* as 'a process of
expanding the real freedoms that people enjoy' (Sen 2000: 1) and by including
not only political freedoms, transparency guarantees and protective security in
his notion of human freedoms, but also economic facilities and social opportunities (4), he considerably broadens the definition of the concept. This has certain consequences. The most important one is that it undermines the frequent
discussions about whether political freedom or gender equality was conducive
to *development* (understood as economic growth). To this, Sen replies: 'this way
of posing the question tends to miss the important understanding that these

substantive freedoms [. . .] are among the constituent components of development' (5). Taking Sen's approach seriously prevents such discussions and their concomitant privileging of the growth of the Gross National Product (GNP) which still take place decades after the Pearson Report (published in 1969 by the UN)[1] has established that economic growth does not automatically lead to poverty reduction.

The critique of narrow growth-centred perspectives is expanded when Sen points out several examples of countries which managed to significantly improve life expectancy without high GNP growth such as Sri Lanka, China before 1978 and the Indian state of Kerala, and inverse cases such as Brazil, South Africa and Gabon where a boost of the latter took place without substantial progress in the former indicator (44–48). His polite style of writing would never allow the author to put it that way, but the book is a slap in the face of all those in development theory and policy who still maintain that a focus on economic growth was the most successful way to reduce poverty and achieve *development* (e.g. Dollar/Kraay 2002).

Even more relevant is that he manages to break up the black box of the state by comparing survival rates of African Americans in the US and Indians in Kerala. Despite the former group being far more prosperous in terms of per-capita income, the latter has better chances of reaching a higher age. The picture becomes more drastic if one narrows the group, e.g. to black men from Harlem (21–23).

Last, but not least, Sen revisits his insights in the study of food policy, pointing out that famines have nothing to do with a general lack of food, but a lot with the 'substantive freedom of the individual and the family to establish ownership over an adequate amount of food' (161), and usually affect 5–10 per cent of the population at most (168). Thus he highlights that famines are a result of unequal distribution of assets. According to him, a functioning multi-party democracy and a free press would be the best methods of famine prevention, since the rulers simply could not afford to let it happen without losing their job, and serious attempts to prevent it by boosting the purchasing power of hard-hit groups were usually successful (178–184).

However, despite these significant merits there are some problematic points in his work which deserve closer attention.

1) *Conceptual confusion.* Regarding the term *development* and its content, Sen is at times ambiguous. There is a lack of conceptual clarity in statement 2) where he writes:

> Freedom is central to the process of development for two distinct reasons. 1) The evaluative reason: assessment of progress has to be done primarily in terms of whether the freedoms that people have are enhanced; 2) The effectiveness reason: achievement of development is thoroughly dependent on the free agency of the people.
>
> (4)

If, as it seems to suggest, *development* is a process different from attaining freedoms or free agency, he is contradicting his earlier argument, because then freedoms are again conducive to some other process (of improvement, growth, etc.) – an argument he strongly criticises elsewhere (5, see above) and one which is incompatible with his view that *development* consists in removing unfreedoms (33). If, on the other hand, *development* consists in attaining freedoms, as he argued earlier, then the sentence basically reads 'The achievement of freedom is dependent on freedom' – a textbook tautology.[2]

2) *All good things go together.* Throughout the book, Sen writes about 'mutually reinforcing connections' (4) between different kinds of freedoms: between political rights and economic opportunities and health care and gender equality and low population growth etc. This assumption dates back to modernisation theory which claimed that all the good things would come with the transition to societies of high mass-consumption (Rostow 1960). But there are numerous empirical observations which do not quite fit into this assumption: nondemocratic states achieving high rates of economic growth (China), high levels of education and health care not leading to economic growth (Cuba), indigenous communities practicing direct democracy but excluding women from it – the list could go on. Obviously good and bad things can occur quite independently.

3) *Benevolent institutions.* In discussing the World Bank's Comprehensive Development Framework (127) or the role of governmental institutions in famine prevention (133), these institutions are implicitly conceived as rational, nonpolitical and benevolent actors pursuing the interest of the poor and waiting to implement the policy recommendations of development theory.[3] This is little more than a convenient fiction neglecting relations of power and institutional interests, assuming that development organisations will in fact work for *development* and nothing else.[4]

4) *Modernisation theory and the equation of development and capitalism.* By contrasting 'elements of "underdevelopment" in some parts of the [Italian] economy' with 'the most dynamic capitalism elsewhere in the same economy' (264), Sen implicitly equates *development* with capitalism – as if the latter would automatically bring the substantive freedoms he writes about earlier. This argument was originally made by modernisation theory, and it is not the only relation to this school of thought. In writing 'there are plenty of examples of the problems faced in precapitalist economies because of the underdevelopment of capitalist virtues' (263) the author reproduces the belief of modernisation theory (e.g. Rostow 1960), that entrepreneurial ethics are a remedy for the problems of societies identified as precapitalist. The problematic aspects of capitalist virtues (eroding communal solidarity, etc.) are not an issue here. Also, modernisation theory's equation of precapitalist and *underdeveloped* economies which neglects the colonial exploitation to which many of these were subjected within global capitalism, remains unquestioned.

5) *Liberal bias.* Even beyond the implicit argumentative structure of modernisation theory, there is an explicit bias towards capitalist relations of production and free markets as the best way to achieve an improvement of living standards or *development* respectively freedom throughout the book. This becomes manifest in categorical statements ('It is hard to think that any process of substantial development

can do without very extensive use of markets' (7) – what about Cuba?), in praise for the hard-core neoliberal Hayek (114) and for microcredits as a best practice of poverty reduction (201), in advocating the freedom that markets bring (ch. 5) without mentioning the unfreedom of those who cannot afford the market prices of urgently needed goods, in chastising 'the political power of those groups that obtain substantial material benefits from restricting trade and exchange' (122) while forgetting about the often far more powerful transnational business lobby groups that benefit from implementing market liberalisations, by confounding economic freedom and economic openness (123) while neglecting the social costs of producers unable to compete with the world market, and in attributing all problems related to market mechanisms to inadequate regulation (142) – reminding me of the saying that 'there is no bad weather, only inappropriate clothing'.

6) *Universalist assumptions.* In his lucid discussion of the problems of cultural relativism (ch. 10), Sen points to numerous different philosophical traditions in Asia, concluding that

> the modern advocates of the authoritarian view of 'Asian values' base their reading on very arbitrary interpretations and extremely narrow selections of authors and traditions. The valuing of freedoms is not confined to one culture only, and the Western traditions are not the only ones that prepare us for a freedom-based approach to social understanding.
>
> (240)

However, his assumption that the capability approach is valid for all cultures raises some questions. Because in postulating that a good life is impossible without 'basic education', 'free media' and 'elections' (242) (as sympathetic as this may seem to most, including myself), he again introduces universalist criteria for evaluating societies which may not be shared by the people concerned. Is the life of indigenous subsistence communities really objectively inferior because it lacks these three elements? A plurality of conceptions of a good life is conceivable.

My argument is that all these flaws (as I see them) are related to the conceptual framework Sen employs, which is the hegemonic framework for dealing with questions of global inequality since the middle of the 20th century: the discourse of development. The use of this framework is contingent, in fact, the situations of 'unfreedom' that Sen describes (undernourishment, premature mortality, discrimination of women, religious violence, tyranny, etc. – e.g. Sen 2000: 3, 8, 20) could easily be framed as questions of economic, social and political inequality – or as questions of justice.

The discourse of 'development'

The perspective to analyse development as a discourse which is presented here builds on the works of Post-Development scholars (Sachs 1992, Ferguson 1994, Escobar 1995 and Rist 1997) as well as on Michel Foucault. According to Foucault (1972), a discourse is a group of statements united by common rules, in particular by rules of formation concerning the objects, concepts, enunciative modalities and thematic choices. While this is not the place for a thorough presentation of the structure of development discourse (see chapters 4 and 5), a brief sketch is certainly necessary. Throughout the following description of the discourse those elements will be highlighted which we encountered in the critical reading of Sen's work.

While the discourse of development as we know it today has been established in the mid-20th century, its roots go back somewhat further. On the one hand to evolutionist thinking of the 19th century (Spencer, Marx, Comte, etc.) which perceived the industrialised capitalist countries of Western Europe to be at the top of an evolution of mankind towards progress and other countries to be backward. On the other hand to Enlightenment thinking and the Saint-Simonians, planning to reform society rationally to reconcile order and progress on the basis of trusteeship and expert knowledge (Cowen/Shenton 1996). Already in the 19th century this intent to improve the social situation of certain groups was a reaction to socialist movements and the intent was to stabilise capitalism by ameliorating poverty. In the first half of the twentieth century, when the idea of *development* was increasingly applied to the European colonies, this intent became even more pressing against the background of the Russian Revolution and anti-colonial movements. Alcalde (1987: 223) concludes that 'The first and broadest function of the idea of development was to give economic activity, particularly foreign economic activity, a positive and essential meaning for the lives of less-developed peoples. . . . the aim was essentially . . . enhancing a mental linkage between capitalism and well-being in the South.' So when Truman (1949), in the context of the Cold War and the dusk of colonialism, announced the first program of *development* to help the *underdeveloped* peoples and simultaneously support the US economy and fight world communism, the explicit *liberal bias* was an important element of the discourse.

During the first post–World War II decades, the picture was clear and the tenets of development discourse were unshaken: there are *developed* and *less developed* countries, the industrialised capitalist countries constituting the former group. So there is a universal scale of comparison, unit of analysis is the state, the West sets the norm and the measure is the GNP. The dominant approach in development theory and policy was *modernisation theory* (e.g. Rostow 1960), which treated subsistence communities and non-Western empires alike as traditional societies in need of capital, technology and modern values. It assumed that traditional societies are *underdeveloped* because they are precapitalist, neglecting the ties which had linked most of them to global capitalism since they had been colonised and implicitly *equating development and capitalism*. Not only Rostow, but also later development theorists (e.g. Menzel 1993: 132) assumed that the process of *development* simultaneously comprised economic growth, modernisation, industrialisation, democratisation, and even redistribution (leading to 'societies of high mass-consumption', as Rostow put it), thus that *all good things go together*.[5]

Already at the beginning of the 1960s, however, it became clear that the transition to these developed societies was not as easy as envisioned by modernisation theory. Economic growth did not necessarily lead to poverty reduction (let alone democratisation), and capitalist modernity did not provide viable livelihoods for everyone. Thus new aspects of the objects (*underdeveloped* countries) gained visibility in development discourse, leading to new strategies of development policy. After the new strategy turned out to be less successful than had been hoped for, the failure led to a new diagnosis of deficiency, a new concept and a renewal of the promise of *development* to overcome poverty and bring affluence (see Figure 4.1). So the rule of formation concerning the objects led to a 'cycle of the clinical gaze', prescribing ever new recipes for the *less developed* countries: rural, endogenous, sustainable, participatory or human development, basic needs, structural adjustment, good governance, mainstreaming gender, ownership, etc. This cycle has led to the proliferation of meanings of the term *development* and to the ensuing *conceptual confusion*. While earlier it was clear that the term denoted economic growth, nowadays anything from female empowerment or biodiversity protection to road building can be the object of a development project. Even on a more abstract level in development theory, the term is used to denote different things: 1) social change in general, 2) social change as a result of capitalist modernity and 3) social change leading to an improvement in the lives of people. And even a brilliant thinker like Sen sometimes gets entangled in this 'web of meanings' (Esteva 1992: 10).

After the end of colonialism, the trusteeship for *development* has been passed on to development institutions, primarily governmental bodies, but also organisations of bilateral or multilateral development cooperation. That these are not necessarily benevolent institutions has been shown in the study of Ferguson (1994), where he portrays the transfer of resources to elites and the increase in bureaucratic power as regular (often unintended) effects of development projects. At the same time, their actions are assumed to be benign because *development* is seen as something positive, aiming at ending poverty or achieving freedom. In the discourse of development, there is usually no place for social conflicts or political struggles, because *development* is seen as a process which benefits the whole society and which consists of technical solutions, e.g. projects resulting in improvements in irrigation, productivity, technology or governance. Thus the question of inequality is removed from relations of power and depoliticised. And development organisations reproduce this discourse: their construction of reality is influenced by the means they have at their disposal: nonpolitical, technical projects. Other solutions to social problems which would entail taking sides in political conflicts, opposing the elite or supporting revolutionary struggles are excluded because they are incompatible with their institutional self-interest and their identity as development organisations. Yet the development organisations discursively produce the image of *benevolent institutions* working for the common good without pursuing any other interest.

One last point to be made concerns the rule of formation of enunciative modalities. The discourse of development inevitably constructs a subject position of the knowing expert who says what a good (*developed*) society looks like and how it can be achieved. Other types of statements appear meaningless within this discourse. Assuming that there is a plurality of visions how a good society looks like, this means that the discourse universalises a particular vision and sub-ordinates others, thus universalist assumptions about one model of a good society contain an authoritarian element. This element was responsible for violence and paternalism in uplifting, educating or *developing* those who were perceived as backward Others. The critique of this authoritarian element has led to conceptual innovations in development policy like participation or empowerment. Yet neither development policy nor theory can do without these *universalist assumptions*, and this is why we find them in the work of Sen as well. If one would reject these assumptions, saying something like: 'People have their own priorities in life and the world is too complex to generalise about processes of social change', one would embrace the plurality of visions and the heterogeneity of reality, but could not any longer provide advice to development institutions. Because they are based on the assumptions that there is just one vision of a good society and that social change occurs everywhere along very similar patterns, which is why it makes sense to send experts to some country in order to provide advice who have never lived there before – but who have a lot of knowledge about *development*.

So it appears that the problematic aspects of Sen's work *Development as Freedom* are related to this discourse of development. And this discourse has been the hegemonic framework for dealing with global inequality since the mid-20th century, defining poverty as a global problem to be dealt with by development project, programmes and organisations (Ferguson 1994, Escobar 1995). Countless aspirations for a better life and a more just society have been framed in this discourse. However, this framework has serious limitations which come to the fore when we examine its contribution to some areas in which debates about global justice take place.

'Development' and justice

Adopting the discourse of development has implications which limit the scope of thought and action concerning global justice. If questions of global inequality are answered with the hegemonic framework of *development*, the 'web of meanings' (Esteva 1992: 10) surrounding the concept suggests that 1) the solutions to global inequality lie in each country's process of social change, 2) these solutions do not require political struggles and transformations of the existing relations of power or capitalist relations of production, 3) these solutions have to be based on expert knowledge and economic growth. Of course critical approaches like the dependency school or world systems theory have questioned these tenets, but the dominant views in the institutions today remain largely untouched by these critiques. However, on this basis better development projects and policies are possible, but a different world order is out of the question. Even if we assume that global capitalism was compatible with global justice (a somewhat questionable assumption according to many definitions of justice), there are at least three areas where urgent questions of justice have been largely ignored by development theory and policy.

1) Reparations for colonialism: After 400 years of conquering, subjugating and exploiting the rest of the planet, there have so far been no reparations from the former colonial powers to the former colonies. This is so despite the fact that reparations, e.g. after the world wars, have been a common feature of international law. However, while the white nations have been willing to pay for their crimes they committed against other white nations, they have not been prepared to do so for their crimes against former colonies.[6] The African World Reparations and Repatriations Truth Commission has estimated the amount of reparations due at US$777,000 trillion. Of course the (substantially lower) financial transfers declared as development aid have sometimes been linked with colonialism, but certainly not all of these transfers have benefited the people in recipient countries – the keywords odious debts and tied aid may suffice here – and it does make a significant difference whether money is given in repayment of a crime or as a benevolent gesture of compassion.

2) Ecological justice: Contrary to the idea that justice can be achieved through *development* in the sense of the poor catching up with the rich, ecological limits demand another kind of justice: namely that the industrialised countries discontinue a way of life based on nonrenewable energy sources and a disproportionate share of resource use and environmental pollution, in particular regarding the question of climate change.[7] Ecological justice could mean that the environment is seen as a public good and that each person must not use more of it than its fair share. And even here, one could talk about historical debts in terms of processes of industrialisation in some countries which have depleted the resources and polluted the environment in such a way that other processes by late-comers are being prevented or rendered irresponsible. But why should some people be entitled to a larger share than others? And is it just to permit oligarchic (or imperial, Brand/Wissen 2011) lifestyles which are possible only if a majority is excluded from them?

3) A cosmopolitan world order: According to a Rawlsian 'veil of ignorance', all people on the world are entitled to the same chance for a decent life. This is in fact not the case, and the coincidence of being born into a slum in São Paulo or an upper-class neighbourhood in Munich determines individual life chances to a considerable extent. This is not only related to social inequality, but also to a nation-state system which severely restricts migration into richer countries and guarantees human rights only for citizens (and even that only in an imperfect manner). Movements for a cosmopolitan citizenship are hardly existent, but some migrants in North Africa and Europe have been organising for a global right to free movement and settlement.[8]

Remembering the critique of universalist assumptions, one might ask: do these struggles not also imply struggles for universal rights? Indeed they do. But here we have to differentiate between universal rights which imply normative judgements on how people should live (to which they could object in the name of self-determination) and universal rights which create conditions for self-determination. In all three areas, any limitation of people's right to self-determination takes place only to protect the rights of others to self-determination, denying rights to exclude people on the basis of their nationality, to consume resources in a oligarchic manner, and to colonise others without compensation.

Of course, the debates and conflicts in these areas have been sketched here only very briefly, but the central point is that Sen's work and in fact the vast majority of development theory and policy remains silent on all three points. Improvements in these areas cannot be expected from development projects based on expert knowledge nor from successful programs of economic growth in income poor countries, but only from changes in political structures as a result of political struggles and social movements. In all three areas pressing questions about global justice are pertinent. And the discourse of development does not provide answers. It is time to overcome this discourse. Struggles for justice should not take the detour of *development*.

Notes

1 http://unesdoc.unesco.org/images/0005/000567/056743eo.pdf (December 17, 2013)
2 A possible line of defence would be if Sen argued that he merely meant that different kinds of freedom are mutually reinforcing each other (4, 37). But then, he first should have been more precise; second, this statement is problematic in itself, as we shall see.
3 At the same time, Sen is quite ready to assume less than benevolent motives in individual actors, taking into account the possibility that some parents keep one child deliberately famished to receive nutritional support (132).
4 To give but one drastic example: The food-for-work programmes which Sen advocates (133) have often been used as political instruments. The most extreme case probably was Guatemala during the 1980s where these programmes (funded by development agencies) were used as a part of the scorched-earth and counterinsurgency policy of the military dictatorship to recruit refugees to build model villages in the vicinity of military camps after their own villages had been destroyed (Schultz 1992).
5 It has to be noted that some conservative (Huntington) or neoliberal (Lal) development theorists did not share this assumption, but saw the necessity for undemocratic governments implementing economic reforms which lead to growth even against the will of the people.
6 This seems to be a case of what Doty (1996: 33–36) calls the Western bond: the differences among former war enemies are overcome by a bond vis-à-vis the non-Western countries.
7 See http://www.climate-justice-now.org/ (March 21, 2014).
8 See their homepage on www.afrique-europe-interact.net (March 21, 2014). Interestingly, they also struggle for a right to stay in their home countries, provided there are opportunities for a secure, dignified and self-determined life, which they frame as fair *development*.

Bibliography

Alcalde, Javier Gonzalo 1987: *The Idea of Third World Development: Emerging Perspectives in the United States and Britain, 1900–1950*. Lanham, MD: University Press of America.
Brand, Ulrich/Wissen, Markus 2011: Sozial-ökologische Krise und imperiale Lebensweise. Zu Krise und Kontinuität kapitalistischer Naturverhältnisse. In: Demirovic, Alex et al. (eds.) *Vielfachkrise. Im finanzdominierten Kapitalismus*. Hamburg, VSA, 79–94.

Cowen, Michael/Shenton, Robert 1996: *Doctrines of Development*. London: Routledge.

Dollar, David/Kraay, Aart 2002: Growth is Good for the Poor. *Journal of Economic Growth* 7(3), 195–225.

Doty, Roxanne Lynn 1996: *Imperial Encounters: The Politics of Representation in North-South relations*. Minneapolis: University of Minnesota Press.

Escobar, Arturo 1995: *Encountering Development: The Making and Unmaking of the Third World*. Princeton, NJ: Princeton University Press.

Esteva, Gustavo 1992: Development. In: Sachs, Wolfgang (ed.) *The Development Dictionary: A Guide to Knowledge as Power*. London: Zed Books, 6–25.

Ferguson, James 1994: *The Anti-politics Machine: 'Development', Depoliticization and Bureaucratic Power in Lesotho*. Minneapolis: University of Minnesota Press.

Foucault, Michel 1972 (1969): *The Archaeology of Knowledge & The Discourse on Language*. New York: Pantheon Books.

Menzel, Ulrich 1993: 40 Jahre Entwicklungsstrategie = 40 Jahre Wachstumsstrategie. In: Nohlen, Dieter/Nuscheler, Franz (eds.) *Handbuch der Dritten Welt. Band I: Grundprobleme, Theorien, Strategien*. Bonn: Dietz, 131–155.

Rist, Gilbert 1997: *The History of Development: From Western Origins to Global Faith*. London: Zed Books.

Rostow, W. W. 1960: *The Stages of Economic Growth: A Non-communist Manifesto*. Cambridge: Cambridge University Press.

Sachs, Wolfgang (ed.) 1992: *The Development Dictionary: A Guide to Knowledge as Power*. London: Zed Books.

Schultz, Susanne 1992: *Guatemala: Entwicklungspolitik im Counterinsurgency-Staat – Das Fallbeispiel Food-for-Work-Projekte*. Diploma Thesis, Free University of Berlin.

Sen, Amartya 2000: *Development and Freedom*. New York: Anchor Books.

Truman, Harry 1949: Inaugural address, January 20, 1949. Online: http://www.trumanlibrary.org/whistlestop/50yr_archive/inagural20jan1949.htm (September 16, 2013).

13 Migration management as development aid?

The IOM and the international migration and development initiative

During the past two decades, traditional development aid has become quite unfashionable or at least lost considerable ground in the debate on North-South relations due to end of the Cold War and the distrust towards interventions in the market mechanisms (see chapter 8). Instead, increasingly prominent issues were (among others) global governance, sustainable development and market liberalisation. The latest trend consists of promoting migration as an engine for *development* in the countries of origin. The International Organisation for Migration (IOM) has summoned an initiative aiming at the improved coordination of the areas of migration and development policy. However, the rights of migrants are not on the centre stage in this initiative.

Migration and development

Since the mid-1980s it has been recognised that global economic inequality has increased in spite of countless development projects and considerable aid flowing to the South. Also, with the end of the Cold War the geopolitical motivation for development aid has mostly disappeared. The traditional patterns of development policy have gradually been pushed aside by new debates and concepts: one party recommended or even prescribed market liberalisation, export orientation, improved investment climate and increased competitiveness, another called for the reform of global economic structures according to social and ecological objectives, for worldwide reregulation and global governance. The latest trend in the *development* debate focuses on highlighting the positive effects of migration for the economies of the countries of origin and promoting 'development through migration' (Thränhardt 2005). The World Bank alone published seven books (IOM/OECD/World Bank 2004; Ozden/Schiff 2005; World Bank 2005; Golding/Reinert 2006; Kuznetsov 2006; Mansoor/Quillin 2006; Wodon 2007) and numerous working papers on this topic within only a few years, and more and more researchers emphasise the economic potential of increased migration from the South to the North.

The concept of 'brain drain', that perceived the emigration of highly qualified experts from poorer to richer countries as a negative factor for the economic development of the former, is increasingly seen as outdated and inappropriate.

So is the enduring practice of sending back migrants after they have completed their studies for example in Germany, which, however, owes at least as much to the fear of rising numbers of foreigners as to the fear of the brain drain. Instead, a 'brain gain' is said to exist: numerous positive impulses for economic growth in the countries of the South are supposed to arise through remittances of migrants to their countries of origin, through the transfer of capital and knowledge, and through the creation of commercial networks instigated by migrants. There are estimates that, for example 60–65 per cent of all FDI in China comes from former emigrants. The rapid development of technology in Taiwan is also based to a significant extent on the know-how of engineers who have remigrated from the US (Hunger 2003: 60f). On the other hand the industrial countries were dependent on immigration due to the aging of their demographic structure, the argument goes, and in the age of globalisation they were competing for the best and brightest from all over the world – a classical win-win-situation. The policy of building ever higher walls around one's country had not quite worked anyway, in the light of high numbers of irregular migrants. And the idea of fighting the causes of migration through increased and improved development cooperation had also not been too successful. Migration, this is the message, should in general be seen less as a sign of crisis, but rather as an opportunity, and migrants less as deficient beings in need of integration, but rather as enriching and useful for our society (Thränhardt 2005: 3f). Migration, it seems, is on its way to become the secret formula for at least slightly *developing* the *less developed* countries while at the same time being beneficial to all parties involved.

The International Organisation for Migration

This view is shared by the International Organisation for Migration (IOM), which recently has presented an International Migration and Development Initiative (IMDI). The IOM (for the following see www.iom.int; Düvell 2002: 101–107; Angenendt 2003: 195f; Antirassismusbüro Bremen 2004; Klemz 2006) is an intergovernmental organisation with 120 member states dedicated to regulating migration. Some other states and several dozen international organisations are observers at the IOM. Originally, it has been founded in 1951 as the Provisional Intergovernmental Committee for the Movement of Migrants in Europe before it was institutionalised two years later as the Intergovernmental Committee for European Migration (ICEM). Its member states were recruited from the allies of the US, and its main task was the transfer of migrants in post–World War II Europe. The ICEM was an instrument in the Cold War and supposed to act as a counterbalance against the shortly before created UN High Commissioner for Human Rights (UNHCR). In order to adapt its name to its increasingly global role, it was renamed in Intergovernmental Committee on Migration (ICM) in 1980 and finally in International Organisation for Migration in 1989. It is concerned with providing logistic support for the transfer of (international and national) refugees and migrants, often in postconflict situations, where it is also involved in humanitarian and reconstruction work and in demobilisation programmes. Other activities of the

IOM include the arrangement of labour migration, above all supporting the relevant countries in the area of recruitment; providing integration aid, repatriation and resettlement assistance, information for potential migrants, capacity building and technical cooperation for police officers and administrative staff, countertrafficking programmes and finally fostering international cooperation in migration policy. The IOM headquarters are located in Geneva, its Technical Cooperation Centre in Vienna. All in all, 6,000 people work for the organisation. The IOM is especially significant in the field of research and knowledge production: it regularly publishes the *World Migration Report*, as well as the series *IOM Migration Research* and the bulletin *Trafficking in Migrants*. Its programmes are financed by voluntary, often tied financial contributions of the member states. It is only to these that the IOM is accountable, it is not authorised by international law or part of the UN system. The IOM itself describes its main task as the 'organized transfer of migrants' and the provision of services in the area of migration at the request of states (IOM 2005a). According to its homepage, the IOM is 'dedicated to the principle that humane and orderly migration benefits migrants and society' (IOM 2005b). In the light of the previous chapters, we can already discern the principle of social technology and a link to trusteeship.

In its public relations work, the IOM draws a positive picture of migration which is not compatible with discourses presenting migration as a threat that northern countries have to protect themselves against – discourses which are prevalent in many European countries. Of utmost importance was, according to this representation, the efficient management and the regulation of migration: irregular migration is described as highly dangerous in several respects. One report from the IOM homepage, for example extensively covers the story of irregular migrants whose dream of a better future ended when they were shipwrecked close to Lampedusa, where 50 of them lost their lives. In contrast to the discourse of pro-migrant organisations, the casualties are not linked with the increasing protection of the EU-border, which leads migrants to use ever more dangerous routes into Europe, but are attributed to criminal traffickers, who had seduced gullible Africans. The latter are nowhere seen as active subjects who, in the face of a bleak future in Africa, had consciously decided to migrate to Europe without legal permit. The vivid portrayal of the 'horrific experiences of those lucky enough to survive the journey', of the terrible scenes when a wave capsized the boat of the migrants almost none of whom could swim, of the endless hours before rescue patrols arrived and of the bodies (Moscarelli 2006) does not provide balanced information on the risks and possibilities of crossing the Mediterranean, but primarily serves the function of deterring potential irregular migrants. It ends by stating

> Knowing that migrants have a very poor knowledge of European immigration laws and virtually no knowledge of the often abusive conditions of the journey they are about to undertake allows IOM and others to devise more effective responses on the dangers of irregular migration. The more effective, the more lives that can be saved.
>
> (Moscarelli 2006)

More effective responses to irregular migration, like enforcing stricter border controls, are in this way constructed as efforts to save lives.

A similar function can be attributed to the posters and brochures published by the IOM in Central and Eastern Europe. They show a half-naked young woman which is literally hooked to the strings of an invisible puppet master. Underneath there are slogans like 'You will be sold like a doll' and 'Do not trust easy money abroad'. (The poster is reproduced in Antirassismusbüro Bremen 2004: 18). Human trafficking and slavery in the sex trade are harsh realities and undeniable dangers for women in Central and Eastern Europe willing to migrate into the West. Still, two objections have to be raised, one concerning the style of presentation, the other its goal. Andrijasevic points to the fact that

> the representation of the body of trafficked women as tricked, wounded and/or broken is far from being innocent; strategies of representation employing inanimate, wounded and mute female bodies reenact the well-known scenario in which female bodies are passive objects of male violence and simultaneously demarcate the borders in which women can be conceived as active actors/subjects.
>
> (Andrijasevic 2005)

The image sends a clear and threatening message: women ought to stay at home, at least if they want to avoid ending in this way. Here again the aim of the presentation is not providing neutral information for an informed decision for or against migration, but the prevention of irregular (and in this case specifically female) labour migration into the more prosperous countries.

This suggests that the struggle against irregular migration is a far higher priority for the IOM than the balanced information for potential migrants. After all, the IOM provides services in the field of migration management for the states that are financing it, it is not a humanitarian organisation. In spite of the rhetoric on the homepage, according to which it seeks to 'uphold the human dignity and well-being of migrants', it sides rather with states preventing migration if there is a conflict between loyalties. This has become unambiguously clear in the project that has become known as the 'pacific solution'. In August 2001 the Australian navy stopped a Norwegian freighter that was going to bring refugees from Afghanistan and Iraq which were shipwrecked before the Australian coast to the nearest harbour. Instead, the refugees were brought to the Pacific island of Nauru and interned in camps. These camps are run by the IOM. Human rights organisations like Amnesty International and Human Rights Watch therefore accused the IOM of being complicit in Australia's breach of the Geneva Convention and expressed concerns regarding the human rights impact of IOM operations (Antirassismusbüro Bremen 2004: 27; noborder network 2002, 2003).

The international migration and development initiative

In September 2006 the IOM initiated a High-level Dialogue on International Migration and Development at the UN General Council to present the IMDI. Representatives of 127 member states participated in the panels and plenary discussions and passed a resolution to continue the dialogue and to implement measures to better link the areas of migration and *development*. Members of the Global Commission on International Migration (GCIM) had approached the IOM with the request to simultaneously address two issues, together with the World Bank: to search for ways to close the gap between labour supply and demand on the one and to promote human resource development on the other hand. The IOM got in touch with the World Bank, but expanded the circle of organisations concerned with the planning debates to include all members of the Global Migration Group (GMG) – the International Labour Office (ILO), the UN High Commission for Refugees (UNHCR), the UN Conference on Trade and Development (UNCTAD), the UN Development Programme (UNDP), the UN Fund for Population Activities (UNFPA), the UN Department for Economic and Social Development (UN-DESA) and the UN Office for Drugs and Crime (UNODC) (IOM 2006b: 1; http://www.un.int/iom/GMG.html). The IMDI is the result of these consultations.

What shape does this initiative take and what are the concrete measures intended? According to the suggestions of the IOM (and the GMG) first of all labour supply and demand ought to be better coordinated. This can be arranged through global databases on labour market trends and labour force profiles, a centralised information source on regional and national migration regulatory frameworks, and policy and programme models for building the capacity of governments to formulate national labour market, human resources development and migration policies in an integrated manner. Additionally, workers are for example to be prepared for the work abroad by language training and courses for cultural orientation, and agreements for the mutual recognition of qualifications are to be negotiated between countries of origin and countries of destination (IOM 2006a: 6–8).

Further, the positive effects of migration on *development* are to be improved. This should happen through increased research and improved data on remittances and their specific effects and the consideration of this knowledge in the conception of developmental and poverty reducing strategies. For example remittances should be made easier and tax incentives for their use in development projects are to be created. Investments by returnees ought to receive support, advice and loans, and the diaspora population is to be better integrated in these strategies (ibid., 9–10).

Finally, safer, more human and orderly labour movements are to be ensured. This is to be achieved by fostering an international dialogue on managed labour migration, by building the capacity of governments to formulate sound policies on labour migration, and by the development of assessment tools and monitoring mechanisms on labour migration policies. Partnerships with the private sector assume a prominent role in this context: a set of nonbinding guiding principles concerning the ethical recruitment and fair treatment of migrant workers is to be elaborated in consultation with business, and those enterprises complying with these principles are to be awarded a quality label. The IMDI also aims to develop a Twinning Programme for Facilitated Mobility between countries of origin and of destination: the former commits itself to respect certain criteria related to combating irregular migration and in exchange obtains visa facilitation or increased labour market access by the latter (ibid., 10–12).

It is emphasised that the IMDI 'would not create any rights of entry or alter any country's right to determine its immigration policy, as this is the sovereign domain of States' (ibid., 3). The IMDI proposal has been outlined slightly more precisely in the debates on the High-Level-Dialogue. As a result, there is a stronger reference to human rights of migrants which are to be protected, but the best way to do so is still seen in 'creating safe and legal channels for orderly migration' and in combating irregular migration (IOM 2006b: 4). The IMDI's task is perceived as providing a frame for coordinating different intergovernmental organisations, avoiding parallel activities and creating synergies. The importance of integrating private actors is stressed once more (ibid., 5). The administrative structure of the IMDI is to be discussed and outlined by a task force comprising all interested organisations of the GMG. The possibility of including representatives of civil society in addition to those of international organisations, governments and the private sector is considered. Projects that are to receive funding have to be agreed on with the governments concerned and they have to be compatible with the development models and poverty reduction strategy papers (PRSPs) of the country in question (ibid., 7).

The IMDI led to the Joint Migration and Development Initiative (JMDI) in 2008, a programme implemented by the UNDP in Brussels in partnership with the EU, the IOM, the UNHCR, UNFPA and the ILO – though funded entirely by the European Commission. Its official aim was to support local authorities and civil society organisations in countries of origin, transit and destination in linking migration and *development*. It involved programmes and projects in the Philippines, Bangladesh, Sri Lanka, Jamaica, Ecuador, ten African and twelve European countries, and, according to Peter Sutherland, Special Representative of the UN Secretary-General for Migration and Development,[1] worked to 'amplify the development benefits of migration' (JMDI 2011: 14).[2]

A new regime of migration and development?

At this stage a well-founded evaluation of the IMDI is difficult, because concrete consequences for migrants are as yet difficult to discern. It has to be seen as positive that restrictive immigration laws are being criticised, and so is the perception of migration as a threat to national security and as a phenomenon invariably causing xenophobia (IOM 2006b: 2). *Development*, on the other hand, is no longer seen as the result of development projects, expert knowledge and loans or investments from the north, but as a consequence of people's own initiative, of the capital and know-how accumulated by former emigrants and returnees – a conception which seems far less paternalistic. From the perspective of migrants, the IMDI certainly includes useful elements. Services like preparatory language courses or a reliable data base on the immigration laws, the possibilities and preconditions in potential countries of destination are among them.

The most significant point may be that the initiative is directed against the privilege of receiving dramatically higher payments than other people simply because one was lucky enough to be born in a country with comparatively high wages. The active defence of this privilege through border regimes supposed to prevent labour migration or linking it with the status of being here illegally and implicitly with the almost complete absence of rights, is challenged by the IMDI. And in contrast to the German Green Card or the mode 4 of the negotiations on trade in services in the WTO the relevant matter is not only the mobility of *highly qualified* labour. From a perspective that perceives nations, peoples and states as historically situated or artificially created constructs and not as natural or fateful communities, this has to be seen as a progressive aspect.

A critical evaluation, however, has to proceed further. It has to be taken into consideration that the collecting of data and information on supply and demand on the labour market will lead to a significant intensification in the visibility and surveillance of people. On top of that, the IMDI links the partial legalisation of labour migration of less qualified workers with an intensified struggle against irregular migration of which the EU's border agency FRONTEX is only the most visible manifestation. It can be presumed that governments which have to fear right-wing populism and correspondent losses in votes will implement especially the latter aspect first and implement it thoroughly. The cracks in the walls will be larger, but the walls higher.

Furthermore, it is obvious according to which principles the restructuring of the migration regime is taking place. The fundamental idea is not a right to move freely that challenges the privileges and wage differentials, but it is the interest of firms and service enterprises in industrial countries in a cheap and flexible labour force. As far as this interest is compatible with the interest of certain people in the periphery willing to migrate, the IMDI surely is bound to have positive consequences for this group. It is clear, however, that the right to migrate will only be granted to those that can be employed (or exploited) in the market, and presumably only as long as their labour is needed in the countries of destination. Two elements of the initiative spoil the positive aspects contained: its primary goal of bridging the gap between supply and demand in the labour market can be reached only if the differences in wages and social security between migrants and domestic labour persist – otherwise the gap would stay the same. So if rights of migrants are put forward by the IMDI, it is exclusively the right to be employed or exploited more cheaply and more flexibly than domestic workers in the north. To be sure: this can be a desirable goal for a large part of the world's population and is to be taken seriously. We still have to bear in mind that in contrast to a universalist, cosmopolitan approach the separation in citizens on the one hand foreign immigrants on the other hand remains untouched here. The idea of equal rights for all is not mentioned anywhere.

The fact cannot be ignored that the situation as a regular (even if only temporary) migrant (who is still systematically being discriminated against in comparison to citizens), is far more comfortable than the situation of an irregular migrant. For the people concerned, it would constitute a significant progress, legally and financially, even if it does not entail completely equal status. But this increase in socioeconomic equality has to be seen in the context of nationally separated labour markets as a means in the conflict between capital and labour. The opening up of the labour market for cheaper and more flexible labour from abroad serves to weaken the position of unionised domestic labour and to fend off their demands. In a somewhat sloppy Marxist formulation one could argue that immigration laws are always strategies in the class struggle.

From the perspective of anti-racist movements it becomes clear that the demand for open borders and equal rights for migrants should not be content with partial successes. Even if immigration models like those envisioned in the IMDI include more legal possibilities for migration and concrete improvements for foreign workers, they nevertheless still operate with a separation alongside national identities and utilise this separation for the disadvantage of both (foreign and national) groups. One group is still being systematically discriminated against, the other has to renounce social rights long fought for. The beneficiaries are the usual suspects. It is politically naive to expect a solution to questions of global social inequality from initiatives like these. The effect of migration management as development aid maybe should not be underestimated, but it is inherently limited.

From the perspective of migration research the IMDI can be interpreted as another sign of a turning of the tide in the migration policy of the OECD countries. This shift does not constitute a complete break with the former policy which was primarily concerned with preventing migration, but rather consists of supplementing it with measures of selective and managed immigration. The development of the EU's regime of migration which was decided on the conference of the European Council in Tampere 1999 provides a telling example. It rests on three elements complementing each other: the extension of the EU's border regime to countries of origin and of transit (through preliminary border controls, repatriation agreements and implementation of stricter migration laws), the intensification of the struggle against irregular migration, and the selective and controlled labour migration (Düvell 2002: 80f, 49). The demographic crisis in the industrial countries serves as a justification for the third element: labour migration is thus conceived as serving the national interest of the country of destination.

From the perspective of development research the IMDI can be identified as a manifestation of the gradual transformation of the development dispositive into a dispositive of globalisation (Ziai 2007). The Herculean task of turning the *less developed* countries into *developed* ones has been given up quite a while ago. Instead, the policy towards the south is more concerned with crisis prevention, liberalisation and access to resources. State interventions in the market aimed at *development*, such as differential treatment or even ODA transfers, are increasingly seen as detrimental. In times of constrained budgets in the north and geopolitical insignificance of the south they are an increasingly anachronistic model, as the transformation of the Lomé-treaty between the EU and the ACP-countries into free trade agreements vividly demonstrate (see chapter 8). The IMDI is a further step in this transformation: its measures – declared as a new form of development policy – include neither financial transfers by governments to improve other states' economies nor market-distorting interventions with the aim of *development*. Development projects are primarily to be financed by the migrants themselves (Kunz/Schwenken 2014). The opening up of the labour markets of the industrial countries, which is at the core of the initiative, corresponds far more to the principles of neoclassical economic theory. Measures for the redistribution of global wealth are envisioned only in a very indirect manner: redistribution will take place as an indirect consequence of an intensified and controlled labour migration from the South to the North which is oriented towards optimised conditions for employment/exploitation by the enterprises in the industrial countries and will probably result in wage decreases and further abolition of the welfare state in the countries of destination. A very special kind of redistribution.

In both areas – migration policy and development policy – neoliberal concepts are gradually pushing aside more traditional approaches (prevention of migration in one, state interventions aiming at *development* in the other area). The convergence of both areas in the new approach of promoting migration management as a new form of development aid therefore has to be analysed as an element of neoliberal globalisation. The possible progressive aspects of the restructuring of the regime of migration should not detract from the fact that its main concern is the interest of enterprises in the North and not the rights of migrants from the South.

Just like the new trend towards microfinance in development policy (Bateman 2010), the focus on the migration-development nexus and the idea of migration working as an engine for *development* has to be interpreted as a new cycle of the circle of diagnosis and promise in development discourse. The new prescription, which is perfectly in line with the neoliberal transformation of the discourse and dispositive of development, recommends letting the poor take care of their poverty themselves by allowing them to migrate into high-income countries and to send remittances to their families at home – of course not in the context of an equal right to mobility, but of controlled labour migration programmes tuned to the needs of the labour markets (i.e. the private sector) of the North. While this interferes with the interests of unions defending the achievements (globally: the privileges) of workers in the North, it does relieve international organisations, states and multinational companies of any responsibility to change existing distributions, relations of power or economic systems in order to combat global poverty. This task is given to the supposedly empowered migrant subjects in the new discursive regime of migration and *development*.

Notes

1 Others may remember him as the last Director General of the General Agreement on Tariffs and Trade (GATT) and the first Director General of the World Trade Organization (WTO), an aggressive proponent of free trade, and a member of the Bilderberg Conference, the Trilateral Commission and the European Roundtable of Industrialists.

2 See also http://www.migration4development.org/content/about-jmdi (March 21, 2015) and https://www.iom.int/cms/en/sites/iom/home/what-we-do/migration—development-1.html (March 21, 2015).

Bibliography

Andrijasevic, Rutvica 2005: Schöne tote Körper: Gender, Migration und Repräsentation in Kampagnen gegen Menschenhandel. In Arbeitsgruppe moving . . . on . . . (eds.) *Handlungen an Grenzen – Strategien zum antirassistischen Handeln*. Berlin: NGBK. Online http://www.policy.hu/andrijasevic/IOM.html (January 3, 2007).

Angenendt, Steffen 2003: Regelung und Vermittlung: Die Rolle internationaler Migrationsorganisationen. In: Thränhardt, Dietrich/Hunger, Uwe (eds.) *Migration im Spannungsfeld von Globalisierung und Nationalstaat*. Leviathan Sonderheft 22, Wiesbaden, 180–202.

Antirassismusbüro Bremen 2004: *Stop IOM! Globale Bewegung gegen Migrationskontrolle*. Bremen.

Bateman, Milford 2010: *Why Doesn't Microfinance Work? The Destructive Rise of Local Neoliberalism*. London: Zed Books.

Düvell, Franck 2002: *Die Globalisierung des Migrationsregimes. Zur neuen Einwanderungspolitik in Europa*. Berlin: Assoziation A.

Golding, Ian/Reinert, Kenneth 2006: *Globalization for Development: Trade, Finance, Aid, Migration, and Policy*. London: Palgrave Macmillan/World Bank.

Hunger, Uwe 2003: Brain drain oder brain gain: Migration und Entwicklung. In: Thränhardt, Dietrich/Hunger, Uwe (eds.) *Migration im Spannungsfeld von Globalisierung und Nationalstaat*. Leviathan Sonderheft 22, Wiesbaden, 58–75.

IOM 2005a: Constitution of the International Organization of Migration. Online http://www.iom.int/en/who/main_constitution.shtml (May 12, 2005).

IOM 2005b: Mission Statement. Online http://www.iom.int/en/who/main_mission.shtml (May 12, 2005).

IOM 2006a: An IOM Proposal for an International Migration and Development Initiative, Draft Concept Paper. Online http://www.iom.int/jahia/webdav/site/myjahiasite/shared/shared/mainsite/media/sp/editorial20061207_dg.pdf (January 2, 2007).

IOM 2006b: International Migration and Development Initiative: Labour Mobility for Development. Online http://www.iom.int/jahia/webdav/site/myjahiasite/shared/shared/mainsite/media/sp/editorial20061207_dg.pdf (January 2, 2007).

IOM/OECD/World Bank 2004: Trade and Migration: Building Bridges for Labour Mobility.

Joint Migration and Development Initiative 2011: *Migration for Development. A Bottom-Up Approach*. Brussels: JMDI.

Klemz, Sascha 2006: Gefangen in den Verhältnissen. Internationale Organisationen im Kampf gegen Zwangsarbeit. *iz3w (Informationszentrum 3. Welt)* Nr. 294, 16–17.

Kunz, Rahel/Schwenken, Helen 2014: MigrantInnen als HoffnungsträgerInnen in der Entwicklungszusammenarbeit? Geschlechterspezifische Subjektivitäten im migration-development nexus. In: Müller, Franziska/Sondermann, Elena/Wehr, Ingrid/Jakobeit, Cord/Ziai, Aram (eds.) *Entwicklungstheorien. Weltgesellschaftliche Transformationen, entwicklungspolitische Herausforderungen, theoretische Innovationen*. Sonderheft 48 der Politischen Vierteljahresschrift. Baden-Baden: Nomos, 323–351.

Kuznetsov, Yevgeny 2006: *Diaspora Networks and the International Migration of Skills: How Countries Can Draw on Their Talent Abroad*. Washington, DC: World Bank.

Mansoor, Ali/Quillin, Bruce 2006: *Migration and Remittances: Eastern Europe and the Former Soviet Union*. Washington, DC: World Bank.

Moscarelli, Simona 2006: La Belle Vita? The Italian Irregular Migration Experience, posted on December 12, 2006. Online http://www.iom.int/jahia/Jahia/featureArticleEU/op/edit/cache/offonce/pid/643?entryID=12320 (January 3, 2007).

Noborder network 2002: IOM in Australia and Nauru, posted on October 9, 2002. Online http://www.noborder.org/iom/display.php?id=157 (January 3, 2007).

Noborder network 2003: Human Rights Watchdogs Condemn IOM, posted on May 13, 2003. Online http://www.noborder.org/iom/display.php?id=243 (May 12, 2005).

Ozden, Caglar/Schiff, Maurice (eds.) 2005: *International Migration, Remittances, and the Brain Drain*. London: Palgrave Macmillan/World Bank.

Thränhardt, Dietrich 2005: Entwicklung durch Migration: ein neuer Forschungsansatz. *APuZ* 27/2005, 3–11.

Thränhardt, Dietrich/Hunger, Uwe (eds.) 2003: *Migration im Spannungsfeld von Globalisierung und Nationalstaat*. Leviathan Sonderheft 22, Wiesbaden.

Wodon, Quentin (ed.) 2007: *Migration, Remittances and Poverty: Case Studies from West Africa*. Washington, DC: World Bank.

World Bank 2005: *Global Economic Prospects 2006: Economic Implications of Remittances and Migration*. Washington, DC: Author.

Ziai, Aram 2007: *Globale Strukturpolitik? Die Nord-Süd Politik der BRD und das Dispositiv der Entwicklung im Zeitalter von neoliberaler Globalisierung und neuer Weltordnung*. Münster: Westälisches Dampfboot.

14 The post-2015 agenda and the Sustainable Development Goals

The persistence of development discourse

As the year 2015 drew nearer, the debate in development policy was increasingly dominated by the agenda which would follow up the Millennium Development Goals (MDGs). Countless reports, proposals and statements were issued and conferences were held on the topic, and even within the UN there was a sometimes bewildering array of global reports on the post-2015 agenda: the Report of the Secretary-General 'A life of dignity for all: accelerating progress towards the MDGs and advancing the UN development agenda beyond 2015' (UN 2013a); the report by the UN Development Group 'A million voices: The world we want' which was based on a global consultation on the post-2015 agenda (UN 2013b); the report of the Open Working Group of the General Assembly on Sustainable Development Goals, which was the outcome of the UN conference on sustainable development titled 'The future we want' (UN 2014a); the report of the High-Level Panel of Eminent Persons on the post-2015 development agenda 'A new global partnership: Eradicate poverty and transform economies through sustainable development' (UN 2014b); and finally the synthesis report of the Secretary-General 'The Road to Dignity by 2030: Ending Poverty, Transforming all Lives and Protecting the Planet' (UN 2014c). And while the one report based not on experts but on more participatory methods states that 'a sense of injustice at the deep inequalities and insecurities permeates all the consultations' (UN 2013b: 17), the others are (although dealing with a comprehensive number of issues) focused on the topic of sustainable development, considering however not only the inclusion of the North into the agenda, but also the question of inequality and the objective of ending poverty.

During this period, the criticisms of the MDG agenda and its continuation increased as well. They concern various issues such as the neglect of gender and empowerment issues (Sen/Mukherjee 2014), the fuzziness of the targets (Vandemoortele 2014: 227), the effects of the focus on numbers and measurable targets (Fukuda-Parr et al. 2014, Lepenies 2014), and the fact that the apparently impressive successes in poverty reduction claimed by the MDG proponents to a great extent came about as a result of tinkering with the international poverty line by the World Bank (Hickel 2014, Pogge/Sengupta 2014).[1] Another criticism was voiced by Ashwani Saith at the British Academy Conference 'After 2015: Development and its Alternatives' where he described the MDGs (and also the

SDGs) as 'a diversion from the significant questions of political economy' (see also Saith 2006). What is lacking so far is a critical assessment of the post-2015 agenda from the perspective of historical discourse analysis and this chapter shall be a first attempt at such an assessment.

Taking the High-Level-Report (UN 2014b), which probably received the most attention, as an object of study, in this chapter I will examine which significant changes and continuities in development discourse can be discerned if we apply the lens of discourse analysis to the text.

The report: eradicate poverty through sustainable development and partnership

The panel assembled by UN Secretary-General Ban Ki-moon in July 2012 was headed by Susilo Bambang Yudhoyono, President of Indonesia, Ellen Johnson-Sirleaf, President of Liberia, and David Cameron, Prime Minister of Great Britain. The other 24 members are described as 'leaders from civil society, private sector and government'[2] – which corresponds to the idea of global governance as outlined by the UN commission (Commission on Global Governance 1995) – and include persons like former IMF Director and German President Horst Köhler; Fulbert Gero Amoussuga, Chair of the African Union and economic adviser to the President of Benin; Izabella Teixeira, Minister of Environment in Brazil; Paul Polman, the CEO of Unilever; Nigerian Minister of the Economy and former World Bank Director Ngozi Okonjo-Iweala; Indian economist Abhijit Banerjee; EU Commissioner for Development Andris Piebalgs; Nobel Peace Prize winner Tawakel Karman of Yemen and Queen Rania of Jordan. The report they submitted is entitled 'A new global partnership: Eradicate poverty and transform economies through sustainable development' and generally employs a vocabulary familiar from many UN declarations and specifically the emphatic variant of the discourse of global governance (Brand et al. 2000) invoking a 'spirit of cooperation', mutual learning ('we have learnt much from each other') and working together 'for the sake of humanity' (UN 2014b: i).

The report starts by praising the achievements of the MDGs but criticises as their most serious shortcoming 'not integrating the economic, social, and environmental aspects of sustainable development' and 'not addressing the need to promote sustainable patterns of consumption and production . . . environment and development were never properly brought together' (v). Instead, we need a 'single sustainable development agenda' (5). Its conclusion is that 'the post-2015 agenda . . . needs to be driven by the five big, transformative shifts' (vi), namely 'Leave No One Behind' (commitment to the excluded, to end discrimination and tackle causes of poverty, 7); 'Put Sustainable Development at the Core' (lower global carbon emissions, moving towards a green economy, investments in sustainable technologies, civil society as watchdogs, 8); 'Transform Economies for Jobs and Inclusive Growth' (sustained growth that can overcome the challenges of unemployment, resource scarcity and climate change, creating opportunities for decent jobs and secure livelihoods, linked with productivity increases, a stable business environment and support for sustainable production and consumption, 8f); 'Build Peace and Effective, Open and Accountable Public Institutions' (recognise peace and good governance as core elements of well-being, transparency and accountability, right to protest and international cooperation, 9); and 'Forge a new Global Partnership' (a new sense of global partnership based on our common humanity and universal principles of human rights, solidarity, etc. and a shared common vision of a better future, 9f). The participants of this partnership (which gave the report its title) are national governments; local authorities; international institutions; business; civil society organisations; foundations, other philanthropists and social impact investors; scientists and academics (10f); and 'people' (12).

Instead of the eight MDGs, the report proposes twelve universal goals for sustainable development, each accompanied by four to six specific targets. The goals are:

1) End Poverty
2) Empower Girls and Women and Achieve Gender Equality
3) Provide Quality Education and Lifelong Learning
4) Ensure Healthy Lives
5) Ensure Food Security and Good Nutrition
6) Achieve Universal Access to Water and Sanitation
7) Secure Sustainable Energy
8) Create Jobs, Sustainable Livelihoods, and Equitable Growth
9) Manage Natural Resources and Assets Sustainably
10) Ensure Good Governance and Effective Institutions
11) Ensure Stable and Peaceful Societies
12) Create a Global Enabling Environment and Catalyse Long-Term Finance. (30f)

According to the report, the new goals need to be specific, measurable, attainable, relevant, and time-bound (13). The reformulation of MDG 8 (Global Partnership for Development) is given particular attention, as it was the only one involving industrialised countries and at the same time very vague and not linked to quantified targets. This reformulation should, according to the report, develop universal targets, quantify them wherever feasible, 'pay more attention to raising, long-term finance for development', 'signal priorities that go beyond aid' and 'infuse global partnerships and cooperation into all the goals' (15).

Before entering into the analysis of changes and continuities in development discourse, some remarkable and – at first sight – progressive elements of the report deserve to be mentioned. One is the explicit mentioning of inequality ('Of all the goods and services consumed in the world each year, the 1.2 billion people living in extreme poverty only account for one per cent, while the richest 1 billion people consume 72 per cent', 4) and gender-based violence ('Every year, one billion women are subject to sexual or physical violence because they lack equal protection under the law', 4), which has often been avoided in similar reports of the MDG era. Another is the significance of immediate action in the context of climate change. Concerning carbon emissions, the report states clearly, 'there is no evidence yet that the upward trend has been slowed or reversed, as it must be if potentially catastrophic changes are to be avoided . . . Changes in consumption and production patterns are essential, and they must be led by the developed countries' (4). Further, it is argued that it was 'unrealistic to think we can help another one billion people to lift themselves out of poverty by growing their national economies without making structural changes in the world economy' (5). This focus on the world economy instead of development cooperation ('Ending poverty is not a matter for aid or international cooperation alone', 5) has been a standard demand of leftist critics for a long time. It is linked to the great responsibility of the *developed* countries, which are called upon to stem tax evasion and illicit capital flows and monitor and control multinational corporations (5). And concerning the measurement of SDG success, the report suggests that 'in all cases where a target applies to outcomes for individuals, it should only be deemed to be met if every group – defined by income quintile, gender, location or otherwise – has met the target' (15). This suggestion would avoid the problem that improvements which have been taking place only for the more privileged parts of the population are designated as improvements, ignoring the situation of those excluded. This suggestion of group- or class-specific targets corresponds not only to the demands of critics like Pogge and Sengupta, who show that behind aggregate poverty reduction in the global economy, an increase of already severe inequality is hidden (2014: 5f).[3] It also corresponds to the demands of the World Bank itself in its report on redistribution and growth (Chenery et al. 1973), as discussed in chapter 9.

Discursive shifts

In comparison to the transformations in the discourse of development analysed in chapters 7 and 8, the shifts that can be analysed in the HLP report on the SDGs are only minor. One could even claim that it contains no discursive elements which have not been present in the history of development discourse already. Mainly, it draws on elements familiar from the debates around global governance, sustainable development and the MDGs. The story lines identified in chapter 11 are present here as well, but to reiterate them would probably be more tedious than surprising. What I intend to do in this section is to trace the shifts which can be observed in historical perspective, before discussing the more significant continuities in the next.

The first obvious shift in comparison to the MDGs concerns the formation of objects. Taking the discourse of sustainability serious, the report claims to focus not any longer on those geographical units defined as *less developed*, but deals with aspects of the *developed* societies. Here, the universal approach of the One World concept or of neoliberalism is manifest. The introductory letter of the co-chairs emphasises that the transformations envisioned are 'applicable to both developed and developing countries alike' (UN 2014b: i) and in the report, sustainable development is described as 'a universal challenge, for every country and every person on earth' (vi) including 'developed and developing countries alike' (5). Nevertheless, the familiar division between *developed* and *developing* countries appears throughout the report. *Developed* countries are called upon to provide development aid, foster new technologies, change their unsustainable consumption and production patterns, and reform the global economy (trade, tax evasion, illicit capital flows) (vi, 3, 4, 5, 8, 10, etc.). *Developing* countries, on the other hand, are as usual the primary objects of policies aimed realising the SDGs (as exemplified in the figures on pages 33, 41, 49), they need 'substantial external funding' (12) and massive infrastructure investments (3), although it is recognised that they are 'much more diverse than when the MDGs were agreed' (10) – which can be seen as a recognition of the critique of the one-size-fits-all approach (see chapter 7). So the binary structures are reaffirmed not only regarding the obligation of the one group of countries to provide aid, but, and this is a new element, also regarding a higher obligation of this group to change its production and consumption patterns. This, at least in theory, enables interventions in the name of sustainable development to be staged in countries of the global North. In practice, such initiatives are hardly existent. However, in the context of climate change, the goals to reduce emissions in industrialised countries (according to the principle of shared, but differentiated responsibilities) are formally comparable to the goals of reducing poverty in poorer countries. This means that the discourse of sustainability – which rose to prominence during the late 1980s and early 1990s and gained increased attention with global warming – has achieved the visibility of industrialised countries in development discourse: they can now be perceived as objects in need of improvement – which beforehand was the dubious privilege of *less developed* countries.

A second discursive shift is that in historical perspective, the SDG report examined here exhibits a little bit of a 1970s-stlye in comparison to the MDG reports analysed in chapter 11. This relates to the elimination of poverty, and the aspects of inequality and justice. Regarding the first issue, the report proposes that 'after 2015, we should move from reducing to *ending* poverty, in all its forms' (vi, emphasis in the original). So after the more modest approach of the MDGs (reducing by half the extreme forms of poverty), a more ambitious goal is being formulated which is somewhat reminiscent of the fervour of the 1970s ('There can be no excuses', vi). As we saw in chapter 11, the International Development Strategy for that decade also envisioned the elimination of all forms of poverty. Apparently, a world without poverty has reentered the terrain of legitimate political visions. Likewise, the issue of inequality is taken up again. The term is mentioned 22 times in the HLP report, whereas it did appear only once (in a quote) in the report of the UN Millennium Project headed by Jeffrey Sachs (UN Millennium Project 2005).[4] A similar picture emerges of we focus on the term justice: only three mentions in 2005 (and of these two in quotes), 30 mentions in 2014. If we take into consideration the absence of any concern with inequality and justice as a characteristic of the neoliberal era (which was a result of the analysis in chapter 9), we could therefore argue that the hegemony of neoliberalism has clearly lost ground within the UN during the past decade. Maybe these issues do not figure quite as prominently on the agenda as in the early 70s, but clearly the discursive ground has shifted: inequality and justice are certainly issues which can legitimately be addressed in the context of the post-2015 agenda. This was hardly or at the very least distinctively less so the case in the MDG context.

However, a note of caution is appropriate in case one is inclined to diagnose the demise of neoliberalism. Concerning economic theory and policy, the case for the benefits of free trade is presented as beyond doubt and self-evident in the report. It stresses the necessity of open markets and free trade and a 'level playing field' (2, 8, 9) and includes it in Goal 12 of the SDGs (43). The elaboration of this goal claims 'Increased trade and access to markets brings more equitable growth and opportunity for all' was 'the surest way to defeat poverty and deprivation' (54) – an unqualified statement that could well come from the heyday of neoliberalism which disregards the substantial evidence to the contrary. The report even postulates that 'we must . . . champion free and fair trade' (vii) – apparently oblivious of the antagonism between the two. While according to classical and neoclassical economics free trade is seen as welfare enhancing precisely because individuals opt for the lowest price and because any distortions and interventions in the market mechanism are banned ('Get the prices right'), fair trade's defining characteristic is the decision not to pay the producers the market price but a fixed one which enables them to live off their work. The ignorance towards such contradictions will be a theme in the next section. For now, we can observe that while there is a new emphasis on the issues of inequality and justice, the central tenets of neoliberalism are still unchallenged in the HLP report. This leads us to focus on the discursive continuities in the history of development policy.

Discursive continuities

The continuities between the SDG agenda and the MDG debates are rather obvious and shall not be discussed here. What is less obvious and will be discussed here are the continuities between the discourse of the current post-2015-agenda and the overarching discursive structures present since the middle of the 20th century. William Easterly, in an article entitled 'The Cartel of Good Intentions' (2002: 236), has already pointed out numerous parallels between the different aid epochs, which he calls the 'stone age' (1950s and 1960s), the 'iron age' (1970s and 1980s), and the 'silicon age' (2000s) of development aid. He demonstrates that numerous ideas and phrases – on the necessity of donor coordination, an increase of aid volume and policy reform; on the desirability of country ownership and debt relief; on the recognition that aid works only in a good policy environment and that reforms are already taking place; and on the intention to increase the emphasis on poverty in development aid – occur in all three epochs.[5] This insight is in stark contradiction to the image of continuous innovation that the development industry constructs and tries to convey. It is, however, perfectly in line with the hypothesis on the diagnostic cycle of the development promise discussed in chapter 4. This cycle consists of a diagnosis of a deficit in the object of development discourse, followed by the prescription of a recipe, a strategy which entails the promise of *development*. The failure to fulfil the promise and reach the state of *development* is followed by an explanation of the failure and a new cycle in which a renewal of the promise takes place. In this way, the development industry can constantly reaffirm its legitimacy, its competence, its good intentions and its effectiveness: 'we've recognized the problem (1) and we know the solution (2) and we're working on it (3) and we're making progress (4)'. This is the message of the discourse of the development industry throughout the epochs. Here, the institutional requirements of aid organisations heavily influence their perception and their discourse, as Ferguson (1994) has so lucidly pointed out in his study of Lesotho and the 'Anti-Politics-Machine' of development aid.[6]

So if there are these general structures to be found in the discourse of development – a claim vehemently disputed by its proponents – then we should be able to identify them in the SDG report of 2014 as well as in Truman's address of 1949. As we have already briefly dealt with a change in the formal structures – namely the formation of objects according to the idea of sustainability – I will focus on structures more related to the content in the following analysis.

Diagnosis: global poverty as a problem

> More than half the people of the world are living in conditions approaching misery. Their food is inadequate. They are victims of disease. Their economic life is primitive and stagnant. Their poverty is a handicap and a threat both to them and to more prosperous areas.
>
> (Truman 1949)

> We are deeply aware of the hunger, vulnerability, and deprivation that still shape the daily lives of more than a billion people in the world today . . ., the 1.2 billion people living in extreme poverty . . . Today, 870 million people in the world do not have enough to eat. Undernourished women give birth to underweight babies, who are less likely to live to their fifth birthday and more likely to develop chronic diseases and other limitations.
>
> (UN 2014b: 4, 40)

The common diagnosis at the foundation of development discourse is that the conditions of living of a large part of world population pose a problem. Hunger and disease are described as obvious manifestations of this problem which is designated as poverty. (It could alternatively be framed as global material inequality or as oppression.)[7] This discursive structure can easily be identified in both texts and illustrates the first continuity. Nevertheless, it has to be mentioned that the diagnosis of the problem is complemented in the SDG discourse by another aspect which is characterised as having potentially catastrophic effects and posing 'perhaps the biggest challenge of all' (UN 2014b: 8) – climate change.

Promise: we can solve the problem today

> For the first time in history, humanity possesses the knowledge and the skill to relieve the suffering of these people . . . we must embark on a bold new program for making the benefits of our scientific advances and industrial progress available for the improvement and growth of underdeveloped areas.
>
> (Truman 1949)

[T]here is a chance now to do something that has never before been done – to eradicate extreme poverty, once and for all . . . We have a historic opportunity to do what no other generation has ever done before: to eradicate extreme poverty by 2030 and end poverty . . . We are convinced that . . . the world possesses the tools and resources it needs to achieve a bold and ambitious vision.

(UN 2014b: 4, 47)

Constructing humanity as a homogeneous subject (devoid of race, gender and class divisions), this second discursive structure postulates that in the present historic moment, we can solve the problem of global poverty by acting determinedly (or boldly). This implies a presentism which neglects the historical capacities of solving the problem 10 years before or after the present moment and thus excludes the question why it has not been done before. Likewise, by ignoring these divisions, it promises that the problem actually can be solved within the current world order and the existing relations of power. The promise thus legitimates this world order and these relations, suggesting that an end to poverty and suffering can be expected in the near future.

Recipe: technical solutions

[O]ur imponderable resources in technical knowledge are constantly growing and are inexhaustible. I believe that we should make available to peace-loving peoples the benefits of our store of technical knowledge in order to help them realize their aspirations for a better life . . . Greater production is the key to prosperity and peace. And the key to greater production is a wider and more vigorous application of modern scientific and technical knowledge.

(Truman 1949)

The resources, know-how and technology that are needed [to eradicate poverty] already exist, and are growing every year. . . . Developed countries . . . can encourage innovation, diffusion and transfer of technology. . . . Scientists and academics can make scientific and technological breakthroughs that will be essential to the post-2015 agenda. Every country that has experienced sustained high growth has done so through absorbing knowledge, technology and ideas from the rest of the world . . . A profound economic transformation can end extreme poverty and promote sustainable development, improving livelihoods, by harnessing innovation, technology, and the potential of business.

(UN 2014b: 18, 10f, 29)

One central recipe which follows from the diagnosis to cure the problem is technical knowledge, which is not portrayed as a scarce, but as an ever-growing resource. Side effects of technology (limited resources, resource extraction, pollution) are not discussed. The solutions are seen to be lying in the field of innovation and progress which corresponds to a construction of the problem as a lack of knowledge and technology. This view excludes a construction of the problem centred around inequality and divisions (according to race, gender, class, etc.) and the corresponding political and conflictive solutions of the problem. Technology is, in the discourse of development perceived as neutral, freely available and beneficial to all. All three perceptions are highly controversial if not dubious in a world where technology is to a large extent owned by private companies and where patents not only exist but are increasingly expanded and enforced.[8]

Recipe: economic growth

> Their economic life is primitive and stagnant. . . . we must embark on a bold new program for making the benefits of our scientific advances and industrial progress available for the improvement and growth of underdeveloped areas. . . . we should foster capital investment in areas needing development. Our aim should be to help the free peoples of the world, through their own efforts, to produce more food, more clothing, more materials for housing, and more mechanical power to lighten their burdens. . . . this program can greatly increase the industrial activity in other nations and can raise substantially their standards of living. . . . Greater production is the key to prosperity and peace.
>
> (Truman 1949)

> The Panel calls for a quantum leap forward in economic opportunities and a profound economic transformation to end extreme poverty and improve livelihoods. There must be a commitment to rapid, equitable growth – not growth at any cost or just short-term spurts in growth, but sustained, long-term, inclusive growth that can overcome the challenges of unemployment (especially youth unemployment), resource scarcity and – perhaps the biggest challenge of all – adaptation to climate change.
>
> (UN 2014b: 8)

The other central recipe which has remained constant throughout the history of development discourse is economic growth in the sense of an increased production of goods and services to be exchanged over the market in the formal economy. (For the criticism of this conception of the economy, see e.g. Ekins/Max-Neef 1992). Comparing the two texts, it becomes clear that on the one hand, economic growth has lost some of its credibility as a recipe for poverty reduction and improvement of livelihoods, so that nowadays it has to be constantly qualified as inclusive and often also sustainable growth. On the other hand, this can be seen in the quote above, it still is assumed to work miracles: overcome unemployment and resource scarcity and poverty in general, while helping people to adapt to climate change.

Credo: harmony of objectives

> All countries, including our own, will greatly benefit from a constructive program for the better use of the world's human and natural resources. Experience shows that our commerce with other countries expands as they progress industrially and economically.
>
> (Truman 1949)

> Countries have resources, expertise or technology that, if shared, can result in mutual benefit. Working together is not just a moral obligation to help those less fortunate but is an investment in the long-term prosperity of all.
>
> (UN 2014b: 10)

The alleged nature of the recipes – technical knowledge and economic growth are beneficial for everyone – allows to maintain the underlying credo of development discourse, namely that all parties involved, *developed* and *developing* countries, will benefit from the program of *development*. This claim is based on two analytically separate tenets: 1) investment and trade will help the poor (through economic growth) and 2) poverty reduction will help the economy (through economic growth) and thereby also the rich will benefit. These tenets also appear regularly in World Bank reports (see chapter 9). If they hold true, there is no need for hard choices between the interests of poor peasants, multinational companies and rich consumers – they all benefit from *development*. Therefore this discursive structure has been used for convincing the governments of poorer countries to keep their markets open to their former colonisers – according to Alcalde, '[t]he first and broadest function of the idea of development was to give economic activity, particularly foreign economic activity, a positive and essential meaning for the lives of less-developed peoples' (1987: 223) – as well as for convincing rich country citizens of the need for development assistance, as it corresponds to their enlightened self-interest, to borrow an oft-used phrase.

This self-interest of the North is linked to improvements in the South not only via the route of investment and markets, but also through the prospect of security and stability.[9] This can be observed in the statements of Truman (1949) that 'their poverty is a handicap *and a threat* both to them and to more prosperous countries' and that 'greater production is the key to prosperity *and peace*' (emphasis added). Whereas at that time, the threat arising out of poverty took the form of communist revolutions, this has for obvious reasons changed since 1989. The security of the North is now increasingly threatened by drugs, migration and – predominantly since 2001 – terrorism. Remarkably, this discursive structure is relatively hard to find in the HLP report – apart from the occasional coupling of 'peaceful and prosperous societies' (2014b: 29).[10] Yet it manifests itself in Goal 11 which clearly states: 'Without development, there can be no enduring peace' (52). According to the report, the privileged should realise that *development* is necessary for a stable and peaceful world order and that there is thus a harmony of objectives regarding poverty reduction and growth. The sustainability agenda and the issue of climate change add a new twist to the credo, which can be seen in the following quote:

> It is sometimes argued that global limits on carbon emissions will force developing countries to sacrifice growth to accommodate the lifestyles of the rich, or that developed countries will have to stop growing so that developing countries can develop – substituting one source of pollution for another. We do not believe that such trade-offs are necessary. Mankind's capacity for innovation, and the many alternatives that already exist, mean that sustainable development can, and must, allow people in all countries to achieve their aspirations.
>
> (UN 2014b: 8)

Just like the harmony of objectives prevents hard choices between reducing poverty and fostering foreign investment, it also allows to combine unlimited growth with sustainability through the belief in technical innovations. Even under the conditions of climate change and global warming – so the credo assumes – there is no need to give up or even limit the resource-intensive lifestyle of the rich. On the contrary, all people can achieve it, due to our unlimited capacity for innovation. This argument appears closer to an act of faith than to a reasonable evaluation in the light of the increasingly alarming reports of the Intergovernmental Panel on Climate Change.[11]

Conclusion: the persistence of development discourse

We have seen that the HLP report, as a representative of the SDG debate, exhibits some features which distinguish it from the older MDG agenda. On the level of content, there is on the one hand a more determined inclusion of issues of inequality and injustice. On the other hand, sustainability and issues of climate change and resource use have (unsurprisingly) taken centre stage in the debate. The latter is also linked to a change in the formation of objects: the industrialised countries of the North finally become conceivable as objects of *development* targets and interventions, although in practice the focus of the report still lies with the *less developed* countries. However, the discursive elements of report found in the report have been present in the debate about development policy at least since the 1990s in the discourses of sustainable development and global governance.

The analysis in this chapter even demonstrated that some central discursive structures to be found in the SDG debate date back to the origins of development aid in the middle of the 20th century. Comparing the HLP report of 2014 with Truman's address of 1949, in which he announced a program of development for the *underdeveloped* areas, we find clear similarities: the diagnosis of global poverty as a problem, the promise of being able to solve the problem, the recipes of technical knowledge and economic growth, and the credo of a harmony of objectives can be found in both texts. While it would be wrong to claim that nothing has changed during these 65 years, the changes are surprisingly minor: these discursive structures manifest themselves in a new form and accommodate past criticisms and current debates to a certain extent, but can still be identified as the same structures which were used after World War II to achieve acceptance for the practices designated as *development* in a capitalist world order. The persistence of development discourse throughout the decades is remarkable.

Notes

1 According to LSE economist Jason Hickel, the World Bank transformed a rise in the numbers of the poor to a substantial decrease by changing the international poverty line on the basis of which the poor were counted from US$1.02 in the purchasing power parity (PPP) of 1985 to US$1.08 in the PPP of 1993 and then to US$1.25 in the PPP of 2008. This resulted in the reduction of the number of the poor by

437 million. On the basis of a more reasonable poverty line of US$2.50 in 2008 PPP, there was an increase of 353 million poor people since 1981, an exclusion of China boosts this number to 852 million people (Hickel 2014). Pogge/Sengupta (2014: 4) also make this point. It is interesting to note in this context that already in the 1990s, Apthorpe wrote: 'Given then that in case after case "absolute" [measurement of poverty with a poverty datum line] proves on re-reading to be close to "negotiable" and "negotiated", one might expect that this mode would have by now disappeared from development policy studies. But this has not happened. . . . The reality is that policy drives the practice of numbering, rather than numbering practice driving the policy.' (1996: 27).

2 http://www.un.org/sg/management/hlppost2015.shtml (January 25, 2015).

3 Pogge and Sengupta show that the share of global household income has risen for the richest 5% from 42.87 to 45.75% between 1988 and 2008, while for the poorest quintile it has fallen from 0.85% to 0.66% during the same period and for the second poorest quintile from 1.52 to 1.43% (2014: 6).

4 Here, I did not count the four mentions of gender inequality, which referred more to discrimination than to economic inequality. Both reports are somewhat comparable in length (UN 2005: 95 pages, UN 2014b: 81 pages).

5 However, it has to be admitted that Easterly is a bit sloppy regarding the separation of these epochs: some of the empirical examples he cites to support his claim about the stone age are from the 1970s and even the early 80s, while one statement allegedly from the iron age is from 1973 (Easterly 2002: 236).

6 '"[D]evelopment" institutions generate their own form of discourse, and this discourse simultaneously constructs Lesotho as a particular kind of object of knowledge, and creates a structure of knowledge around that object. Interventions are then organised on the basis of this structure of knowledge, which, while "failing" on their own terms, nonetheless have regular effects, which include the expansion and entrenchment of bureaucratic state power, side by side with the projection of a representation of economic and social life which denies "politics" and, to the extent that it is successful, suspends its effects. The short answer to the question of what the "development" apparatus in Lesotho does, then is . . .: it is an "anti-politics machine" . . . An academic analysis is of no use to a "development" agency unless it provides a place for the agency to plug itself in, unless it provides a charter for the sort of intervention that the agency is set up to do. An analysis which suggests that the causes of poverty in Lesotho are political and structural (not technical and geographical), that the national government is part of the problem (not a neutral instrument for its solution), and that meaningful change can only come through revolutionary social transformation in South Africa has no place in "development" discourse simply because "development" agencies are not in the business of promoting political realignments or supporting revolutionary struggles. . . . For an analysis to meet the needs of "development" institutions, it must do what academic discourse inevitably fails to do; it must make Lesotho out to be an enormously promising candidate for the only sort of intervention a "development" agency is capable of launching: the apolitical, technical "development" intervention' (Ferguson 1994: xivf, 68f).

7 Another alternative, suggested by neopopulist Post-Development approaches, would be to differentiate between frugality (a simple life characterised by a lack of goods not necessary for survival and well-being) and destitution (a lack of means of survival resulting from processes of pauperization and the expansion of market economy) as two fundamental different kinds of poverty (Rahnema 1992).

8 For a critique of the view that technology is neutral and beneficial to all, see especially the work of Ivan Illich.
9 On this issue, see above all the work of Mark Duffield (2007, 2014).
10 It occurs much more frequently and explicitly in the statements of bilateral development agencies more concerned with convincing citizens of the North of the usefulness of development assistance. Explaining its fundamental purpose, the German Ministry for Economic Cooperation and Development claims that: 'The large problems of our time do not stop at national borders. . . . Conflicts in other countries also endanger the security of people in Germany. . . . Development cooperation helps to prevent crises and cope with conflicts' (BMZ 2013).
11 See also Wuppertal Institut 2005, Latouche 2011 and Paech 2012.

Bibliography

Alcalde, Javier Gonzalo 1987: *The Idea of Third World Development: Emerging Perspectives in the United States and Britain, 1900–1950*. Lanham, MD: University Press of America.

Apthorpe, Raymond 1996: Reading Development Policy and Policy Analysis: On Framing, Naming, Numbering and Coding. In: Apthorpe, Raymond/Gasper, Des (eds.) *Arguing Development Policy: Frames and Discourses*. London: Frank Cass, 16–35.

BMZ 2013: Warum brauchen wir Entwicklungspolitik? Online http://www.bmz.de/de/was_wir_machen/ziele/grundsaetze/index.html (June 12, 2013).

Brand, Ulrich/Brunnengräber, Achim/Schrader, Lutz/Stock, Christian/ Wahl, Peter 2000: *Global Governance. Alternative zur neoliberalen Globalisierung?* Münster: Westfälisches Dampfboot.

Chenery, Hollis/Ahluwalia, Montek S./Bell, C.L.G./Duloy, John H./Jolly, Richard 1973: *Redistribution with Growth: Policies to Improve Income Distribution in Developing Countries in the Context of Economic Growth*. Oxford: Oxford University Press.

Commission on Global Governance 1995: *Our Global Neighbourhood*. Oxford: Oxford University Press.

Duffield, Mark 2007: *Development, Security and Unending War: Governing the World of Peoples*. London: Polity.

Duffield Mark 2014: *Global Governance and the New Wars: The Merging of Development and Security*. London: Zed Books.

Easterly, William 2002: The Cartel of Good Intentions: The Problem of Bureaucracy in Foreign Aid. *Policy Reform* 5(4), 223–250.

Ekins, Paul/Max-Neef, Manfred 1992: *Real-Life Economics: Understanding Wealth Creation*. London: Routledge.

Ferguson, James 1994 (1990): *The Anti-politics Machine: Development, Depoliticization and Bureaucratic Power in Lesotho*. Minneapolis: University of Minnesota Press.

Fukuda-Parr, Sakiko/Ely Yamin, Alicia/Greenstein, Joshua 2014: The Power of Numbers: A Critical Review of Millennium Development Goal Targets for Human Development and Human Rights. *Journal of Human Development and Capabilities* 15(2–3), 105–117.

Hickel, Jason 2014: Die Millenniumslüge. Die Erzählung von der abnehmenden Armut ist falsch. In: *Informationsbrief Weltwirtschaft & Entwicklung* 09/2014, 2–4. Also as 2014: Exposing the great 'poverty reduction' lie. Online: http://www.aljazeera.com/indepth/opinion/2014/08/exposing-great-poverty-reductio-2014812115907 29809.html (January 11, 2015).

Latouche, Serge 2011: *Vers une société d'abondance frugal: Contresens et controverses sur la décroissance*. Paris: Mille et une Nuits.

Lepenies, Philipp 2014: Die Politik der messbaren Ziele. Die Millennium Development Goals aus gouvernementalitätstheoretischer Sicht. Lehren aus der Fixierung globaler Entwicklungsindikatoren. In: Müller, Franziska/Sondermann, Elena/Wehr, Ingrid/ Jakobeit, Cord/Ziai, Aram (eds.) *Entwicklungstheorien. Weltgesellschaftliche Transformationen, entwicklungspolitische Herausforderungen, theoretische Innovationen.* Baden-Baden: Nomos, 200–224.

Paech, Nico 2012: *Befreiung vom Überfluss: Auf dem Weg in die Postwachstumsökonomie.* München: Oekom.

Pogge, Thomas/Sengupta, Mitu 2014: Rethinking the Post-2015 Development Agenda: Eight Ways to End Poverty Now. *Global Justice. Theory, Practice, Rhetoric* 7, 3–11.

Rahnema, Majid 1992: Poverty. In: Sachs, Wolfgang (ed.) 1992: *The Development Dictionary: A Guide to Knowledge as Power.* London: Zed Books, 158–176.

Saith, Ashwani 2006: From Universal Values to Millennium Development Goals: Lost in Translation. *Development & Change* 37(6), 1167–1199.

Sen, Gita/Mukherjee, Avanti 2014: No Empowerment Without Rights, No Right Without Politics: Gender-equality, MDGs and the Post-2015 Development Agenda. *Journal of Human Development and Capabilities* 15(2–3), 188–202.

Truman, Harold 1949: Inaugural address of President Harry S. Truman, January 20, 1949.

UN 2013a: *A Life of Dignity for All: Accelerating Progress Towards the Millennium Development Goals and Advancing the United Nations Development Agenda Beyond 2015.* Report of the Secretary-General. Document A/68/202.

UN 2013b: *A Million Voices: The World We Want: A Sustainable Future With Dignity for All.* New York: UNDP.

UN 2014a: *Open Working Group Proposal for Sustainable Development Goals.* Document A/68/970.

UN 2014b: *A New Global Partnership: Eradicate Poverty and Transform Economies Through Sustainable Development. The Report of the High-Level Panel of Eminent Persons on the Post-2015 Development Agenda.* New York: United Nations.

UN 2014c: *The Road to Dignity by 2030: Ending Poverty, Transforming All Lives and Protecting the Planet. Synthesis Report of the Secretary-General on the Post-2015 Agenda.* New York: United Nations.

UN Millennium Project 2005: *Investing in Development. A Practical Plan to Achieve the Millennium Development Goals. Overview.* New York: United Nations Development Programme.

Vandemoortele, January 2014: Post-2015 Agenda: Mission Impossible? *Development Studies Research* 1(1), 223–232.

Wuppertal Institut für Klima, Umwelt, Energie 2005: *Fair Future: Begrenzte Ressourcen und globale Gerechtigkeit.* Munich: C.H. Beck.

Part IV

Conclusion

15 Conclusion

The contribution of discourse analysis to development studies

Having followed the history of the term *development* through various decades and issues, it is now time to take stock of the analysis and contextualise it within the research on discourse in development studies. This research is relatively novel and has (except for a few early starters) emerged during the 1990s (see e.g. Escobar 1985 and 1995, Sachs 1990 and 1992, Manzo 1991, Nederveen Pieterse 1991, Ferguson 1994, Crush 1995, Moore/Schmitz 1995, Apthorpe/Gasper 1996, Cooper/Packard 1997a, Grillo/Stirrat 1997) and has continued to draw attention in the 2000s (Abrahamsen 2000, Biccum 2002 and 2006, Karagiannis 2004, Oommen 2004, Stein 2004, Eriksson Baaz 2005, Groves/Hinton 2005, Mosse/Lewis 2005, Smith 2006, Duffield 2007a and 2014, Li 2007, Greenstein 2009, Cornwall/Eade 2010, Griffiths 2010). However, there were numerous books on the history of development theory and the idea of *development* in earlier decades (e.g. Alcalde 1987, Arndt 1987, Nisbet 1969) without using the term discourse which became popular only in the – often somewhat superficial – reception of the works of Michel Foucault.

While a relatively recent article claims that 'the study of discourses about *underdevelopment* appears to have been neglected by discourse analysts' and that 'analysis that examines dynamics of power through the study of speech, text and images has not broken through into mainstream development studies and remains a marginal field of analysis in critical IDS' (della Faille 2011: 215f), a closer look casts doubt on this claim. This doubt not only rests on the number of works listed above, but also on their presence in academic debates. While development agencies on the one hand and established scholars in development theory have usually not at all been keen to take these new approaches serious, the quotes in google scholar certainly cannot testify a marginalisation: while both Jeffrey Sachs' *The End of Poverty* and William Easterly's *The White Man's Burden* – two of the best-selling and oft-quoted books in development studies during the last decade – have been quoted a little under 3,000 times, Escobar's Encountering Development has (in February 2015) over 7,000 quotes.[1]

So, judging from this admittedly narrow evidence, discourse analysis in development studies seems at least to inspire debate. While this strand of research is too vast to be comprehensively paraphrased and evaluated here, this chapter will nevertheless try to deal with the contribution of discourse analysis to development studies. It will do so by 1) summing up and discussing frequent points of criticism towards discourse analysis in development studies, 2) highlighting important points of selected texts of this research and articulate their contribution in the light of this critique and 3) specify what the preceding chapters have to add to the state of the research.

The critique of discourse analysis in development studies

> The critical point is not to make the easy claim that poststructural critics [i.e. discourse analysts] of development theory overstate their position, but to argue that the analysis of discourse, with its linking oppositional theoretical traditions because they 'share the same discursive space' (i.e. oppose one another!) is prone to this kind of overgeneralization. . . . because it diverts attention away from the 'international and class relations' and material contexts expressed in discourses, hence merging conflicting positions (PAR and World Bank) into a single developmental discourse, or condemning modernity as a whole rather than, for example, capitalist versions of modern consumptive life.
>
> (Peet 1999: 156)

Peet is probably among the most outspoken critics of discourse analysis in development studies, but similar concerns have been raised as well by numerous writers from different perspectives (Gasper/Apthorpe 1996: 4, Kiely 1999: 36 and 41f, Blaikie 2000: 1034, Nederveen Pieterse 2010: 115f and 2011: 239, to name but a few; see also Peet 1999: 154–56). Their main arguments can be summed up in the following points:

1)   The focus on discourse risks losing sight of materiality. By concerning itself primarily with questions of representation, language and identity, discourse analysis neglects material questions of poverty and survival in capitalism. And these material relations are what counts (or should count) in development studies.
2)   The critique of development discourse in the singular homogenises different, even opposing discourses into a single monolithic entity. This ignores crucial political differences.
3)   Foucauldian approaches to discourse analysis construct a pervasive and all-powerful discourse, thereby losing track of questions of agency. Subjects are reduced to cogs in the machine.
4)   Therefore, the critique of discourse is unable to provide political alternatives. Sometimes, the issue of epistemological relativism (all discourses are equally valid on their own terms, one cannot distinguish between true and false discourses) is raised, which would also lead to political inertia.

In order to evaluate the contribution of discourse analysis to development studies, these four points have to be examined more closely.

Losing sight of materiality

As a first step, it has to be conceded that discourse analysis in development studies is concerned primarily with issues of representation, but with the representation of material inequality and of the attempts to ameliorate it. So unless one assumes that the representational practices (development discourse) and the material practices (development policy) are entirely unrelated, there is obviously some degree of relevance of the former for the latter. By proponents of discourse analysis in development studies, this degree is assumed to be considerable. Escobar claims that:

> As a discourse, development is thus a very real historical formation, albeit articulated around a fictitious construct (underdevelopment) and upon a certain materiality (the conditions baptized as underdevelopment), which must be conceptualized in different ways if the power of development discourse is to be challenged or displaced. To be sure, there is a situation of economic exploitation that must be recognized and dealt with. . . . There is also a certain materiality of life conditions that is extremely preoccupying and that requires effort and attention. . . . Changing the order of discourse is a political question that entails the collective practice of social actors and the restructuring of existing political economies of truth.
>
> (Escobar 1995: 53, 216)

In this perspective, a change in the order of discourse is a necessary component of a larger transformation and a progressive change in the materiality of life conditions is possible only if discursive transformations take place. So it is not the case, to use the words of Christine Sylvester, that discourse analysis in development studies 'does not tend to concern itself with whether the subaltern is eating' (1999: 703), but that the problem is seen as a larger complex of power relations in which representational and material practices can only be transformed together. But although they differ regarding the importance of representation, the concern for material inequality is as present with the discourse analysts as it is with the critics warning of losing sight of materiality.

However, and this is the second step, a closer look reveals that the examination of material inequality in some of the best-known examples of discourse analysis in development studies is superficial at best. A much-criticised passage of Escobar's introduction reads:

> [I]nstead of the kingdom of abundance promised by theorists and politicians in the 1950s, the discourse and strategy of development produced its opposite: massive underdevelopment and impoverishment, untold exploitation and oppression. The debt crisis, the Sahelian famine, increasing poverty, malnutrition and violence are only the most pathetic signs of the failure of forty years of development. . . . most people's conditions not only did not improve but deteriorated [during the era of development].
>
> (Escobar 1995: 4f)

Here we observe again that Escobar sees discursive and material practices as closely interlinked in *development*. But the sweeping statements about impoverishment and increasing malnutrition etc. are in no way supported by empirical evidence or more detailed analysis of the role of development discourse in the debt crisis or the Sahelian famine. And they ignore, as numerous critics have pointed out (e.g. Kiely 1999: 37), the rise in living standards on average at least regarding standard indicators like life expectancy and school enrolment, which has taken place during the era of development in the Third World. According to UN figures, average life expectancy at birth in *less developed* countries rose between 1960 and 1996 from 46 to 62 years (Thomas 2000: 7).[2] A critical position may now investigate the distribution of this progress in the richer and poorer segments of these countries, examine in how far this progress is linked to interventions in the market mechanism, or even dispute that life expectancy should be seen as a crucial indicator of a good life, arguing that a shorter life as a happy and self-reliant subsistence farmer lived in communal solidarity and dignity is closer to this ideal than a longer life as an unhappy wage labourer living in competition to others and constant fear of unemployment and deprivation. But to talk about deteriorating conditions without engaging these questions can be seen as an inadequate treatment of issues of material inequality.

Nevertheless, there are also analyses of development discourse which have been based on thorough empirical studies not only of discursive but also of material practices, and it is no coincidence that these are often the most interesting because they illuminate the specific interrelation between the two. This is the case when Ferguson (1994) contrasts the discursive construction of Lesotho by the World Bank as a rural subsistence economy with the reality of many of the designated farmers being in fact migrant wage labourers in South African mines – a fact which he explains with the institutional necessities of constructing the problem of Lesotho's poverty in such a way that development projects improving agricultural productivity actually make sense. A more realistic agenda for improving living standards of the poor in Lesotho, namely supporting workers' struggles in South Africa, was inconceivable for organisations involved in *development*. Another example is provided by Mitchell (1995) who shows that USAID constructs itself as a rational consciousness outside of Egypt while in fact being a powerful actor in the country working to channel heavily subsidised grain from US producers to the country which allowed higher meat consumption of more prosperous classes while at the same time demanding an end to subsidies of the national state. Despite acting as an interested party for international and national classes, the agency engaged in necessary self-deception on the level of discourse which enabled it to maintain its material practices. So, and this is the last step of the argument, the combination of the analysis of discursive and material practices which some authors engage in has not only produced original and convincing research but has also demonstrated that a focus on discourse need not lead to losing sight of materiality.

Homogenisation and overgeneralisation

A common critique is that already talking about development discourse in the singular unduly homogenises a very diverse field of statements and vastly different concepts – simply put, it even ignores the differences between capitalist development and socialist development. In general, one can reply that it may well be worthwhile to explore (differences notwithstanding) the striking commonalities of even these two discourses: the emphasis on technological progress, economic growth and the privileging of modern, scientific forms of knowledge – as was done by Ivan Illich, whose critique could be applied to both kinds of modern societies. Yet we have to be more specific than that.

Probably the most sophisticated critique of this point is provided by Gasper who argues that 'a plurality of practices [in "development"] requires a plurality of concepts' (1996: 170). Taking the examples of Ferguson and Escobar, who both argue that 'bureaucratic control is an essential component of the deployment of development' (Escobar 1995: 145; see also Ferguson 1994: 255), Gasper correctly points out that '[t]his "development" then seems to exclude free-marketeers and important approaches prominent in the 1980s and 1990s' (Gasper 1996: 169). Indeed one central point in what Toye (1987) has called the 'counter-revolution in development theory and policy' of neoliberalism was to dismantle the developmental state and its bureaucracy. One could, however, argue that these neoliberal policies in fact constitute a significant departure from development discourse, as I have done in chapter 8. Yet Gasper has a point when he writes that 'these and other authors . . . give to an ideal type of one part of development discourse (often a different ideal type per author) the status of a description of the whole', leading to 'oversimplification and misrepresentation of complex discursive fields' (Gasper 1996: 169). In this context, he points to Moore (1995) whose identification of equity, democracy and sustainability as the core concepts of development discourse might have been plausible for the 1990s (and even then not all would agree – what about the market?), but certainly not for the 1960s.[3]

Gasper also takes issue with Ferguson's (and others') hypothesis that depoliticisation (see section 2) was a central element of development discourse and argues that this description 'do[es] not fit the language of political conditionality or human rights', trying to make the point that the heterogeneity of development discourse is ignored. Obviously the discourse of good governance which rose to prominence during the 1990s (after the end of the Cold War!) addresses political issues and at first sight does not seem compatible with the hypothesis. Yet if good governance is defined as 'sound development management' (World Bank 1992: 1) or as 'the manner in which power is exercised in the management of a country's economic and social resources for development' (World Bank 1992: 3), politics is reduced to a technical matter: 'what the tethering of politics to governance does is to marginalise questions about authentic degrees of democratisation within both government and society, in favour of issues of functional utility related to development performance. The effect, ultimately, is to de-politicise policy debates while still casting them within a normative framework which subordinates democracy to development' (Schmitz 1995: 74f). So following Schmitz (1995) as well as Abrahamsen (2000) and Mkandawire (2010), one could see good governance (at least the way it was deployed in development policy since the 1990s in the context of structural adjustment) precisely as a depoliticised version of politics.[4] Therefore in this case Gasper's point is not a convincing rejection of the attempt to generalise about development discourse.

So Gasper is right about warning of overgeneralisation if one writes about the discourse of development in the singular. Yet overgeneralisation is not a necessary feature of such writing. Of course there is a bewildering array of different historical, geographical and thematic contexts and one should always be aware of that. But generalisation is the stuff that theory is made of, the element that sets it apart from mere description or history. And I would argue it is not only possible, but even necessary to reflect which discursive structures Truman's point 4, World Bank reports of the 1980s and current reports on the Sustainable Development Goals have in common.

Questions of agency

It is true that theoretical works based on Foucault are conventionally strong on structures and weak on agency. However, not all studies of discourse in development studies belong to this camp.[5] The frequent reference to Truman's inaugural address as the starting point of development discourse (e.g. in the works of Escobar, Sachs or Esteva) already implies an emphasis on individual agency which is difficult to reconcile with Foucaults earlier very structuralist writings. Further, for those analyses belonging to the camp of Post-Development, it can be observed that by pointing to the rejection of development discourse and resistance to development projects in social movements and indigenous communities in the South, they do attribute agency to those often seen as the passive objects of this discourse.

Yet regarding the fact that these people are sometimes seen as manipulated by the 'ideology of development' if they do not resist (e.g. Rahnema 1997), one might point to the fact that this is a rather narrow conceptualisation of agency: either being manipulated by a discourse or explicitly resisting it. James Scott (1985, 1990) has shown that poor people's agency often takes other and more subtle forms than outright resistance – which is a dangerous option for the weak. In development studies, few people have analysed the transformations and appropriations of development discourse by subjects in the South. If these are taken into account, *development* does no longer *merely* look like a technocratic discourse allowing to uphold the colonial division of labour, but as a discourse which *also* enables unions, parties and anticolonial movements in the South (and later the heads of state of the independent states) to pose demands and make claims regarding social and economic progress which could not be dismissed out of hand by colonial officials and Northern politicians (see chapter 6 and Cooper 1997: 84).

One interesting example of an indigenous engagement with development discourse is provided by Wainwright (2008) who examines the Maya in Belize's Toledo district and the discourse of Mayanism describing them and constructing their identity as nonmodern since colonial times and legitimising interventions in their way of life. He focuses in particular on the Maya atlas, an attempt at

countermapping in which the Maya portray their land and their culture, opposing attempts to assimilate and settle them. Wainwright shows, however, that
this atlas includes discursive elements from nationalism, international law and
sustainable development, and how their self-representation blanks out ambiva-
lences and hybridities – in fact, is even shaped by a romantic Mayanism. External
influences visible in everyday life of Maya communities such as rice, wage labour,
chain saws and Christianity, do not appear in the atlas. 'The meaning of what
constitutes "Maya" space in the Atlas is produced through a set of exclusions'
(Wainwright 2008: 257), also concerning gender relations and marital violence.
Thus even in explicitly resisting the discourse of those who define their way of
life as *less developed*, the Maya atlas betrays the influence of these discourses of
colonialism and *development*, excluding all that they have actually appropriated
from the Western modernisers in terms of discursive and material practices and
attempting to conform to the image of the noble savages. Here, discourse analysis
in development reveals an exertion of agency in the South which simultaneously
denies its own agency.

Political alternatives

The greater part of analyses of discourse in development studies is visibly concerned with a critique of relations of power and often also with the promotion
of political alternatives. These alternatives take different shapes. While Escobar
outlined the 'defence and promotion of localized, pluralistic grassroots movements' (1995: 215), Rist, when answering the question 'What is to be done?',
broadened the range of possibilities to 'self-organization', 'finding new ways of
social linkage' and collectively 'secure [one's] existence' (1997: 243), but also
considered constructive and deconstructive criticism of the existing order as
legitimate alternatives (242–248).

The most interesting and thoughtful answer to the same question was in my
view given by Ferguson:

> 'What is to be done?' demands first of all an answer to the question, 'By whom?'
> Often, the question was put to me in the form 'What should they do?' . . .
> The 'they' here is an imaginary collective subject . . . Such a 'they' clearly
> needs to be broken up. The inhabitants of Lesotho do not share the same
> interests or the same circumstances, and they do not act as a single unit. . . .
> the interests represented by governmental elites . . . are not congruent with
> those of the governed . . . There is not one question – 'what is to be done' –
> but hundreds: what should the mineworkers do, what should the abandoned
> old women do, what should the unemployed do, and so on. It seems, at the
> least, presumptuous to offer prescriptions here. The toiling miners and the
> abandoned old women know the tactics proper to their own situation far
> better than any expert does. Indeed, the only general answer to the question,
> 'What should they do?' is: 'They are doing it!' . . . A second, and apparently
> less arrogant, form of the question is to ask . . . 'what should we do?' But once

again, the crucial question is, which 'we'? . . . What should we scholars and intellectuals working in or concerned about the Third World do? . . . One of the most important forms of engagement is simply the political participation in one's own society that is appropriate to any citizen. This is perhaps particularly true for citizens of a country like the United States, where – thanks to an imperialistic power projected across the globe – national politics powerfully impacts upon the rest of the world.

(Ferguson 1994: 280f, 282, 285f)

In this section, Ferguson does not only suggest counterhegemonic alternative points of engagement, he also soothes those worried about the neglect of class (and gender!) by pointing to the relations of oppression concealed by a national collective and at the same time reveals the presumptuousness of outside experts on *development* advising poor people around the world what they should be doing. So discourse analysis in development studies does seem capable of reflecting upon and providing political alternatives.

While all the arguments listed in this section should not be interpreted to refute the points of criticism for any and all contributions to discourse analysis in development studies (far from it), the general point to be made here is that if they occur it has nothing to do with the approach itself – contrary to what Peet claims in the quote at the beginning.

Significant arguments of discourse analysis in development studies

Having dealt with the criticisms voiced against it, we now attempt to assess the contribution of discourse analysis in development studies. In order to do so, I will reiterate the arguments of some key works in this section which I deem significant. I maintain that these approaches have yielded crucial insights for development studies in regard to the following features of at least orthodox development discourse as articulated by most development agencies and mainstream scholars:

1) Naturalisation
2) Othering
3) Legitimisation
4) Hierarchisation
5) Depoliticisation
6) Appropriation.

Naturalisation and the universal scale

The first and maybe most fundamental achievement discourse analysis in development studies provides is the insight that the categories and strategies of *development* imply a certain perspective which is contingent – in contrast to being the natural and normal way of seeing things. That societies can be compared according to their level of *development*, that there are *developed* and *less developed* countries, and that the latter can be found in Africa, Asia and Latin America and are in need of *development*, development experts, development projects and development aid provided by the former, are assumptions that are by no means self-evident. Discourse analysis has shown that they belong to a certain historical and geopolitical context – the aftermath of World War II and the beginning Cold War, although of course there are predecessors in colonial development (Hodge et al. 2014) and 19th century social policy and post-Enlightenment social engineering (Cowen/Shenton 1996). As Ferguson describes it:

> Like 'civilization' in the 19th century, 'development' is the name not only for a value, but also for a dominant problematic or interpretative grid through which the impoverished regions of the world are known to us. Within this interpretative grid, a host of everyday observations are rendered intelligible and meaningful. The images of the ragged poor of Asia thus become legible as markers of a stage of development . . . Within this problematic, it appears self-evident that debtor Third-World nation states and starving peasants share a common 'problem', that both lack a single 'thing': 'development'.
> (Ferguson 1994: xiii)

Escobar agrees that the discourse of development has 'created a space in which only certain things could be said and even imagined' (1995: 39) and goes on to point out 'even today most people in the West (and many parts of the Third World) have great difficulty thinking about Third World situations and people in terms other than those provided by the development discourse' (1995: 12), terms like poverty, malnutrition, illiteracy, etc. Now the point of discourse analysis is not to claim that these terms are pure fantasy and have no empirical referent in these regions, the point is that other terms which also have empirical referents do not form part of the discourse, the representation of reality is partial and structured according to certain stereotypes, excluding those parts which do not fit. The question of which stereotypes we are talking about will be answered in the subsection on Othering. But regardless of their content, there is already a problematic implication in any talk about *development*, about *more* and *less developed* countries. According to Esteva, '[developed] is a comparative adjective, whose base support is the assumption, very Western but unacceptable and indemonstrable, of the oneness, homogeneity and linear evolution of the world', using one fragment of the world 'as a general point of reference' (1992: 11f). Thus the discourse of development assumes a consensus on what is seen as *developed*, progressive and desirable. If one were to take serious the talk that 'people have to decide for themselves what they see as development' (see chapter 7), this universal scale would disappear and we could not compare societies unless they had explicitly agreed to one scale.

Now to what extent the discourse of development really limits what can be said and establishes a universal scale of measurement for all societies, cannot be examined here empirically. But that this question can be posed at all is an achievement of discourse analysis in development studies. It introduced the linguistic turn into the thinking about global inequality and North-South relations, enabling us to question the very basic categories of our discipline.

Othering and the problematisation of deviance

The naturalisation of the Self enables the problematisation of the Other. The universal scale allows to measure and compare according to a certain norm. In development discourse, this is no neutral endeavour, but inextricably linked with the construction of the Self as superior, as the norm, and the Other as inferior, as deviant. Based on this Eurocentric scale, the majority of humanity was defined as *underdeveloped* through development discourse: 'they ceased being what they were, in all their diversity' and were burdened with the challenge to 'escape from the undignified condition called underdevelopment' (Esteva 1992: 7).[6] As we have seen in chapter 3, the discourse of development evolved out of colonial discourse, but employed similar binaries describing 'us' and 'them'. And yet it is not quite correct to reduce the shift from the 'civilized/barbarian dichotomy' to that of 'development/underdevelopment' (Duffield 2007b: 228) to a 'shift in vocabulary' (Biccum 2002: 49) – the recognition of the sovereignty of formerly colonised peoples is not a trifle. We are faced with the 'emergence of an international discourse that reproduces the dualism of the colonial relationship without its explicit racism and without its reliance on the direct exercise of political power by an imperial government' (Cooper 1997: 83f). However, in both discourses, the Other is seen not only as inferior, but as a backward version of the Self. Nandy identified this discursive operation as the 'transformation of geo-cultural difference into historical stages' (Nandy 1992: 146). Consequently, our own 'modern' society, in the words of Manzo, 'was placed in hierarchical opposition to other areas of the globe which remained "traditional," that is, less cosmopolitan, less scientific, less secular, less rational, less individualist, and less democratic. They were defined solely in relation to the West, the foundational source of "development," as an inferior or derivative form' (Manzo 1991: 10).

Escobar has described this process of Othering as an 'infantilization of the Third World' (1995: 30) in analogy to the view that these backward peoples need tutelage and education, and as a 'medicalization of the political gaze' (1995: 30) as they were, in the new discourse, perceived not as biologically inferior but as stricken by disease, malnutrition, and so on. He contends that *development* 'proceeded by creating "abnormalities" (such as the "illiterate", the "underdeveloped", the "malnourished" . . . which it would later treat and reform' (1995: 41). This latter activity will be dealt with later, here we are mainly concerned with the problematisation, which also according to Li takes place through 'identifying deficiencies' (Li 2007: 7). All of this of course implies that the problem lies with the deviance from the norm in the non-West (the lack of capital, technology and modern values, see Escobar 1995: 162), not with the norm, i.e. the West itself: that the West may have had something to do with the problems in the South, is ruled out in this problematisation. This is in part due to a methodological nationalism in liberal development discourse[7] which sees each country as a kind of container unrelated to others – 'a free-standing entity, rather than a particular position within a larger arrangement of transnational economic and political forces' (Mitchell 1995: 147) – and in part due to 'an elision of colonial relations of power' (Biccum 2002: 44), neglecting the historical entanglements which allowed Europe's rise.

It has to be mentioned again that what has been described here are dominant structures, but is not an accurate description of anything that has been said and written in development policy, let alone theory. Nevertheless, even in the 21st century we find processes of Othering in development discourse which are remarkably similar to earlier, colonial representations of the South. Examples for this are Eriksson Baaz's analysis of interviews with white development aid workers in Tanzania, who consistently characterise 'the Africans' as unreliable, passive, irrational and 'situated at a different stage of development and Enlightenment' (2005: 167) or Bendix's (2013) critique of the racist imagery used in poster campaigns of the German ministry for development cooperation.

Legitimisation and the promise of betterment

One central function of development discourse is legitimisation through the promise of betterment, but the object of legitimisation varies depending on the specific discourse. In the discourse of immanent development (according to Cowen/Shenton, 1996, concerned with the evolution of capitalist society), the issue is the legitimisation of capitalism and private enterprise; in the discourse of intentional development (concerned with planned interventions), the issue is the legitimisation of these interventions and the development apparatus, and in both cases the secondary object is the existing political and economic order on the national or international level.

In both liberal and interventionist development discourse, the legitimisation works via the promise to improve the lives of *less developed* people, to solve the problem of poverty and ameliorate the deficiencies identified in the diagnosis, either through investments and the market or through projects and planned interventions in the market (economic growth, technological progress and modern values feature in both versions). In both cases, criticisms concerning the failure of the promise to deliver in the past are repelled by a mechanism which can be called the shifting of signifiers. It builds on the polysemy of the term *development* (see chapter 10): one the one hand, the term refers to a transformation towards a modern, capitalist, industrial economy, on the other, to an improvement in living standards and reducing poverty. By shifting between the two meanings, it can now be argued that the remedy to poverty is a transformation towards a capitalist economy even though this transformation might cause or contribute to the impoverishment of some part of the population: they are poor (i.e. lack *development* in the second sense) so they need to be integrated into the capitalist world market (i.e. *development* in the first sense) (Ferguson 1994: 15, 55).[8] This shift also allows for what Gasper (1996: 150) calls the 'beyond criticism gambit': 'Negative experiences of industrialization or capitalism or whatever then become excused as not real examples, not "real development"; and the concept of "development" can live on as at the same time a definite programme and an untarnishable promise' (Gasper 1996: 149). The actions of development organisations by definition bring *development* and if they do not, then something went wrong in the implementation, but the policy or programme itself is 'not to blame' (150).[9]

Together with the legitimacy provided by expert knowledge, the polysemy of *development* enables the reformulation of the promise even after obvious failure. The meaning of the term can be shifted to include new aspects. After the Pearson report had shown clearly that development policy's growth strategy had not reduced poverty and inequality during the 1960s, the World Bank discovered the rural poor as a new target group and redefined *development* as rural development, adding new integrated rural development projects to its standard infrastructure projects. In the words of Sachs:

> The logic of this conceptual operation is obvious enough: the idea of development was not abandoned; indeed, its field of application was enlarged. Similarly, in rapid succession, . . . the eradication of poverty, basic needs, women, and, finally, the environment, were swiftly turned into problems and became the object of special strategies. The meaning of development exploded, increasingly covering a host of contradictory practices. . . . So, development has become a shapeless, amoeba-like word. . . . Development thus has no content, but it does possess a function: it allows any intervention to be sanctified in the name of a higher, evolutionary goal.
>
> (Sachs 1990: 6; see also Esteva 1985 and 1992, Escobar 1995: 58)

Here, the legitimising function of the promise is spelled out clearly. The reformulation and renewal of the promise of betterment by the apparatus of development has been described by Duffield as an 'institutional "Groundhog day" in which every decade or two similar pronouncements are repackaged by a new generation of aid administrators and presented afresh as the way forward' (2007: 227). While Duffield describes this promise as a decidedly 'liberal strategisation of power' (231, 227), Berger (1974) has shown already in the 1970s that such a painting of a bright future to legitimate the negative sides of the current political and economic order has been a feature of both capitalist and socialist regimes in the South.

For the development apparatus of the West, the promise requires that the solutions offered match the problematisation in order to be credible: 'The West possesses the expertise, technology and management skills that the non-West is lacking. This lack is what has caused the problems of the non-West' (Mitchell 1995: 156). Thus the promise is dependent on a privileged type of knowledge, and this brings us to the next point.

Hierarchisation and the expert knowledge of trustees

While the problematisation has identified deficiencies in 'less developed' societies and the promise has announced their remedy, the claim to be able to do so is based on expert knowledge on how to achieve *development*. This in turn requires a hierarchisation of different types of knowledge (and sometimes also cultures and values), with one type (universally applicable expert knowledge) being privileged and the other (local, unscientific knowledge) denigrated (DuBois 1991: 7). Taking up the category of trusteeship (Cowen/Shenton 1996: ixf, 25, 31), Li argues that development experts and aid workers 'occupy the position of trustees, a position defined by the claim to know how others should live' (2007: 4f) – of course not with the intent to dominate them, but to *develop* them, to enhance their capacities and improve their lives. Escobar also contends that within the discourse, development professionals should be entrusted with the management of social life identified as *underdeveloped* because their 'specialized knowledge allegedly qualified them for this task' (1995: 52). This power entrusted to them relies on this knowledge which consists in the ability of the development professionals to ascertain procedures for diagnosis and treatment of the *underdeveloped* (Apthorpe 1996: 20).

Yet while this knowledge about *development* presents itself as technical and neutral, Cooper and Packard (1997b: 19) remind us that 'development is fundamentally about changing how people conduct their lives, and the very claim to technical knowledge is in itself a political act.' Assuming that *development* is about improvement and a good life, Berger (1974: 35, 45) concurs: 'People who speak of development should frankly admit that they are engaged in the business of ethics and, at least potentially, of politics. . . . Development is not something to be decided by experts, simply because there are no experts on the desirable goals of human life.'

But what if experts rightly claim that their knowledge leads to an improvement in the lives of their beneficiaries? And the latter willingly accept the advice of the experts? Here, the characteristic (and controversial) position of Foucauldian discourse analysis is illustrated by DuBois (1991): after the lifestyles of the beneficiaries have become transparent, experts proscribe safer, more efficient, healthier and generally better ways of doing things (1991: 21). As a result of these disciplinary techniques at the micro-level,

> an accompanying and unspoken hierarchization is produced between the ways, in general, of performing tasks in the two cultures as these introductions multiply. The hierarchization of cultures that characterizes the categorization of 'developed' and 'developing' nations is not imposed from the top down but is the sum (effect) of a multiplicity of localized hierarchizations or judgments regarding economic, political, social, and cultural aspects. Finally, even though many of the norms erected by relations of disciplinary power in the context of development are based not on the discourse of the human sciences but on that of the natural sciences (and therefore 'really are true') – boiling drinking water to kill bacteria, using fertilizer to increase yields, and so on – the effects mentioned above are still produced.
>
> (DuBois 1991: 22)

So even if the knowledge is correct, a hierarchisation takes place. This hierarchisation is the result of the general structure of development discourse that the

problems of *underdevelopment* are located in the South, while the North possesses the knowledge to solve these problems – experts are sent only in one direction and development cooperation is not designed as intercultural exchange,
although one can think of indicators and social problems where the latter might
well make sense for the North: suicide rates, drug abuse, treatment of the elderly,
etc. (DuBois 1991: 25).

Now one may perfectly well adopt the ethical position that engendering power
relations and subordinating local knowledge and culture is legitimate if the introduction of scientific practices can save lives – but at least one should be aware of
these effects and implications, in particular for the production of *developed* identities supposedly part of a superior culture as well as *less developed* identities supposedly part of an inferior culture (1991: 25). These effects are what leads Escobar to
the hypothesis that the institutionalisation of development discourse in agencies
producing and circulating knowledge about the Third World 'has been able to
integrate, manage, and control countries and populations in increasingly detailed
and encompassing ways' (Escobar 1995: 47) and DuBois to the statement that
'one may understand the process of development as the increased governance
of the Third World' (1991: 28). However, what both seem to neglect somewhat
is the question of agency already mentioned in the first section of this chapter.
Therefore, processes of appropriation and hybridisation need to be discussed as
well. But before that, we have to turn to the political consequence of the claim
that the knowledge about *development* is merely technical: the depoliticisation of
conflicts.

Depoliticisation and the common interest

The discourse of development, at least the one employed by most development
agencies, assumes that *development* is something that benefits everyone and therefore no one can object to, something removed from conflicts over political and
economic questions. Simply put, this discourse wants to help the poor without
hurting the rich (on a national and international level). It has to do so in order
to gain support and legitimacy, but in doing so neglects an analysis of the structural causes of poverty and depoliticises the conflicts and divisions in society. The
most explicit articulation of this insight comes from Ferguson, who explains the
distortions he finds in development discourse's representation of Lesotho through
institutional necessities:

> An academic analysis is of no use to a 'development' agency unless it provides
> a place for the agency to plug itself in, unless it provides a charter for the sort
> of intervention that the agency is set up to do. An analysis which suggests that
> the causes of poverty in Lesotho are political and structural (not technical
> and geographical), that the national government is part of the problem (not
> a neutral instrument for its solution), and that meaningful change can only
> come through revolutionary social transformation in South Africa has no
> place in 'development' discourse simply because 'development' agencies are

not in the business of promoting political realignments or supporting revolutionary struggles. . . . For an analysis to meet the needs of 'development'
institutions, it must do what academic discourse inevitably fails to do; it must
make Lesotho out to be an enormously promising candidate for the only sort
of intervention a 'development' agency is capable of launching: the apolitical, technical 'development' intervention.

(Ferguson 1994: 68f)

Ferguson goes on to argue that '[b]y uncompromisingly reducing poverty to a
technical problem, and by promising technical solutions to the sufferings of the
powerless and oppressed people', the discourse of development was 'the principal
means through which the question of poverty is de-politicised in the world today'
(256). And although development projects are always concerned with the transfer of resources and social restructuring which benefits some groups more than
others and thus with political questions, the development apparatus denies its
political role and functions as an 'anti-politics machine' (256).

This argument is supported by numerous other analyses of development discourse. Mitchell, in his analysis of USAID in Egypt, finds that the organisation
is 'a central element in configurations of power within the country' but 'must
imagine itself as a rational consciousness standing outside the country' – a necessary self-deception to maintain its role as a neutral provider of technical knowledge (Mitchell 1995: 149). Mitchell investigates the exclusions and silences in
USAID's analyses and concludes: 'Questions of power or inequality, whether on
the global level of international grain markets, state subsidies, and the arms trade,
or the more local level of landholding, food supplies and income distribution, will
nowhere be discussed' (156). These exclusions illustrate 'the necessary limits of
development discourse' (ibid.).

A more recent study by Li (2007) of development projects in Central Sulawesi
in Indonesia confirms Ferguson's and Mitchell's findings. The project documents
neglected political-economic causes of poverty and reframed social and environmental problems 'in terms amenable to a technical solution' (2007: 126). And
even when police and army collaborated with illegal practices of timber extraction, sabotaging the sustainability objectives of the project, the development
agencies were not interested: 'refractory findings suggesting that "the government" is not dedicated to the public good cannot be processed by the development machine' (134). Li empirically identifies three limitations of development
agency discourse, all contributing to depoliticisation: the assumption that the
state apparatus can be made to work in the public interest, the ignorance of
experts to the power relation implicit in their positioning and the credo that
capitalist enterprise and the search for profit can only be a solution to poverty,
not a cause (267, 275).

Escobar agrees that development discourse (by what he calls professionaliza-
tion) 'remove[s] problems from the political and cultural realms to the more neutral realm of science' (1995: 45) and similarly concludes that 'the problem [of rural
poverty] is thought to be characterized by exclusion from markets and state policy,

not by exploitation within the market and the state' (150). In the words of Rist (1997: 78), it 'presented "development" as a set of technical measures outside the realm of political debate (utilisation of scientific knowledge, growth of productivity, expansion of international trade)' serving the 'common good'. Moore (1995: 22) stresses that *development* usually functions as a catch-all phrase capturing goals and aspirations of all parties and Gasper remarks that the discourse works through the 'concealment of divisive issues' (Gasper 1996: 151). *Development* thus is, since Truman, in everyone's interest: we as donors (or investors) can help the poor and at the same time pursue our economic or geopolitical interest. Rist identifies the 'yoking together of solidarity and self-interest' as 'one of the basic elements in "development" discourse, as a way of convincing both those who emphasised the "humanitarian imperative" and those who focused on national interest' (1997: 91). If the argument is not based on investment and markets, it is based on the crises in the South which have to be prevented or contained through development aid before we in the North are affected negatively by drugs, migrants or terrorism: 'In fostering "their" development, we improve "our" security' (Duffield 2007: 225; see also Sachs 1999: 20–23). The argument about the enlightened self-interest sounds familiar: *development* benefits everyone and no one can object to it, it manifests the common good. That is why the transfer of resources to Village Development Committees made up of members of the ruling party in the Thaba-Tseka development project in Lesotho and the ensuing theft and sabotage elicited contradictory reactions: while a chief remarked that 'development has many enemies here', an oppositional informant commented 'politics is nowadays nicknamed development' (quoted in Ferguson 1994: 247).

Against such an 'amoeba word' that 'denotes nothing while claims the best of intentions' (Sachs 1990: 6), discourse analysis can be a useful tool, as Cornwall has pointed out, if we apply what Cornwall calls constructive deconstruction: 'the taking apart of the different meanings that these words have acquired. . . . in development discourse. . . . this process can bring into view dissonance between these meanings. If the use of buzzwords as fuzzwords conceals ideological differences, the process of constructive deconstruction reveals them.' (Cornwall 2010: 14)

Appropriation and the hybridisation of development discourse

The last feature of development discourse to be discussed here is one that is often neglected in the analyses cited above and one which corresponds to the critical comments on the question of agency in the first section. It concerns the transformation of the discourse through 1) its appropriation through actors in the South and 2) the effects of the critique articulated by discourse analysis in development studies.

Regarding the appropriation, it can be observed that although the discourse of development was initiated by Western actors concerned about access to raw materials and markets in the South, it would be myopic to assume that all Southern actors employing this discourse were manipulated and pursuing someone else's interest. Analysing colonial development in Africa in the 1940s and 1950s,

Cooper (1997: 84f) has shown that although the discourse of development 'was originally supposed to sustain empire', it 'did not simply spring from the brow of colonial leaders, but was to a significant extent forced upon them, by the collective actions of workers'. Once it was articulated,

> developmentalist arguments . . . were something trade union and political leaders in Africa could engage with, appropriate, and turn back. The framework allowed them to pose demands in forms that could be understood in London and Paris, that could not be dismissed as 'primitive'. Political parties could assert that true development required sovereign control over a development apparatus . . . Much as one can read the universalism of development discourse as a form of European particularism imposed abroad, it could also be read . . . as a rejection of the fundamental premises of colonial rule, a firm assertion of people of all races to participate in global politics and lay claim to a globally defined standard of living.
>
> (Cooper 1997: 84)

So, and this is important to note regarding the contribution of discourse analysis to development studies, development discourse did *not only* function as a discourse of hierarchisation and depoliticisation, but it *also* worked (as has also been shown in chapter 6) as a discourse of claims and rights for those who were designated as deficient and inadequate by it. Ferguson (2006: 186) has remarked that many people pointing to a lack of *development* or modernity in their context are referring to inadequate socioeconomic conditions or a low standard of living. Here, we can conclude, development discourse provides a language to criticise material inequality and articulate 'expectations of modernity' (Ferguson 1999). Abandoning the promise of *development* as in neoliberal discourse leaves them without a prospect of material improvement and a 'de-developmentalized' global hierarchy (Ferguson 2006: 189, see chapter 8).

This insight may also shed new light on the possibility of resignifying the term *development*. Contrary to the position taken in chapter 5, Cornwall argues that Laclau's notion of chains of equivalences between signifiers may prove to be useful here:

> *Used in a chain of equivalence with* good governance, accountability, results-based management, reform *and* security, . . . *words like* democracy *and* empowerment *come to mean something altogether different from their use in conjunction with* citizenship, participation, solidarity, rights, *and* social justice. . . . *Thinking of words in constellations rather than in the singular opens up further strategies for reclaiming 'lost' words, as well as salvaging some of the meanings that were never completely submerged.*
>
> (Cornwall 2010: 15)

So would it be a strategy for reclaiming *development* to use it in a constellation with *hospitality, degrowth, sharing, autonomy* and *commons*? I have no answer here, but remain doubtful.

A second point has to be made, and this concerns the transformations in development discourse which came about as a result of its critique. Often linked with postcolonial and Post-Development approaches, discourse analysis in development studies has become somewhat influential in academia (not policy) during the past two decades. As a consequence, almost every introduction to the field of development studies at least mentions and often engages with its critique. A striking example to me is the new edition of the Development Reader (Chari/Corbridge 2008). While in the first edition (Corbridge 1995), one out of 27 texts came from one of the three mentioned approaches, in the new edition there are nine out of 54 – a more than fourfold increase. As mentioned in the beginning, the work of Escobar is a top contender for the highest number of quotes in development studies. And still discourse analysis perceives itself as marginalised (della Faille 2011) – why? Eriksson Baaz (2005) gives the following answer. Of course the critics have been influential and even the development industry does not remain entirely unperturbed by their arguments, but at the same time this means that a decisive critique is more difficult to maintain if one has to admit that the establishment has adopted some of the critique. So it is easier for the critics to portray themselves as marginalised in order not to compromise the severity and appropriateness of their critique of the development apparatus:

> [B]y placing the critics of development [solely] outside the development industry [they] tend to neglect the workings and influence of their own critique. . . . any influential, successful critique adopted by the mainstream Other will destabilize the opposing identity (as an alternative inherently different from the mainstream). The neglect of influence and simplistic representations of development practitioners can thus be seen as, partly, reflecting a destabilized, threatened identity, which feeds a need to distance the alternative, critical Self further from the mainstream Other.
>
> (Eriksson Baaz 2005: 169f)

So while it does make a lot of sense for discourse analysis in development studies to examine how institutions like the World Bank have adopted once oppositional concepts like sustainability and empowerment, robbing them of their critical edge, an equally useful task is to investigate how critical concepts managed to unsettle and change institutional practice. What is decried as co-optation by the establishment can from another perspective be seen as a first step in the struggle for change, as changing the terrain of discourse to one's advantage (Cornwall 2010: 13).

Added value? Some conclusions

So what has the research in this book, what have the arguments of the preceding chapters added to the state of the art outlined above? I believe that the archaeological and genealogical attempts undertaken here yielded some added value, and that this contribution can be (incompletely) summed up in the following points:

1) On the general level it could be shown that despite early programmes of colonial development and despite continuities regarding the binary division between the progressive Self and the backward Other, the Eurocentric evolutionism and the social technology linked to the notion of trusteeship, the discourses of colonialism and *development* can be described as separate discourses in the area of North-South relations. In the new discourse, the explicitly racist element (they are unable to govern themselves) is abandoned and the trusteeship for the *development* of the (former) colonies is given over to national elites. Also, the objects of discourse are constituted more in the area of economic geography (*underdeveloped* regions) and less in that of biology (uncivilised peoples). The new discourse was far more attractive to people in the South because it offered to those designated as backward the opportunity to catch up in the economic race on their own through modernisation, industrialisation and growth – although supported by investment, technology and aid from the West (chapters 3 and 4).

2) The analysis of rules of formation showed the existence of mechanisms within the discourse of development which those who employ the discourse are usually unaware of. The most notable among these is the subject position which comes about as a result of the rules of the enunciative modality of the discourse: anyone speaking in the discourse occupies the subject position of someone who knows what *development* is and how to achieve it. As *development* is concerned with a desirable state of society, this subject position automatically subordinates other visions of such a state and thus invariably contains an authoritarian element. Knowledge about *development* therefore is knowledge about the deficiencies of others' ways of life and involves political claims presented as technical knowledge ('this is how you should live' or the slightly less arrogant 'this is how we should live') (chapters 4 and 5).

3) The analysis has further affirmed and specified two significant points which have been made before. While Sachs (1990), Esteva (1992), Escobar (1995), Easterly (2002) and Duffield (2007b) have made the point about the recurrent promise of development discourse to fight poverty, the archaeological analysis has yielded that the appearance of objects in the discourse is regulated according to a pattern which renders visible ever new aspects of these objects identified as deviant according to the Western norm. These new aspects become the object of treatment and reform, allowing an articulation of recipes and a reformulation of the promise. Failure of the strategy is explained by an inadequate implementation, but soon also leads to research highlighting a new aspect responsible for the failure and allowing a reformulation of the promise. There is a recurrent cycle of diagnosis – prescription and promise – disappointment – new diagnosis, etc. in which the development industry produces new concepts and strategies regularly (chapter 4).

4) The second point made before concerns the characterisation of the *development* concept as an amoeba, i.e. to the argument that the frequent redefinitions let the term appear shapeless or devoid of any precise content (Esteva 1985 and 1992, Sachs 1990). The analysis has affirmed that the signifier

development can be linked to any signified, to any activity, if and as long as it assumes the form of a technical, nonpolitical intervention in the interest of the poor (chapter 10).

5) One point neglected in most critical research on development discourse is the appropriation of the concept by Southern actors. An analysis of the appropriation of the discourse by elites in the decolonising and postcolonial states showed that its results had different political effects on the national and the international level. While the technocratic and authoritarian principle of trusteeship was affirmed on the national scale, it was challenged and rejected on the international level. This illustrates a theoretical point made by Foucault (1978: 100): the tactical polyvalence of discourses (chapter 6).

6) Regarding the inclusion of oppositional concepts in the discourse of development agencies in the context of its transformation after the crisis of development in the 1980s, my research has examined the effects of the concepts of participation, sustainability and heterogeneity on the discourse of development workers. Because the new concepts were at odds with some of the basic rules of formation of the discourse, they led to incoherence and contradictions in the interviews. For example: the critique of top-down procedures in development projects has led to the inclusion of participatory principles, but taking seriously these principles (manifest in sentences like 'the people have to decide themselves what *development* is for them') is at odds with the discursive practice of defining *development* (chapter 7).

7) Regarding another aspect of the transformation of development discourse, we could observe clear differences between the discourse of development and the discourse of neoliberalism and globalisation. While the former assumed two different kinds of subjects in international politics (*developed* and *underdeveloped* countries) and correspondingly special rules in trade for the weaker kind, the latter knows just one kind and accordingly just one set of rules. The new discourse is no longer dedicated to the principle of social technology (aiming at the transformation of *less developed* into *developed* regions), but to the principle of adjustment to the demands of the world market. Interventions in the market mechanism, which are standard tools in developmental states and development aid, are seen as ineffective and damaging in the neoliberal discourse. This also means that the promise of 'developing the less developed regions', which was linked to the vision of global socioeconomic equality, has been abandoned in neoliberalism (chapter 8).

8) Historical analyses have exemplified the massive shift in the representation of North-South relations and the struggle against poverty between the 1970s and the 2000s as a result of the influence of neoliberal discourse. They have also shown the emergence of a neoliberal discourse of development that combines the inevitability and benevolence of market-based strategies of one discourse with the insistence on financial transfers and the necessity of development institutions of the other discourse – although the assumptions of these discourses actually contradict one another. The research has illustrated different variants of this discourse in different reports of the World Bank and the UN (chapters 9 and 11).

9) Finally, the historical comparison between Truman's speech of 1949 and an SDG report of 2014 has shown that through the concept of sustainability, industrialised societies today also become conceivable as objects of intervention in the discourse (although not yet in practice). But it has also demonstrated the persistence of certain structures of development discourse (the diagnosis of global poverty as a problem, the promise to be able to solve the problem today, the recipes of technical knowledge and economic growth and the credo of a harmony of objectives) over a period of more than six decades (chapter 14). In this light, Escobar's diagnosis (1995: 42) that 'although the discourse has gone through a series of structural changes, the architecture of the discursive formation laid down in 1945–55 has remained unchanged, allowing the discourse to adapt to new conditions' may fail to explore the transformations discussed above, but still appears surprisingly plausible.

Regarding the contribution of discourse analysis to development studies, my opinion is that it has beyond doubt convincingly pointed out the relations of power implicit in the discourse and at its best (Ferguson 1994, Mitchell 1995, Li 2007, Wainwright 2008) showed the entanglement of capitalism, state, the development apparatus and development discourse; the limitations of the discourse caused by institutional necessities and material interests as well as the limitations of the practice caused by discursive boundaries.

To the critics of discourse analysis, one point must be conceded: We must not stop at deconstruction and provide alternatives. Even if the current discourse of development includes Eurocentric, depoliticising and authoritarian features, it is the most influential discourse in which claims to material improvements for the poorer classes can be articulated today. The challenge remains to construct the problem of global economic inequality in a way that is devoid of these features, in a way that offers more political and more progressive possibilities of engaging the problem. For if theory does not serve to overthrow all those conditions in which humans are abased, enslaved, abandoned, contemptible beings (Marx 1844: 18) and to contribute to building more humane conditions – how can we justify it in a world like this?

Notes

1   So in this respect, Nederveen Pieterse (2011) is right in rejecting della Faille's marginalisation hypothesis. Yet when he supports his counterclaim that development studies has experienced the linguistic turn and that 'all critical development scholars use discourse analysis, except for quantitative scholars and empiricists and policy specialists' (2011: 237), he is excluding three substantial groups plus all noncritical scholars – which might together well add up to a majority. Empirical studies of this question may be helpful.

2   The rise is even more impressive regarding the time span from 1950 and 2010: from 42 to 67 years (UN 2012: 4).

3   He also points to Manzo's (1991) argument that the idea of the modern West as a model of achievement which would allegedly be disproven by non-Western

(countermodernist) models of development. This is not quite convincing: trying to catch up with and overtake the West (Gasper mentions Japan and South Korea) does imply adopting the model and one would have to look closely in which aspects another path (he also mentions Mugabe and Nyerere) has been taken.

4   'Good governance thus simply became one more instrument for ensuring the implementation of adjustment programmes. Because macroeconomic policies were sacrosanct, it was important that the democratic institutions that might come with good governance were not used to undermine economic policy. This was ensured by introducing institutional reform that effectively compromised the authority of elected bodies through the insulation of policy technocrats and the creation of "autonomous" authorities' (Mkandawire 2010: 267).

5   In an earlier work (Ziai 2004) I showed that while Post-Development approaches are often seen as exemplars of discourse analysis inspired by Foucault, their theoretical approaches are closer to a traditional critique of ideology.

6   See also Shreshta (1995) for a first-hand experience of being deprived of dignity through development discourse.

7   Of course, the great achievement of dependency and world-system approaches in development theory has been to overcome this methodological nationalism.

8   Already Rostow's modernization theory implicitly employed this discursive mechanism by defining poor countries as traditional, i.e. precapitalist, excluding the possibility that poverty may be a result of an inclusion into the capitalist world-system on subordinate terms.

9   The World Bank's defence of structural adjustment is a good example of this (see also chapter 9).

Bibliography

Abrahamsen, Rita 2000: *Disciplining Democracy: Development Discourse and Good Governance in Africa*. London: Zed Books.

Alcalde, Javier Gonzalo 1987: *The Idea of Third World Development: Emerging Perspectives in the United States and Britain, 1900–1950*. Lanham, MD: University Press of America.

Apthorpe, Raymond/Gasper, Des (eds.) 1996: *Arguing Development Policy: Frames and Discourses*. London: Frank Cass.

Arndt, Heinz Wolfgang 1987: *Economic Development: The History of an Idea*. Chicago: University of Chicago Press.

Bendix, Daniel/Glokal e.V. 2013: The Big Five as Dangerous as Ever: German Development Cooperation, Colonial-Racist Imagery, and Civil Society's Response. *Critical Literacy: Theories and Practices* 7(2), 48–57.

Berger, Peter L. 1974: *Pyramids of Sacrifice: Political Ethics and Social Change*. New York: Anchor Books.

Biccum, A. R. April 2002: Interrupting the Discourse of Development: On a Collision Course with Postcolonial Theory. *Culture, Theory & Critique* 43(1), 33–50.

Biccum, A. R. April 2006: Development and the 'New' Imperialism: A Reinvention of Colonial Discourse in DFID Promotional Literature. *Third World Quarterly* 26(6), 1005–1020.

Blaikie, Piers 2000: Development: Post-, Anti-, and Populist: A Critical Review. *Environment and Planning* 32(6), 1023–1050.

Chari, Sharad/Corbridge, Stuart (eds.) 2008: *The Development Reader*. London: Routledge.

Corbridge, Stuart (ed.) 1995: *Development Studies: A Reader*. London: Edward Arnold.

Cooper, Frederick 1997: Modernizing Bureaucrats, Backward Africans, and the Development Concept. In: Cooper, Frederick/Packard, Randall (eds.) *International Development and the Social Sciences: Essays on the History and Politics of Knowledge*. Berkeley: University of California Press, 64–92.

Cooper, Frederick/Packard, Randall (eds.) 1997a: *International Development and the Social Sciences: Essays on the History and Politics of Knowledge*. Berkeley: University of California Press.

Cooper, Frederick/Packard, Randall 1997b: Introduction. In: Cooper, Frederick/Packard, Randall (eds.) *International Development and the Social Sciences: Essays on the History and Politics of Knowledge*. Berkeley: University of California Press, 1–41.

Cornwall, Andrea 2010: Introductory Overview – Buzzwords and Fuzzwords: Deconstructing Development Discourse. In: Cornwall, Andrea/Eade, Deborah (eds.) *Deconstructing Development Discourse: Buzzwords and Fuzzwords*. Bourton: Practical Action, 1–18.

Cornwall, Andrea/Eade, Deborah (eds.) 2010: *Deconstructing Development Discourse: Buzzwords and Fuzzwords*. Bourton: Practical Action.

Cowen, Michael P./Shenton, Robert W. 1996: *Doctrines of Development*. London: Routledge.

Crush, Jonathan (ed.) 1995: *Power of Development*. London: Routledge.

della Faille, Dimitri 2011: Discourse Analysis in International Development Studies: Mapping Some Contemporary Contributions. *Journal of Multicultural Discourses* 6(3), 215–235.

Duffield, Mark 2007a: *Development, Security and Unending War: Governing the World of Peoples*. London: Polity.

Duffield, Mark 2007b: Development, Territories, and People: Consolidating the External Sovereign Frontier. *Alternatives* 32(2), 225–246.

Duffield, Mark 2014: *Global Governance and the New Wars: The Merging of Development and Security*. London: Zed Books.

DuBois, Marc 1991: The Governance of the Third World: A Foucauldian Perspective on Power Relations in Development. *Alternatives* 16(1), 1–30.

Easterly, William 2002: The Cartel of Good Intentions: The Problem of Bureaucracy in Foreign Aid. *Policy Reform* 5(4), 223–250.

Eriksson Baaz, Maria 2005: *The Paternalism of Partnership: A Postcolonial Reading of Identity in Development Aid*. London: Zed Books.

Escobar, Arturo 1985: Michel Foucault and the Relevance of His Work to the Third World. *Alternatives* 10(3), 377–400.

Escobar, Arturo 1995: *Encountering Development: The Making and Unmaking of the Third World*. Princeton, NJ: Princeton University Press.

Esteva, Gustavo 1985: Development: Metaphor, Myth, Threat. *Development: Seeds of Change* 3, 78–79.

Esteva, Gustavo 1992: Development. In: Sachs, Wolfgang (ed.) *The Development Dictionary: A Guide to Knowledge as Power*. London: Zed Books, 6–25.

Ferguson, James 1994: *The Anti-politics Machine: 'Development', Depoliticization and Bureaucratic Power in Lesotho*. Minneapolis: University of Minnesota Press.

Ferguson, James 1999: *Expectations of Modernity: Myths and Meanings of Urban Life on the Zambian Copperbelt*. Berkeley: University of California Press.

Ferguson, James 2006: *Global Shadows: Africa in the Neoliberal World Order*. Durham, NC: Duke University Press.

Foucault, Michel 1978 (1976): *The History of Sexuality. Volume 1: An Introduction*. New York: Random House.

Gasper, Des 1996: Essentialism In and About Development Discourse. In: Apthorpe, Raymond/Gasper, Des (eds.) *Arguing Development Policy: Frames and Discourses*. London: Frank Cass, 149–176.

Gasper, Des/Apthorpe, Raymond 1996: Introduction: Discourse Analysis and Policy Discourse. In: Apthorpe, Raymond/Gasper, Des (eds.) *Arguing Development Policy: Frames and Discourses*. London: Frank Cass, 1–15.

Greenstein, Ran 2009: Alternative Modernity: Development Discourse in Post-apartheid South Africa. *International Social Science Journal* 60(195), 69–84.

Griffiths, Claire 2010: *Globalizing the Postcolony: Contesting Discourses of Gender and Development in Francophone Africa*. Plymouth: Lexington.

Grillo, R. D./Stirrat, R. L. (eds.) 1997: *Discourses of Development. Anthropological Perspectives*. Oxford: Berg.

Groves, Leslie/Hinton, Rachel (eds.) 2005: *Inclusive Aid: Changing Power and Relationships in International Development*. London: Earthscan.

Hodge, Joseph/Hödl, Gerald/Kopf, Martina 2014: *Developing Africa: Concepts and Practices in Twentieth-Century Colonialism*. Manchester: Manchester University Press.

Karagiannis, Nathalie 2004: *Avoiding Responsibility: The Politics and Discourse of European Development Policy*. London: Pluto.

Kiely, Ray 1999: The Last Refuge of the Noble Savage? A Critical Assessment of Post-development Theory. *European Journal of Development Research* 11(1), 30–55.

Li, Tania Murray 2007: *The Will to Improve. Governmentality, Development, and the Practice of Politics*. Durham, NC: Duke University Press.

Manzo, Kate 1991: Modernist Discourse and the Crisis of Development Theory. *Studies in Comparative International Development* 26(2), 3–36.

Marx, Karl 1844: Zur Kritik der Hegelschen Rechtsphilosophie. In: Marx, Karl/Engels, Friedrich (eds.) 1978: *Ausgewählte Werke in sechs Bänden, Band I*. Berlin: Dietz, 9–25.

Mitchell, Timothy 1995: The Object of Development. America's Egypt. In: Crush, Jonathan (ed.) *Power of Development*. London: Routledge, 129–157.

Mkandawire, Thandika 2010: 'Good Governance': The Itinerary of an Idea. In: Cornwall, Andrea/Eade, Deborah (eds.) *Deconstructing Development Discourse: Buzzwords and Fuzzwords*. Bourton: Practical Action, 265–268.

Moore, David 1995: Development Discourse as Hegemony: Towards an Ideological History 1945–1995. In: Moore, David/Schmitz, Gerald J. (eds.) *Debating Development Discourse: Institutional and Popular Perspectives*. Basingstoke: Macmillan, 1–53.

Moore, David/Schmitz, Gerald J. (eds.) 1995: *Debating Development Discourse: Institutional and Popular Perspectives*. Basingstoke: Macmillan.

Mosse, David/Lewis, David (eds.) 2005: *The Aid Effect: Giving and Governing in International Development*. London: Pluto.

Nandy, Ashis 1992: *Traditions, Tyranny, and Utopias: Essays in the Politics of Awareness*. Delhi: Oxford University Press.

Nederveen Pieterse, Jan 1991: Dilemmas of Development Discourse: The Crisis of Developmentalism and the Comparative Method. *Development and Change* 22(1), 5–29.

Nederveen Pieterse, Jan 2010: *Development Theory*. 2nd ed. London: Sage.

Nederveen Pieterse, Jan 2011: Discourse Analysis in International Development Studies. *Journal of Multicultural Discourses* 6(3), 237–240.

Nisbet, Robert 1969: *Social Change and History: Aspects of the Western Theory of Development*. Oxford: Oxford University Press.

Oommen, Tharaileth Koshy 2004: *Development Discourse: Issues and Concerns*. New Delhi: Regency.

Peet, Richard/Hartwick, Elaine 1999: *Theories of Development*. New York: Guilford Press.

Rahnema, Majid 1997: Development and the People's Immune System: The Story of Another Variety of AIDS. In: Rahnema, Majid/Bawtree, Victoria (eds.) 1997: *The Post-development Reader*. London: Zed Books, 111–129.

Rist, Gilbert 1997: *The History of Development: From Western Origins to Global Faith*. London: Zed Books.

Sachs, Wolfgang 1990: The Archaeology of the Development Idea. *Interculture* 23(4), No. 109, 1–37.

Sachs, Wolfgang (ed.) 1992: *The Development Dictionary: A Guide to Knowledge as Power*. London: Zed Books.

Sachs, Wolfgang 1999: *Planet Dialectics. Exploration in Environment and Development*. London: Zed Books.

Schmitz, Gerald 1995: Democratization and Demystification: Deconstructing 'Governance' as Development Paradigm. In: Moore, David/Schmitz, Gerald J. (eds.) *Debating Development Discourse: Institutional and Popular Perspectives*. Basingstoke: Macmillan, 54–90.

Scott, James C. 1985: *Weapons of the Weak: Everyday Forms of Peasant Resistance*. New Haven, CT: Yale University Press.

Scott, James C. 1990: *Domination and the Arts of Resistance*. New Haven, CT: Yale University Press.

Shreshta, Nanda 1995: Becoming a Development Category. In: Crush, Jonathan (ed.) *Power of Development*. London: Routledge, 266–277.

Smith, Malinda 2006: *Beyond the 'African Tragedy': Discourses of Development and the Global Economy*. Aldershot: Ashgate.

Stein, William 2004: *Deconstructing Development Discourse in Peru*. Lanham, MD: University Press of America.

Thomas, Alan 2000: Poverty and the 'End of Development'. In: Allen, Tim/Thomas, Alan (eds.) 2000: *Poverty and Development Into the 21st Century*. Oxford: Oxford University Press, 3–22.

Toye, John 1987: *Dilemmas of Development. Reflections on the Counter-revolution in Development Theory and Policy*. Oxford: Blackwell.

UN Department of Economic and Social Affairs 2012: *World Mortality Report 2011*. New York: United Nations.

Wainwright, Joel 2008: *Decolonizing Development: Colonial Power and the Maya*. Oxford: Blackwell.

World Bank 1992: *Governance and Development*. Washington, DC: Author.

Ziai, Aram 2004: The Ambivalence of Post-development: Between Reactionary Populism and Radical Democracy. *Third World Quarterly* 25(6), 1045–1061.

Index

For Product Safety Concerns and information please contact our EU representative GPSR@taylorandfrancis.com Taylor & Francis Verlag GmbH, Kaufingerstraße 24, 80331 München, Germany